Careerism
and Intellectualism
Among
College Students

Patterns of Academic
and Career Choice
in the Undergraduate Years

Herant A. Katchadourian
John Boli

with the assistance of

Nancy Olsen
Raymond F. Bacchetti
Sally Mahoney

Careerism
and Intellectualism
Among
College Students

San Francisco • London • 1985

CAREERISM AND INTELLECTUALISM AMONG COLLEGE STUDENTS:
Patterns of Academic and Career Choice in the Undergraduate Years
  by Herant A. Katchadourian and John Boli

Copyright © 1985 by: Jossey-Bass Inc., Publishers
                       433 California Street
                       San Francisco, California 94104

&

                       Jossey-Bass Limited
                       28 Banner Street
                       London EC1Y 8QE

Library of Congress Cataloging-in-Publication Data

Katchadourian, Herant A.
  Careerism and intellectualism among college
students.

  Bibliography: p. 311
  Includes index.
  1. Stanford University—Students—Attitudes—
Case studies.   2. Vocational interests—California—
Stanford—Case studies.   3. Learning and scholarship—
California—Stanford—Case studies.   4. Student
aspirations—California—Stanford—Case studies.
I. Boli, John (date).   II. Title.   III. Title:
College students: patterns of Academic and career
choice in the undergraduate years.
LD3036.K37   1985   378'.1981   85-45058
ISBN 0-87589-662-2

Manufactured in the United States of America

The paper in this book meets the guidelines for
permanence and durability of the Committee on
Production Guidelines for Book Longevity of the
Council on Library Resources.

JACKET DESIGN BY WILLI BAUM

FIRST EDITION

Code 8534

The Jossey-Bass
Higher Education Series

Foreword

Universities, it has been said, are devoted to the careful and scholarly examination of human institutions—except themselves. That description is not exactly true; there are good studies of the history of universities, of their role in society, even of their organization and management. But it is not exactly unfair, either, because surprisingly little useful knowledge exists on at least one critical feature of the university's mission: in what ways, and how much, do they affect the lives and capacities of the students they enroll?

When Herant Katchadourian was appointed vice-provost and dean of undergraduate studies at Stanford in 1976, little information existed either on the course-taking behavior of Stanford students or on the relationship between their aspirations and the choices they made as undergraduates. He and a group of colleagues decided to examine both these questions: the first, through a detailed and careful study of course selection and curricular paths taken by an entire year-class of Stanford students; and the second by examining, through questionnaires and in-depth interviews, the aspirations and choices of a large cohort of their classmates. The study was begun during the presidency of one of us (R.W.L.) and completed during that of the other (D.K.).

The "Cohort Study," as the second venture soon came to be called, attracted a lot of attention from the Stanford administration as it progressed. Some of our ablest colleagues were recruited to act as interviewers, and soon they were interrupting staff meetings with fascinating accounts of the hopes, fears, and unusual capacities of their interviewees. Out of these anecdotes, it almost seemed that a typology was crystallizing—although the categories were not fully defined and named until the analysis was over. At different points in the study, we both became convinced at least of this: that a remarkable amount of thoughtful, experienced, and enthusiastic labor was being invested in an effort to understand our undergraduate students as a population.

The results are, at least to us, fascinating. From our total of about fifty years' experience with Stanford students, as faculty members and administrators, we experience as we read this book quick surges of recognition, delight, or—occasionally—dismay. For us, the typology carries conviction. Whether it will surprise others, we do not know; we could not even say whether the categories are ones that seem intuitively obvious. But they do seem real, and we think our colleagues will find them equally recognizable.

But at a more fundamental level, how broadly applicable will these findings be? It is not easy to say. In one sense, Stanford is typical of a small number of private research universities with highly selective undergraduate student bodies. Their applicant groups show a good deal of overlap, and it is easy to think of all of them as representing the same limited pool of bright and ambitious young Americans.

Furthermore, the lines that separate one kind of American university from another are not clear and distinct. One of the glories of our nonsystem of higher education is that the pecking order is forever being debated, attacked, and altered. On any of a very large number of campuses one will find students not unlike those at Stanford; no university, no group of universities has a monopoly on talent or ambition.

On the other hand, it is easy to forget that even the most "national" of American universities are highly regional as far as the origin of their undergraduate student bodies is concerned. Harvard and Stanford each draws nearly half its students from a radius of 500 miles from the campus; students from the Northeast and Middle Atlantic states are a small minority at Stanford, just as students from the Rocky Mountain and Pacific states are at Harvard. There is still powerful regional heterogeneity in this country; and what impact that has on the behavioral characteristics of Stanford undergraduates as compared with, say, those at an Ivy League college is difficult to know. We think we are safe in predicting that some of our colleagues at other institutions will find this a recognizable portrait, and that others will firmly assert that it has no relevance to their institutions whatever. We only hope the disagreements are energetic enough, and clear enough, to encourage further studies.

Finally, we return to the question with which we started this brief foreword. In the study that follows, our colleagues have told us a great deal about the lives and the capacities of undergraduate students in one university. Behind the choices they make and the aspirations they cite, one sees the institution—sometimes lurking indistinctly in the background, occasionally jumping into clearer focus. One wants to ask: What is Stanford doing to, and for, these young people? Is it adding wisdom, capacity, value? Or is it more like a benign landlord, renting out rooms to the best and the brightest and helping them hear lectures and find books? If the former, how can it do better? And if the latter, should it do more, and if so, how?

Even the most enthusiastic and believing reader will not find clear answers to these questions. How much value universities actually add to their students is an abiding mystery. This study does not solve it; but without a greater understanding of our students— their hopes, the ways in which they work, the ways in which they change—we won't even know where to begin.

September 1985   Donald Kennedy
                                    President, Stanford University

                                    Richard W. Lyman
                                    President, Rockefeller Foundation

To the students who participated in the cohort study
—be they Careerists, Intellectuals, Strivers,
or Unconnected—
this book is gratefully and affectionately dedicated.

Preface

There is widespread and mounting concern among educators that careerism and consumerism pervade American higher education. Students seem to have become passive participants in the educational enterprise, concerned primarily with the occupational advantages derived from a college education rather than focused on the intrinsic and intellectual benefits to be obtained from such learning.

The research study on which this book is based was initiated to learn about the academic experiences of students at Stanford University in order to enhance the quality of undergraduate education. We have written this book because what we have learned about careerism and intellectualism in college holds the promise of being useful to a far broader range of institutions than just our own.

A great deal of current literature on college students is either purely quantitative or merely anecdotal. Our work integrates a solid quantitative base with a rich set of interview reports. The quantitative data anchor the interview materials while the interviews add personal meaning and interest to the statistical abstractions. The heart of the book is a typology of academic orientations which is new and conceived differently from existing typologies in higher education. It has a firm empirical base and an analytical derivation. We have found it to be an excellent conceptual tool for characterizing the similarities and differences in how college students make academic and career choices.

The basic issues in higher education have been reiterated for so long that it is hard not to repeat what has already been said. But the voices of the students themselves have been largely missing from these discussions; they ring loud and clear in the following pages. Our aim throughout is to bring the reader face to face with real, live, young men and women in college.

Who Should Read This Book?

We have written this book for several groups. Scholars and investigators of college student development will find in this report a study of unusual depth and comprehensiveness. Academic administrators, such as presidents, provosts, academic vice-presidents, deans, department heads, and others involved in formulating and implementing educational policy will find much food for thought in these pages. Student affairs practitioners, career counselors, academic advisors, deans of students, directors of residential education, and others can derive from it many useful tools for their work.

Finally, we fervently hope that the primary actors in the educational enterprise—students and faculty—will take an interest in our work. They are the ones who in the final analysis are most likely to benefit from it. Anyone who has been to college may find the experience of our students useful in putting his or her own educational and occupational life in perspective.

Overview of the Contents

The first two chapters set the context. Chapter One addresses the concepts of careerism and intellectualism in college, provides historical background, and outlines current concerns over the issue of rising careerism and waning intellectualism.

Chapter Two focuses on the study itself—its background, methodology, and conceptual framework. We introduce our typology of academic orientations and compare it to other typologies in higher education.

Chapter Three deals with the undergraduate experience as a whole by focusing on the special characteristics of each of the four years and tracing the paths of change and challenge followed by students in their undergraduate careers.

The next four chapters constitute the heart of the book, where each of the four types of students is given detailed treatment. Chapter Four deals with Careerists; Chapter Five, with Intellectuals; Chapter Six, with Strivers; and Chapter Seven, with the Unconnected. We examine the students' background characteristics, choices of major and career, attitudes toward liberal education, extracurricular and social lives, and academic successes and satisfactions. Each chapter ends with a balance sheet summarizing the positive and negative aspects of each orientation.

Chapter Eight concludes the text with a review of our findings, their significance, and a set of recommendations based on them.

We have made a conscientious attempt to document our major conclusions in the text, but not every sentence carries the supporting data strapped to its back. Most of the quantitative information is presented in a set of tables in the appendixes. The reader will also find there a detailed discussion of our sample and methodology, descriptions of the questionnaires used and issues related to coding the questionnaires, and an explanation of how the typology was constructed. For readers who are not acquainted with Stanford, the appendixes also contain a succinct description of those aspects of the university that are particularly germane to undergraduate education.

We have made liberal use of interview reports to illustrate and document various points in the text. These are set in different type and consist of direct quotes from students and interviewers as well as paraphrases of interviewer comments. We also provide more general descriptions of student types in a set of four profiles in each of the four chapters dealing with the typology categories. These come early in each chapter and are not keyed to any particular section (although we do refer to some particular profiles at a number of points). The profiles can be read at any time and are not meant to break the flow of the main text.

We have written this book to be read, indeed to be enjoyed. We hoped it will stimulate similar efforts in other institutions and that those who undertake such efforts will benefit from them as much as we have.

Background of the Study and Acknowledgments

Literally hundreds of people have contributed to the study on which this book is based. We are first and foremost grateful to the students who for four years diligently and candidly shared their educational experiences with us. They are the true authors of this book. We are no less indebted to the members of the interviewing team who, in addition to their demanding schedules and without remuneration, took on the arduous task of eliciting and recording the students' information. Their contributions went beyond furnishing us with interview reports; they also helped us formulate the questions and interpret the answers that inform this book. The members of the interviewing team, in addition to ourselves, are listed below, along with their titles at the time of the study:

James Adams, Associate Dean and Professor of Engineering;
Mary Lou Allen, Director, Instructional TV Network;
Raymond G. Bacchetti, Vice-Provost for Management and Director of University Budgets;
Parker Beverage, Associate Director and Dean of Transfer Admissions;
John Bunnell, Associate Dean of Admissions;
Sylvia Castillo, Assistant Dean of Student Affairs;
Griselda Castro, Assistant Dean of Student Affairs;
Anne Coxon, Director, Academic Information Center;
Jean Fetter, Associate Dean of Graduate Studies;
Tania Granoff, Director of Academic Advising;
Fred Hargadon, Dean of Admissions;
Peggy Kent, Assistant Director, Academic Information Center;
James Lyons, Dean of Student Affairs;
Sally Mahoney, Associate Provost and University Registrar;
Elizabeth Meyer, Director, Academic Information Center;
Michelle Moore, Recorder;
Nancy Olsen, Coordinator of the Cohort Study, Office of the Dean of Undergraduate Studies;
Stephen Peeps, Admissions Officer;
Lowell Price, Associate Provost for Management and Budget;
Melanie Reeves, Assistant Dean of Undergraduate Studies;
Beverly Scott, Assistant Dean of Undergraduate Studies;
Debra Von Bargen, Associate Director and Dean of Transfer Admissions;

Timothy Warner, Assistant Provost for Management and
Budget;

Bill Washburn, Research Coordinator, Office of the Dean of
Undergraduate Studies.

When the study began, Richard W. Lyman was president and
Donald Kennedy was provost of Stanford University; when it ended,
Donald Kennedy was president and Albert H. Hastorf was provost.
Their interest and support in our work was a welcome source of
sustenance. The project was carried out largely with institutional
support and with a generous grant from the Spencer Foundation,
for which we are most grateful.

The study was initiated and directed by Herant Katchadourian. Bill Washburn, who was at the time a graduate student in the
Stanford School of Education, coordinated the project at its
inception in 1976. He was subsequently joined by Nancy Olsen,
who took on the primary staff responsibility for the cohort study.
In 1980, Washburn left to take a position elsewhere and Olsen
became a consultant to the project. Their duties were taken up by
John Boli who coordinated the study until its completion.

Throughout the progress of our work, Raymond Bacchetti
and Sally Mahoney took active roles in its various aspects. Along
with the staff members named above, they constituted a "kitchen
cabinet," providing much valued guidance and support.

John Boli, assisted by Nancy Olsen, had primary responsibility for the analysis and use of the questionnaire data and Herant
Katchadourian for the interview material. The text was written in
close collaboration by Herant Katchadourian and John Boli. Nancy
Olsen, Raymond Bacchetti, and Sally Mahoney offered ongoing
advice and criticism throughout the writing of the book. Since
many of their thoughts and words are incorporated into the text,
their names are listed on the title page along with ours. We also
benefited from the advice of Lincoln Moses and James March, who
advised us in the selection of our sample, and the comments of Lewis
Mayhew, JB Lon Hefferlin, Peter T. Ewell, Donald Kennedy, Albert
Hastorf, James Lyons, and Debra Wilson.

Annette Holcomb, Margaret Hernandez, Andrea Garwood, and Nancy Bovee served as research secretaries at successive phases of the project, and Laurie Burmeister typed the final versions of the manuscript. For their dedicated and competent work we express our gratitude.

Stanford, California   Herant A. Katchadourian
September 1985   John Boli

Contents

The Authors

Herant A. Katchadourian is professor of psychiatry and behavioral sciences at Stanford University. He received his B.A. and M.D. degrees from the American University of Beirut, Lebanon, in 1954 and 1958, respectively, and his residency training in psychiatry at the University of Rochester, New York (1958–1961). From 1976 to 1981 he served as vice-provost and dean of undergraduate studies and for the next three years as vice-provost for undergraduate education at Stanford. His publications include *Fundamentals of Human Sexuality*, 4th edition (1985); *Biology of Adolescence* (1977); *Human Sexuality—Sense and Nonsense* (1972). He is the editor of *Human Sexuality: A Comparative and Developmental Perspective* (1979) and the author of various book chapters and articles in the fields of cross-cultural psychiatry, sexuality, and the human life cycle. Katchadourian is a member of the Alpha Omega Alpha medical honor society. He has been chosen four times Outstanding Professor and Class Day Speaker by graduating Stanford seniors and has received the Richard W. Lyman Award from the Stanford Alumni Association.

John Boli is research coordinator, Office of Undergraduate Research, and research associate, Department of Sociology, at Stanford University. He studied sociology at Stanford, earning his B.A. degree in 1970, his M.A. degree in 1973, and his Ph.D. degree in 1976. He has taught at San Francisco State University, the University of Santa Clara, San Jose State University, and Stanford University. A member of the American Sociological Association and the American Educational Research Association, he has presented numerous papers at the annual meetings of those bodies. His publications in the sociology of education have appeared in the *American Educational Research Journal, Sociology of Education,*

Comparative Educational Review, and several edited volumes. Boli has also published articles on the rise of the modern state, the development of human rights ideology, cross-national studies of constitutions, and the work of Jacques Ellul. His current research focuses on the rise of mass education in nineteenth-century Western Europe and the global institutionalization of educational ideology in the twentieth century. He also writes political novels and science fiction.

Principal Collaborators

———————————— ··✦∞✦·· ————————————

Nancy Olsen is a research and editorial consultant and a bookseller. She earned her B.A. degree in sociology in 1960 from the University of Minnesota. She received her M.A. degree in 1966 and her Ph.D. degree in 1971, both from Cornell University, in the field of human development and family studies. Olsen has taught at the University of Santa Clara, Oregon State University, and Stanford University. She has published research papers in the *American Journal of Sociology*, the *Journal of Marriage and the Family*, and other periodicals.

Raymond F. Bacchetti is vice-provost for management, director of university budgets, and a lecturer in the School of Education at Stanford University. He received his A.B. degree in business administration in 1956 and his Ed.M. degree in 1959, both from Rutgers University. He received his Ph.D. degree in education in 1968 from Stanford University. A former school board member and currently a Trustee of the Foothill-DeAnza Community College District, Bacchetti's professional interests lie in management theory and practice in higher education. He has taught this topic in the United States, Australia, England, and New Zealand, and has published several articles on higher education. In 1982, he was given the Kenneth M. Cuthbertson Award for Exceptional Service to Stanford University.

Sally Mahoney is associate provost and university registrar at Stanford University. She received her A.B. degree in English from San Francisco College for Women in 1961 and did graduate work in English literature at Stanford University. She served in the Office of the Dean of Student Affairs at Stanford from 1964 to

1970 before becoming assistant provost and director of summer session. She was appointed associate provost and university registrar in 1973.

Careerism
and Intellectualism
Among
College Students

Patterns of Academic
and Career Choice
in the Undergraduate Years

1

The Careerism
Versus Intellectualism
Controversy

Who would have thought that over a mere decade or so careerism would replace radicalism as the central concern of educators? The dominant image of the 1960s college student was a disheveled, surly, and alienated youth tearing away at the fabric of higher education. The 1980s image is a tidy, cheerful, and self-centered student milking higher education for all it is worth to get ahead in the world. Such stereotypes are misleading if generalized, but they are not meaningless if they capture the spirit of the times.

The college student of today is, in some ways, the answer to the prayers of teachers and parents of yesterday. Yet there is mounting alarm that the true purposes of higher education are being subverted. The villain in this unfolding drama is "careerism," its victim "intellectualism." The word *career* (derived from Latin for "vehicle") refers to the pursuit of achievement in public, professional, or business life. Though more prestigious than trade or labor, a professional career fulfills the same fundamental task of earning one's daily bread. The pursuit of a career is considered laudable while *careerism* has a pejorative ring to it, connoting excess.

Intellectualism is harder to explain. The dictionary definition as "devotion to the exercise of intellect or to intellectual pursuits" is not very revealing. The parallel with careerism is also

1

problematic. We commonly refer to careerists but not to intellectualists (which the Oxford Dictionary defines as "a devotee of the intellect or understanding"). Not only is intellectualism a more nebulous concept than careerism, it also strikes most people as more of a luxury—not the bread but the butter of higher learning.

The assumption underlying current discussions in higher education is that rising careerism has been accompanied by waning intellectualism. As careerism increases, so the thinking goes, the concern for liberal education diminishes, for students can hardly be expected to combine the pursuit of careerist and intellectual commitments simultaneously. But are we necessarily dealing here with a zero-sum game? The answer to this question is crucial since the remedies one chooses, assuming that remedies are called for, will heavily depend on it.

In response to these concerns there is a broad movement afoot to reaffirm the importance of intellectual values in education and stimulate student interest in liberal learning (Shulman, 1979; Hendrix and Stoel, 1982; Keller, 1982). These efforts focus on strengthening teaching in the liberal arts and the humanities, often referred to as the core of our Western cultural heritage. Typical measures taken include increasing general education requirements, emphasizing the humanities in distributional requirements, and strengthening core curricula. El-Khawas (1985) shows that over 90 percent of four-year colleges and universities have taken some such action in recent years. At their best, such efforts reflect a serious commitment to liberal education. More often, lip service is paid to keep in step with the rhetoric of the times but genuine reform and renewal are not achieved.

Ample survey data exist to support the statement that rising careerism among college students has been accompanied by waning intellectualism. But we are not convinced that rising interest in vocational preparation is, in itself, a lamentable development. Only when it compromises fundamental educational purposes does it become problematic. To isolate careerism as the villain in higher education is naive, betraying a lack of historical perspective. Since its Sumerian origins in 6000 B.C., education has always had a central vocational purpose. Even if one believes that careerism is bad, to add a humanities requirement here and a cultural survey course there will hardly stem the careerist tide. As long as careerism is pitted against intellectualism, the outcome is regrettably but surely predictable. Rather than engage in such an unequal struggle, we need to find ways of making liberal learning and career preparation complementary, not competitive; while retaining its distinct purposes, each ought to serve the needs of the other as well.

A flurry of recent books explores the meaning of student careerism, its causes, consequences, and probable future course (Gaff and others, 1980; Levine, 1980b; Boyer and Levine, 1981; Riesman, 1981; Gamson and others, 1984). Yet most of this literature deals with the effects of careerism on *institutions* of higher learning. The authors typically develop one of two themes: Either they offer advice as to how colleges can convince prospective students that their programs are sufficiently career related to meet their vocational expectations, or they argue from a loftier position that the colleges should not too eagerly nurture student careerism because of the risk of neglecting their historical mission of fostering intellectual development and liberal learning.

By contrast, there is very little research that relates to the *student* perspective on careerism. The voices of students are largely missing from these learned debates. What does the rise of careerism mean to undergraduates themselves? How does it affect their educational choices, their personal relationships and social activities, their level of contentment with their college experience? Most important, what is the impact of careerism on liberal education and the pursuit of intellectual virtues?

The particular contribution of our study lies in its emphasis on the student perspective. We have tried to elucidate what undergraduates think about these issues, and we have found that their opinions vary widely. Some are unabashedly in favor of pursuing career interests, whatever the cost to the rest of their education, while others balk at this prospect and are intent on putting their educational purposes ahead of vocational aims. There are those who would like to get the best of both worlds, while others seem reluctant to connect to either. The following excerpts from interview reports illustrate these attitudes:

Edward is very much oriented to vocation, job security, and building a future free from financial restraints. He expressed little satisfaction with the experience of going to college but a great deal of satisfaction with the prospects that come with college certification at graduation. Edward wants a job that pays very well and he wants as much competitive edge in the job market as he can possibly get out of a place like Stanford. So he will choose the sort of major that will advance these aims and will have nothing to do with courses in the humanities. College is a place where one does hard work, not a place where one relaxes or enjoys what one is doing.

Sally conveys a real excitement about her academic life in college. After many of her classes she would come out and be absolutely "soaring." In thinking about what kinds of things really make her happiest, she's found that it's the times when she's either reading something she's very interested in or when she's writing something that she really thinks is worthwhile. For her, the epitome of a well-educated person is a well-read person.

During his senior year in high school Jim developed a budding interest in law and felt that a liberal arts background would be a good way to prepare for that goal. But now he wages an internal battle with himself between preparing for law school by fighting to get good grades and taking courses for their sheer enjoyment. He concludes that the best deal will be finding a happy medium. So far, history fits the bill pretty well, as it is both enjoyable and good preparation for law school.

Linda isn't sure she wants a career, and if she is to have one, she wants many careers—she can't see doing something "forever." She has faith that something will come along that interests her and doesn't want to plan too much in her life . . . looks ahead only six months ("I'm going to live a long life and there's no reason to press it right now"). Planning too much wrecks all the surprises and runs the risk of disappointments if plans do not work out.

The central purpose of this book is to investigate the meaning and significance of intellectualism and careerism for college students themselves. We discuss the factors that shape the academic and career attitudes of college students, showing that parents, teachers, peers, and academic background are important determinants. We examine students' choice of major and career, their academic performance, and their levels of satisfaction with the college experience to see what difference careerism and intellectualism make with respect to these variables. We finally seek to understand how colleges and universities can fulfill their educational mission more effectively in light of the answers we have to these questions.

The study on which this volume is based has as its subjects several hundred undergraduate students at one of the leading educational institutions of the country, Stanford University. Neither the institution nor the students are representative of the entire range of the American educational establishment, which includes close to twelve million young men and women enrolled in over three thousand institutions of higher learning pursuing one or another of fifteen hundred separate degrees. On the other hand, the issues we focus on are so fundamental that with the appropriate correctives, what we have to say should be highly relevant to the enterprise of higher education as a whole. By taking a close-up view of the lives of these young women and men, we hope to shed light on the meaning of career preparation and liberal learning for college students everywhere.

Historical Background

Many fundamental questions of educational philosophy and purpose have remained unchanged over the centuries. In ancient Greece the more utilitarian aims of education advocated by the Sophists were already in conflict with the pursuit of the purer truth by Plato's academy. In American history the supporters of a broad, liberal education and the champions of "practical" training for utilitarian purposes have been at loggerheads since at least the late eighteenth century, when mathematics and natural philosophy (in the process of breaking down into distinct disciplines such as physics and chemistry) became established curricular elements in the colonial colleges; it was feared at the time that these practical pursuits would deflect students from the true purpose of education, which was knowledge of the Divine Being (Rudolph, 1977).

Though everyone is in favor of liberal learning, it is far from clear what such learning should consist of. Should it have something of everything or be more selective? Should it rely on the tested and true or the current and innovative? Should its core be classics or computer science? Because science and technology are more "practical," there is a tendency to minimize their role in liberal education. Fingers are easily pointed at engineers for being narrow, but are humanists who are scientific illiterates any broader?

The liberal arts have been closely associated with the humanities throughout much of the history of higher education. The historical background of this association as described in the report of the Commission on the Humanities (1980, pp. 63-65) is worth quoting at length:

> Until well into the nineteenth century, the humanities dominated an undergraduate curriculum whose vocational, educational, and social purposes were in harmony. The early American college had three basic aims: to train young men for the clergy or political leadership; to develop the mental discipline and moral and religious habits appropriate to a cultivated gentleman, whatever his vocation; and to maintain, through induction into the traditions of classical culture, a small elite of the educated in a predominantly agricultural society. These goals, educators thought, could be achieved through studies in the literature, history, and culture of Western antiquity, combined with religious instruction. Through the humanities the early college expressed its faith in the coherence of knowledge, in a single cultural tradition, and in the community of the learned.
>
> Revolutionary intellectual and social changes weakened that faith. The explosion of knowledge in the second half of the nineteenth century scattered the fields of academic inquiry beyond the reach of a single curriculum or small faculty. To impose order on this fragmentation, newborn universities divided into schools, departments, disciplines, and specialties. Universities also took on a new responsibility for higher education: research, the pursuit of new

knowledge for its own sake and for the benefit of society. The sciences gained a prominence in the universities that has never been challenged. Humanistic learning also profited from the new emphasis on research, but in the curriculum the division and subdivision of knowledge eroded common ground formerly occupied by the humanities.

Founded as institutions where, in the words of Ezra Cornell, "any person can find instruction in any study," the new universities also expanded the social mission of higher education. They did not educate an elite as socially exclusive or all-male as the earlier colleges had. Studies preparing students for skilled occupations, formerly relegated to apprenticeships, found their way into the curriculum, especially at the comprehensive land grant institutions established by the Morrill Act of 1862. Vocational training in college education attracted new students and taught new technologies required by a society growing rapidly in population and industry.

As new arts and sciences arose and utility rivaled cultivation, liberal education was redefined as a synthesis of new studies and old ideals. The curriculum became a catalog—much as we know it today—of branches of knowledge and kinds of expertise needed by society. Colleges and universities entered the twentieth century offering an emporium of courses in place of the old curriculum of humane studies. Organization of the undergraduate course of study into the major and electives reflected the increasingly specialized character of knowledge and gave students freedom to follow their own interests. Undergraduate education was called liberal insofar as institutions required students to take survey courses in the major fields of knowledge and satisfy distribution requirements.

The humanities remained an essential part of liberal learning through the first half of this century. They claimed far less of the curriculum than previously, but institutions still looked to them to fulfill inherited ideals of liberal education. One of these was civic: the humanities helped prepare students for responsible participation in society. A second ideal was personal: the humanities offered spiritual and emotional enrichment. Liberal education, which became widely known as general education, usually included requirements in humanities. Through survey courses in Western culture, for example, many institutions expected generations of students to shape their civic and personal values. Surveys of the Western tradition also provided a common educational experience—another traditional ideal of liberal education—for an increasingly diversified student body.

Following the Second World War, the population of colleges began to change character through the extension of educational opportunities to new social groups, thereby making the notion of a common culture a tenuous proposition. The idea and ideals of Western cultural traditions came under frontal attack by the student radical movements of the 1960s. Combined with the demand for greater student autonomy and academic choice, they led to the cutback of curricular requirements and the further loss of the ideal of a coherent and common educational experience.

Current Issues

The current dilemma is generally seen as a matter of preventing the tide of vocationalism from overwhelming what is left of the tradition of liberal education. To understand this problem we need to clarify further the aims that these two ostensibly competitive components of higher education are expected to serve.

The objectives of career preparation are considerably clearer than those of liberal education. There is little ambiguity, for instance, in the more technically oriented training provided in areas like engineering and earth sciences. There is no pretense that such technical study will in itself constitute a liberal education. The situation is more complicated with respect to the broader program of study within which such career preparation is embedded. Are the general education courses, such as in literature, that these students take intended to make them better engineers by teaching them "communication skills," or is such education superimposed on the engineering curriculum for nonvocational purposes? Do the faculty of these programs value such courses in and of themselves, or do they suffer them only insofar as they provide a substantive base for professional work (see Dressel and Mayhew, 1954)?

Even more ambiguous is the case where undergraduate programs serve the purposes of preprofessional education. The best example is the set of demanding courses required for admission to medical school. They neither constitute a form of liberal education in themselves nor are they a part of medical training. As individual courses they are an integral part of the education of students in departments like biology and chemistry. But as a sequence of requirements, their avowed purpose is to prepare students for the future study of medicine. The extent to which this constitutes the best preparation for the future study and practice of medicine is far from clear (Thomas, 1979). Yet these requirements exert an enormous influence in shaping the undergraduate experience of premedical students; indeed, they are the most critical hurdles the students must clear to get into medical school.

Schools of law and business do not have comparable requirements for preprofessional study. In principle, any four-year college program can equip students for graduate study in these fields. However, student-generated expectations, if not the reality, of what admission committees are looking for create certain constraints on academic choices. It is thus no wonder that students heading for business school are likely to major in economics and those aiming at law often take up political science. There is obviously nothing wrong with these choices, as such. Problems arise, however, when such choices are made on utilitarian or tactical grounds rather than being based on interest in the subject matter.

Lest we take the linkages between preprofessional education in college and professional school training as preordained, we must recall that it was not until the twentieth century that the training of the majority of doctors and lawyers came to be preceded by a college education. Before then, most of these professionals entered practice either by way of apprenticeships or through study in specialized schools that coexisted with the colleges. No one would argue that better-educated students do not make better professionals; but in aiming to become better professionals, are students having their liberal education shortchanged?

Even without vocational considerations, the aims of liberal learning are hard to define, though many have tried (see, for instance, the volumes sponsored by The Carnegie Council on Policy Studies in Higher Education, such as The Carnegie Foundation for the Advancement of Teaching, 1977; Rudolph, 1977; and Levine, 1978).

The mandate of liberal education is so broad that it is ultimately based on the larger expectation of how one should live one's life. Its components include: instilling the requisite rudiments for common discourse; transmitting the universals of human culture; providing an integrating experience underlining the unity of knowledge; providing general knowledge of the world around us; preparing students for participation in a democratic society; developing a means of achieving one's human potential; obtaining the knowledge necessary for a satisfying private life; and so on (Levine, 1978, pp. 3–4). Liberal education is aimed at providing learning common to all students by exposure to a defined body of knowledge and an emphasis on "first principles." Simultaneously, there has been the expectation that such learning will train the mind, teach the student the principles involved in generating and evaluating knowledge, and provide "the discipline and the furniture of the mind," as phrased by the Yale Report of 1828.

The aim of all these conceptions of liberal education is the production of an "educated person." Yet clearly, the image of who is an educated person varies with the concept of liberal education in use (Bouwsma, 1975). The current understanding commonly attributes to the educated individual three basic properties: a fund of general knowledge, an intellectual perspective on the world, and career competence.

Students have their own views on the matter, as expressed in the following excerpts from essays our subjects were asked to write in their senior year on their conception of what is an educated person.

"Not an easy question. I don't think schooling makes you an educated person. To me, an educated person is anyone who can think, reach conclusions given information, understand new concepts. I've met people from all different backgrounds (farmers, mechanics, and so on) who don't have college degrees but are still very perceptive people. The only difference between them and college-educated people is the vocabulary they use to make their points."

"An educated person should have an understanding of the world, philosophy, history, the arts, science, math, and literature. I feel that an educated person is a kind of Renaissance person. He should be able to speak a foreign language. He should be well rounded. Yet, I also feel that being educated means one should know at least one of these areas well. Of course there are certain skills that an educated person must have, such as the ability to think, analyze, and write clearly, but I think that there is a difference between an educated person and one who simply knows a skill. Educated implies a greater cultivation of the individual."

"An educated person is one who has developed her or his analytical capabilities, focusing on one discipline but with an inkling of understanding of many. This understanding should extend to life and the world outside academia. An educated person is not one who is so rational and intellectual that his or her humanitarian and spiritual perspectives on life are blunted or ignored, but rather understands the balance necessary to achieve an understanding of herself or himself alone, and in relation to others."

"An educated person understands what it means to be a human being. . . . The primary task of education is not to prepare people for vocations or professions but rather to help them understand themselves. It is a lifelong process and therefore there is no person who is completely 'educated.'"

Distinguished educators have insistently made the point that the aims of technical and liberal education are inseparable, though they may be in conflict. Robert Maynard Hutchins wrote: "There is a conflict between one aim of the university, the pursuit of truth for its own sake, and another which it professes too, the preparation of men and women for their life work. This is not a conflict between education and research. It is a conflict between two kinds of education. Both kinds are found in all parts of a university . . . professional training is given in almost every department, and the pursuit of truth for its own sake may occasionally be met even in a professional school" (Hutchins, 1936, p. 33). Alfred North Whitehead addresses the same issue as follows: "The antithesis between a technical and liberal education is fallacious. There can be no adequate technical education which is not liberal, and no liberal education which is not technical: that is, no education which does not impart both technique and intellectual vision" (Whitehead, 1929, p. 74).

It would be a mistake to imagine that any undergraduate institution of higher education has ever been exclusively devoted to either liberal education or professional training; as Jencks and Riesman (1968, p. 199) have phrased it, "The question always has been *how* an institution mixed the academic with the vocational, not *whether* it did so." Even the most cynical students do not say that they want nothing from college but a good job, just as not even the most idealistic students claim to have no concern whatsoever for their future careers. So what is the problem? The problem is one of relative emphasis. The current concern is that the balance has tipped too far toward vocationalism, a shift that has occurred only recently.

The Shift Toward Careerism in the Late 1970s

Over the past fifteen years much has been said and written about the increase in careerism among college students and the corresponding decline in intellectualism. We will outline the dimensions of the problem based on three bodies of evidence: the American Council on Education's (ACE) annual surveys of incoming freshmen (American Council on Education, 1966–1970,

1971-1972; Cooperative Institutional Research Program, 1973-1983); the statistics on bachelor's degrees granted by higher education institutions, compiled by the National Center for Education Statistics (1982); and a series of surveys conducted by The Carnegie Commission on Higher Education and the Carnegie Council on Policy Studies in Higher Education (the "Carnegie Surveys" of 1969, 1976, and 1978, described in Levine, 1980a).

   Student Goals and Reasons for Attending College. Among all freshmen entering college in 1967, the most commonly endorsed goal was "developing a meaningful philosophy of life" (83 percent). Second was "becoming an authority in my field" (68 percent), followed by "helping others in difficulty" and "keeping up with political affairs." A decade later, much had changed. The most important goal now was becoming an authority in one's field (75 percent), followed by helping others in difficulty (65 percent). Developing a philosophy of life had fallen to third place, and it was no more important than raising a family (59 percent) and being very well-off financially (58 percent). The drop in concern with developing a philosophy of life was enormous—some twenty-three points—while keeping up with politics fell eleven points. Meanwhile, being well-off financially increased by fifteen points. Figure 1 captures the most important changes among these indicators of student life goals.

   By 1983 these trends had become even more accentuated. Developing a philosophy of life was down to just over half its 1967 level and had become only the seventh most important goal. Becoming an authority in one's field and being very well-off were the most important goals (endorsed by 72 percent and 69 percent of freshmen, respectively), followed by raising a family. Helping others in difficulty had declined to its 1967 level, while obtaining peer recognition and succeeding in one's own business were clearly on the rise. Keeping up with politics was endorsed by just over a third of the students in 1983, compared to over half the students in 1967.

   Concerns about career and personal advancement clearly came to dominate student goals by 1983, while intellectual and social concerns became much less important. In addition, the artistic and cultural commitment of students also decreased during

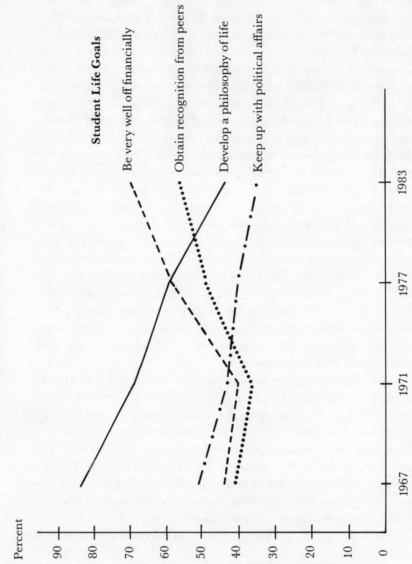

Figure 1. Indicators of Waning Intellectualism and Rising Careerism Among Entering College Freshmen, 1967–1983.

Student Life Goals

Be very well off financially

Obtain recognition from peers

Develop a philosophy of life

Keep up with political affairs

Percent

90
80
70
60
50
40
30
20
10
0

1967   1971   1977   1983

Source: Data from American Council on Education, 1966–1970, 1971–1972; and Cooperative Institutional Research Program, 1973–1983, freshman surveys for all students.

this period. The goals of "writing original works" or "creating works of art" were endorsed by 29 percent of all students in 1967 and 23 percent in 1983. We have examined, separately, the figures for freshmen in all private universities and in highly selective private universities (which include Stanford). The same trends hold for those institutions, though they are somewhat less pronounced than the overall national pattern.

ACE's surveys of incoming freshmen also inquire into the reasons for going to college. In 1971, the most common reason given for attending college was to "get a better job" (74 percent), followed by "learn more about things" (69 percent) and "gain a general education" (60 percent). By 1977 there had been an increase in virtually all items, indicating that students were endorsing more goals but not just career-related items. By 1983, however, we find that educational concerns had fallen to near their 1971 levels, getting a better job remained a prominent item, and the desire to make more money had continued to increase.

These figures point to a clear increase in careerism during the 1970s but no concomitant abandonment of the goals of liberal education. By the early 1980s, students were only modestly less likely to endorse educational goals than personal success goals. This was particularly true of freshmen entering the more selective private universities.

Choice of Major and Career. National trends in student choices of academic majors (based on data produced by the National Center for Education Statistics) show that the 1970s saw tremendous shifts in the distribution of students across major fields; the humanities and most of the social sciences suffered huge losses, while business, engineering, and other career-oriented disciplines expanded. Between 1970–71 and 1976–77, for example, bachelor's degrees declined by 36 percent in English, by 30 percent in foreign languages, and by 24 percent in the social sciences, while the number of undergraduate degrees increased in business by 32 percent and in communications by 115 percent (Roemer, 1980). These trends continued through the years our cohort of students was at Stanford: By 1979–80, business degrees had increased by 64 percent over 1970–71, communications degrees by 165 percent, engineering degrees by 39 percent, and computer science degrees by

370 percent. On the other hand, there were declines of 44 percent in English, 42 percent in foreign languages, and 33 percent in the social sciences (National Center for Education Statistics, 1982). Some of the more important of these changes are presented in Figure 2.

To a certain extent, the trends of the 1970s represented only reversals of the trends in the 1960s, when students became increasingly disenchanted with technical and business-oriented majors and rushed headlong into the social sciences and liberal arts. For example, engineering's share of all degrees did not return to its 1961 level until about 1977–78, while sociology's share of all degrees did not decline to its 1961 level until about 1979–80 (U.S. Department of Health, Education and Welfare, 1961; National Center for Education Statistics, 1982). Further, not all liberal arts disciplines suffered declines; the fine and applied arts expanded considerably throughout the 1970s. But on the whole the movement toward occupationally linked majors was so marked that by 1981–82 many of these disciplines were granting a larger proportion of all degrees than at any time since national statistics began to be assembled.

These trends are very consistent with those revealed in the ACE freshman surveys regarding students' intended fields of study (Astin, 1982). It appears, therefore, that student intentions before entering college are consistent with the degrees they earn at graduation.

An important sex difference characterizes these trends. Astin (1982) shows that much of the change in student choice of major reflects changes on the part of women, not men. For example, between 1966 and 1981 interest in business majors increased from 16 percent to 23 percent for men, but from 7 percent to 21 percent for women. In 1971 among private university students 22 percent of women and 43 percent of men cited the goal of being very well-off financially as a reason for attending college; by 1983 the figure for women had almost tripled to 63 percent, while for men it had less than doubled, to 72 percent. In virtually all dimensions the responses of women have changed to resemble those of men far more than men's responses have changed to resemble those of women.

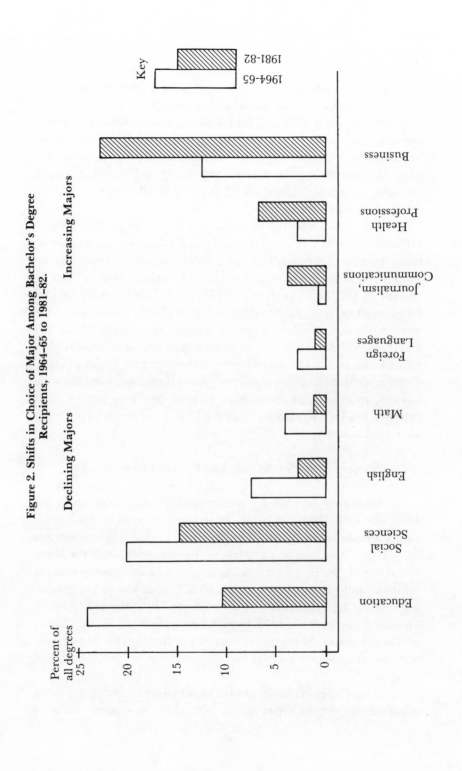

Figure 2. Shifts in Choice of Major Among Bachelor's Degree
Recipients, 1964-65 to 1981-82.

When we consider the career choices of students (Figure 3), the only national data available deal with career intentions in college, not actual career choices after college. The ACE surveys show that between 1972 and 1981 business careers became twice as popular (rising from 10 percent to 20 percent) with college freshmen, with engineering also on the increase (to 11 percent after a low of 5 percent in 1974). Careers in primary and secondary school teaching, which accounted for 22 percent of all career choices in 1967, fell to 6 percent in 1981.

The aspirations of entering freshmen for graduate study declined considerably after the early 1970s following a period of rapid increase. For example, among private university freshmen the proportion planning to obtain a doctoral-level degree rose from 32 percent in 1966 to 55 percent in 1973, but by 1981 this figure had fallen to 44 percent. This decline occurred chiefly among men, not women; the aspirations of women expanded enormously until 1975 and then leveled off, while those of men declined fairly steadily after 1972 (Astin, 1982). The decline reflects the changing career plans of entering freshmen: Fewer students planned on becoming doctors, lawyers, professors, or researchers. Instead they were interested in getting a master's-level degree (often a M.B.A.) or getting a job right after graduation.

Student Attitudes, Values, and Political Orientations

Changing patterns in intellectualism and careerism in the 1970s and early 1980s can be placed in the context of broader social values and attitudes expressed by students. Levine (1980a) contrasts an age of "community ascendancy" in the 1960s with the more recent age of "individual ascendancy" of the 1970s, arguing that the outlooks and values of individuals tend to conform to the general tenor of the age in which they live. Levine faults the self-centered, me-first attitudes of the 1970s (which Lasch [1979] called the culture of narcissism) for the declining interest in education for its own sake and the heightened interest in education as an instrument for success.

All of this evidence points to widespread changes having occurred in the post-Vietnam era, with shifts in student choice of

Figure 3. Shifts in Choice of Career Among College Freshmen, Fall 1966 to Fall 1981 (Percentage of All Careers).

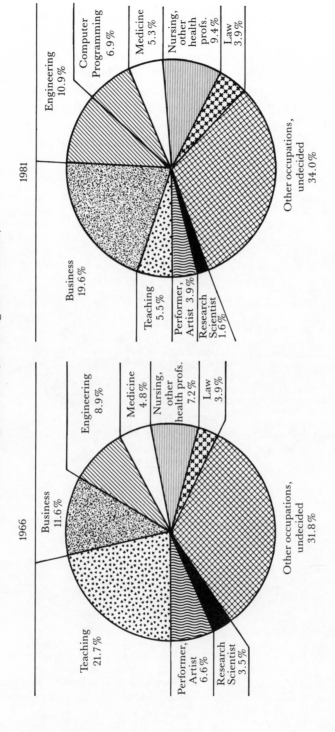

major, educational aspirations, career intentions, political attitudes, and other areas constituting a broad and coherent set of trends. These trends emphasizing preparation for careers and a relative neglect of liberal education, which many in higher education now view as problematic, form the focus of our own research, which is presented in the following chapters.

2

⸺⸻⸺

Four Types
of Students: Careerists,
Intellectuals, Strivers,
and the Unconnected

To observe the movements of a crowd, it is best to watch it at a distance. But to learn about the movements of individuals within it, one must get into the crowd itself. The trends we reviewed in Chapter One characterize large populations of students. We certainly need to understand these general patterns of change, but they tell us little about the impact of careerism and intellectualism on the experiences of individual college students—how they react to various external influences, how they choose majors and careers, and the degree to which they succeed in achieving their educational goals. To learn about these matters, we will rely on the experience of several hundred Stanford students whom we studied over a period of four years.

Study of Undergraduate Experience at Stanford

The Study of Undergraduate Experience at Stanford, on which this book is based, was initiated in 1977. It was part of a broader effort by the Office of the Vice-Provost and Dean of Undergraduate Studies to provide Stanford faculty and administra-

21

tors with an informational base on issues pertaining to undergraduate education.

The position of the Dean of Undergraduate Studies was created in 1970 as a result of the Study of Education at Stanford (Steering Committee, 1969). The Dean's responsibilities were to include "continuing review of Stanford's education of undergraduates, to support and maintain what is good, to aid in the renovation of what is inadequate, and to stimulate and assist educational innovation" (p. 10). To these ends, the Dean's office initiated two projects in 1976 to evaluate the experiences of undergraduates. One of these, the Senior Survey, is intended to function as a quality-control device. The questionnaire is mailed to all graduating seniors each year and seeks their assessments of various facets of the undergraduate program, faculty, staff, as well as their assessments of their own abilities across a wide range of knowledge areas. The second project, the Statistical Study of the Curriculum (usually referred to as the Curriculum Study), conducted in collaboration with the Office of the Registrar, is an ongoing effort designed to monitor the course choices and classroom performance of students, using their academic transcripts as a data base.

Both of these efforts have proven useful, but neither of them affords an opportunity to learn about individual students in more detailed ways through face-to-face encounters. The Study of Undergraduate Experience was initiated to provide such an opportunity. It set out to investigate, through questionnaires and yearly interviews, the academic and career choices of a cohort of freshmen (hence, the Cohort Study) throughout their four years at Stanford.

The methodology of the Cohort Study is presented in detail in Appendix II; it can be briefly summarized as follows. We chose a 20 percent random sample of incoming freshmen (320 students) from the class of 1981. The students were interviewed individually and given a detailed questionnaire in the spring of each year from 1977 until graduation. To represent more fully the graduating class under study, we added 50 sophomore and 50 junior transfer students to the sample in the appropriate years, bringing the total study population to 420 students. The transfers completed the same questionnaires as the other students, as well as an addendum at the time they started at Stanford asking them to explain why they transferred and to compare Stanford with their prior institution. Students who left Stanford before graduation were followed up to determine their reasons for leaving and their status at the time that their former peers in the Cohort sample graduated from Stanford.

Purposes of the Study. In designing the Cohort Study we cast a wide net to learn about many facets of undergraduate education. Our central purpose was to investigate how undergraduates make academic and career choices. We wanted to understand the academic predispositions students brought to college and how those predispositions were shaped by the college experience. We were also interested in knowing about the special experiences of the various components of the undergraduate population. How does being a woman or a member of an ethnic minority affect one's undergraduate experience? How are the choices of courses and majors influenced by the academic orientation of students? How are career choices made? What are the critical areas where the institution can intervene more effectively to enhance the undergraduate experience?

Though the issues surrounding vocational training and liberal learning were central to our concerns, we did not set out to study careerism and intellectualism, nor did we start searching for a typology of students. It was only after all the information was in and we were trying to make sense of the mountains of data we had gathered that we began to focus on what has now come to be the main substance and orientation of this book. So we can neither be congratulated for successfully testing a hypothesis nor suspected of finding what we set out looking for.

Questionnaires. The questionnaires sought information on a wide range of topics, many of which we will not deal with here. With respect to the central issues of the college years, such as the factors that influence students in their choice of major or the characteristics students find desirable in prospective careers, the same questionnaire items were repeated each year. Other sections of each questionnaire were geared to particular issues salient in only one of the four years; for instance, in the freshman questionnaire the issue of adapting to college received special attention, while in the senior questionnaire the issue of developing career plans was given special prominence. We shall discuss here the questionnaire items that were most relevant for constructing the typology. Further details relating to the questionnaires are given in Appendix II.

Interviews. The interviewing team consisted of some twenty-five senior- and middle-echelon administrators (two of whom were also members of the faculty) drawn from offices intimately involved with undergraduates, such as the Office of the Vice-Provost and Dean of Undergraduate Studies, the Office of Admissions, the Office of Student Affairs, and the Office of the Registrar. These individuals brought to the study a vast amount of knowledge and experience with undergraduates that was invaluable for eliciting interview data as well as analysis and interpretation of our findings. The interviewers were assigned to students on the same basis that freshmen are assigned to academic advisers, namely, by initial area of academic interest: the natural sciences, social sciences, humanities, engineering, and premedical studies. The interviewers assigned to a given group usually came from a cognate educational background. Each interviewer stayed with his or her original set of fifteen or so students, irrespective of any subsequent shifts in the students' interests.

The interview formats for the four years varied considerably, partly by design and partly by default. During the first year of study our intention was primarily to obtain global impressions. The interviewers were given guidance with respect to the general areas to explore, but they were not given a specific set of questions to probe. The resulting interview reports were therefore wide-ranging but not well focused.

With the sophomore year the interviews were made more structured. Six broad areas were identified, with many subdivisions (Appendix II). We thereby sought to focus on discrete issues that we thought would be particularly germane for the sophomore year; we also hoped to obtain more uniformity in the interview reports. In subsequent years we relaxed this structure slightly because the interviewers found the sophomore-year approach too restrictive; in the junior and senior interviews, general areas were identified and sample questions were supplied for each area but interviewers were free to stray into areas that had special relevance for their students.

This semistructured format produced the most interesting and useful interviews.

We have used the material from the interview reports quite extensively. All comments attributed to students are quoted directly and all of the quotations are authentic. We have changed the names of students and removed self-revealing details to protect their anonymity. To help maintain some sense of authenticity with respect to names, we have switched names, often relying on more common names and excluding unusual ones. Within a given chapter, a student who is quoted or referred to more than once carries the same assigned name each time. But the same name may be used to designate different individuals in different chapters (thus, there may be a Careerist "John," as well as a Striver "John").

In dealing with the interviewer comments, we have quoted and paraphrased their comments as well as constructed student profiles and statements in our own words based on their information.

Other Sources of Data. The Senior Survey and the Curriculum Study, previously mentioned, provide broad, longitudinal contexts within which to view the findings of the Cohort Study.

For the years that these three projects were concurrently in progress, their findings have been closely integrated. Thus, although the Senior Survey questionnaire is ordinarily administered anonymously, the respondents who were subjects in the Cohort Study identified themselves. This made it possible for us to use a number of items from the Senior Survey to measure student satisfaction with the undergraduate experience and the degree to which students felt they had succeeded in substantive academic areas.

Similarly, the Curriculum Study files supplied us with the full transcripts of the Cohort students, so that we could generate such academic variables as grade point average, proportion of units taken in courses of a given type, and the like. A full description of the data base, the types of analyses made possible by the Curriculum Study, and a five-year overview of findings is given in Boli, Katchadourian, and Mahoney (1983). We are also preparing a five-year retrospective analysis of the findings of the Senior Survey (Katchadourian and Boli, forthcoming).

Study Sample

The 20 percent random sample of 320 students closely matched the rest of the freshman class with respect to all available background variables including gender, ethnicity, high school background, Scholastic Aptitude Test (SAT) scores, and preliminary academic interests. The material presented in Chapters Four through Seven is based solely on this original cohort of students who entered Stanford as freshmen—they are the students we have in mind when we refer to the study sample. The transfer students will be discussed only in Chapter Three.

Some 57 percent of the students in the sample were men and 43 percent were women, the usual sex ratio at Stanford over the past two decades. Caucasians comprised 82 percent of the total; Asian Americans, Blacks, and Chicanos and other Hispanics comprised 6 percent each, for a total of 18 percent minority students. A small percentage, less than 3 percent, of the students in these groups were from foreign countries.

Most of the students came from public high schools, but a substantial minority (28 percent) came from private schools. They had very high SAT scores, with a mean verbal score of 600 and a mean mathematics score of 654, as compared to national mean scores of 429 and 470. These students did very well in high school; 24 percent were ranked number one or two in their graduating class, although an equal proportion were ranked lower than number fifteen.

For a number of other background characteristics we have information only for the sample but not the rest of the class, but we assume that the sample was representative in these dimensions also. The families of our subjects were of very high socioeconomic status: Eighteen percent of them had yearly family incomes (in 1981) of $100,000 or higher, 57 percent had incomes of more than $50,000, and only 24 percent under $30,000. Their parents were highly educated: Eighty-two percent of the fathers and 62 percent of the mothers were college graduates, and 48 percent of the fathers had advanced degrees. Using Hollingshead's categories (Hollingshead and Redlich, 1958) of occupational classification, we find that 66 percent of the fathers were major professionals or executives (16 percent doctors, 22 percent corporate executives, 9 percent college professors, 6 percent lawyers) and an additional 20 percent were lesser professionals or executives (including 7 percent engineers). Only 14 percent were minor professionals, clerical workers, or skilled blue-collar workers.

Clearly, these students are by no means typical of the entire American student population. Stanford undergraduates come from high-status families and they have done exceptionally well in high school, both in their academic work and in their extracurricular activities. It is therefore fair to ask if findings based on a Stanford sample are applicable elsewhere, or even if findings based on the class of 1981 are applicable to the class of 1985. We believe they are.

First, Stanford students are quite typical of the students in highly selective private universities as a whole, and they are not much different in most respects from the students in private universities in general—in the ACE freshman surveys, their attitudes, goals, career and major choices, and family backgrounds are remarkably similar to those of these larger student populations. Second, Stanford's undergraduate program is structured in ways quite comparable to the programs at other private universities, and in many respects it is not markedly different from the undergraduate programs at most public universities. Hence, Stanford and its students are probably a good deal less distinctive than popular images may suggest, and the experiences of Stanford students have a great deal in common with those of students at other institutions.

As to whether the findings for the class of 1981 apply to more recent cohorts of students, the answer is both yes and no. Our work with the Senior Survey and other studies reveals that change occurs only very slowly, in general; student attitudes, choice of major, course selections, and other activities look very much the same from one year to the next. Some things are indeed changing, such as the proportion of ethnic minorities in the freshman class (18 percent in 1977, up to 25 percent in 1984), but we think that such change is largely overwhelmed by the constancy of the general ethos of the university and the normal inertia that characterizes student academic and career orientations.

If our study had attempted to ascertain the precise proportion of students with various academic orientations, such as the percentage of students with an exclusively careerist orientation or the percentage who make liberal education their primary focus in college, we would have had more cause for worry since such proportions are bound to change. Instead we are concerned with the elucidation of general trends and the development of a typology of academic orientation that helps us understand students and improve their education, which are more general issues with broad ramifications. Hence we feel confident that the insights we have gained from the class of 1981 are quite generally applicable to other graduating classes, at least up to now.

Our Typology of Academic Orientation

One may get the impression from the brief description of the sample that the Stanford undergraduate population is highly homogenous. With respect to some variables, such as their records of high school performance, that is true. But when one gets to see these students at closer range, their differences become much more salient; at the intimate range of individual lives, the diversity is almost bewildering. Some specific examples will illustrate this.

Many of our students come from the metropolis of Los Angeles; but Barbara came from a California desert community of only fifteen people, of whom five were members of her own family. One student grew up in a Park Avenue apartment, others in the barrio. Steven spent all but one weekend of his junior year on trips home, to the beach, and flying to various vacation spots; Debra worked during all of her vacations to relieve her father of the parental obligation specified in her work study package. Many students work at standard college jobs like hashing; Michael was an accomplished jet engine mechanic specializing in DC-8s and DC-10s. It is not unusual for some students to party through the night; Jeremy worked as a forklift operator on the night shift for two years. Many athletically inclined students rarely go indoors; a few students hardly ever see the sun. Roger was socially awkward and probably did not have a single date; Maria was happily married by her junior year.

The majority of undergraduates led relatively uneventful and happy lives. But among our sample, there were also students who faced turmoil and tragedy: One young man was shot in a holdup while working in a gas station; a young woman was sexually assaulted by a group of men; an athlete became a quadriplegic through a spinal injury; another student succumbed to a fatal illness. The brother of one student mutilated himself in a psychotic fit; other students suffered through painful parental divorces and assorted family crises. Before the end of her junior year Sandra's parents had divorced, her older brother had been hospitalized for alcoholism, her younger brother had embraced religion in a bizarre way, her younger sister was discovered to have breast cancer, and Sandra broke up with her long-term boyfriend (yet she could still say to the interviewer, "It has been a good year, verging on great").

With the matrix of these life experiences, students exhibited a rich variety of academic and career choices. Subjects in our sample majored in over forty academic areas. They chose from a catalogue of several thousand courses and planned to go in dozens of career directions. While four out of five wanted to be doctors, lawyers, engineers, or go into business, others included an ornithologist headed for South America and a casino manager headed for Reno; one student yearned to be president of the United States, another a pianist on a cruise ship to Tahiti.

To investigate the issues outlined in Chapter One, we have tried to impose some order on this remarkable diversity through a typology based on students' attitudes with respect to career preparation and liberal education in college. We will describe our typology of academic orientation in some detail in a moment, but it is important to raise first some precautions in interpreting it.

Every typology is arbitrary to some extent because it is an external pattern imposed on social reality, and ours is no different in this respect. By classifying individual students into four distinct types, we have severed the naturally occurring linkages between them. Like trees that have been plucked out of the earth and placed in planters, the normal intermingling of roots and commonality of soil that sustains them is thereby lost. We must live with the fact that classifying individuals makes them sharper at the boundaries, more stereotyped, and less real. Yet we hope that our typology does not do undue violence to social reality and that the types of students we identify are easily recognizable and familiar to all.

Questionnaire Basis of the Typology. The typology was developed on the basis of questionnaire data after all data collection was completed. The interview material was therefore neither used in developing the typology nor could the typology have influenced the perceptions of the interviewers in any way.

The typology is based on two scales that measure respectively the careerism and intellectualism of students. The scales are, in turn, built on a number of disparate items from the questionnaires; they are listed in Table 1. Further details on the methodology of constructing the typology are given at the end of Appendix II.

The variables selected for the scales are theoretically related to the concepts of intellectualism and careerism, and each of the two sets of variables has high intercorrelations among the variables it includes. We had expected that the careerism and intellectualism scales would be negatively correlated with each other—students high in careerism would be low in intellectualism, and vice versa. Given the picture we have drawn in Chapter One, this expectation appears to be almost tautological. But in fact our two scales turned out to be unrelated to each other (Pearson's $r = 0.10$). This means that from the point of view of students, careerism and intellectualism are not mutually exclusive or necessarily in conflict. An undergraduate can be high in careerism and either high or low in intellectualism, and vice versa. This is one of our most important findings, to which we shall return time and again. The key issue it points to is that rising careerism does not doom intellectualism as a matter of principle. Rather, the question is how well students can manage to combine the simultaneous goals of career and intellectual interests.

A scattergram showing the distribution of students in a grid cross-tabulating the careerism and intellectualism scales is shown graphically in Figure 4. It is clear from the scattergram that the two scales are largely independent of one another; the students are widely dispersed across the grid, and knowing a student's intellectualism score provides little aid in predicting the student's careerism score. This observation applies to both men and women.

Table 1. Items Used in the Intellectualism and Careerism Scales.

Intellectualism Scale	*Careerism Scale*
Reasons for attending college:	
Learning to think critically	Specialized preparation for future
Exposure to different viewpoints	career
General liberal education	Acquisition of marketable skills
Developing ethical and moral	Preparation for graduate/
values	professional school
Developing artistic and esthetic	Establishing professional contacts
taste and judgment	for the future
Making friends	Future financial security
Developing skills in dealing with	Acquiring technical/
people	preprofessional skills
Characteristics desired in a major:	
Interesting subject	Step toward graduate school
Intellectually challenging	Useful in career field
Good teaching	Many career options
Departmental faculty accessible to	
students	
Characteristics desired in a career:	
Requires creativity and originality	Social status and prestige
Intellectually challenging	Job security
Service to others	High income
Opportunities to work with people	Public recognition

In building a typology from scales of questionnaire items added together, one cannot avoid using some set of arbitrary cutting points to differentiate one type of student from another. To minimize the misclassification of students that such arbitrary points can produce, we first divided each of the scales in thirds. In this scheme, one third of the students are classified as *low*, one third as *medium,* and one third as *high* on the intellectualism scale. This process is repeated for the careerism scale, classifying one third of the students as low, medium, or high in careerism. By cross-tabulating the two variables we produced a nine-cell grid, as shown in Figure 5. Students in the four corner groups are the extreme cases in a statistical sense; they give the highest or lowest careerist and

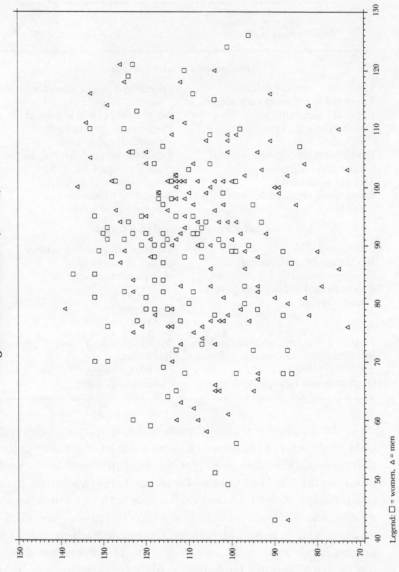

Figure 4. Cross-Tabulation of Careerism and Intellectualism Scales, Original Cohort Students (N = 236).

Legend: □ = women, △ = men

Figure 5. Schematic Representation of the Typology (Nine Cell).

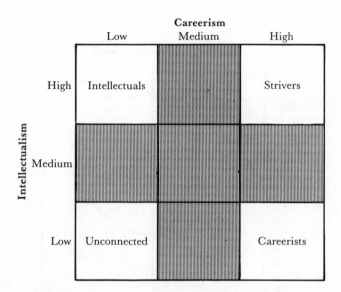

intellectualist responses. These students approximate the hypothetical "pure" types within each category and we shall refer to them as the *core groups*.

The core groups define the four basic academic orientations of our typology. They consist of students who rate *high* on the careerism scale and *low* on the intellectualism scale; *low* on the careerism scale and *high* on the intellectualism scale; *high* on both scales; and *low* on both scales. We have called these groups *Careerists, Intellectuals, Strivers,* and the *Unconnected,* respectively, with some reservations that we shall express shortly.

If we use only the students in the core groups for our data analyses, there is little chance that they will be misclassified. But this stringent approach is costly because it excludes more than half the subjects from further consideration. If we divide the careerism and intellectualism scales at their respective medians (instead of in thirds) we can then classify all students into one of the four types (Figure 6; please disregard the circle in the center for the moment). This approach is certain to misclassify some students because the

Figure 6. Schematic Representation of the Typology (Four Cell).

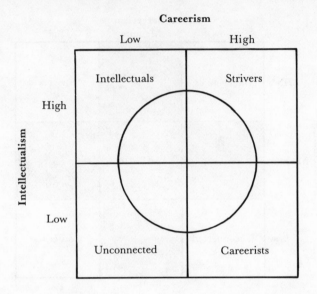

Careerism

difference between high intellectualism and low intellectualism, for instance, is but a single point at the median. This shortcoming is compensated, however, by the inclusion of sixty or so students within each category, which makes possible more extensive statistical analyses.

If the students outside the core within each category were significantly different in their academic orientation from those within the core, their inclusion in the data analyses would result in a serious distortion of what each of these types is supposed to represent. Fortunately, as we proceeded with the data analysis we discovered that the more inclusive model using all students yields results that are very similar to those obtained with the core groups. In no case are the conclusions derived from the larger groupings at variance with those based on the core group data only. We therefore decided to use the more inclusive model as the basis of all of our statistical analyses, presented in Chapters Four through Seven. The tables for all these analyses are presented in Appendix IV.

Problem of Labels. A special burden of all classificatory systems is the need for appropriate labels. The most forthright designations for our typology would be descriptive, such as the High Careerism/Low Intellectualism group. But since such labels are clumsy and drab, we have, after much searching, settled on Careerist, Intellectualist, Striver, and the Unconnected.

These designations, while serviceable, are far from perfect, as we shall discuss in subsequent chapters dealing with these four categories. The ideal label should represent accurately and succinctly the key characteristics of a given group without carrying strong positive or negative connotations. If there are labels that could better achieve this task with respect to the four types we have constructed, we have not found them. When we look at the labels used in other typologies, we find we are in good company, though that is small comfort.

We do take heart, nonetheless, from the fact that our labels are attached to reasonably discrete entities that have a clear empirical base. When we call someone a Careerist, we mean that the student scores high on one set of variables and low on the other. Though we have chosen these labels with an eye to their commonly understood meanings, readers should not be distracted by the connotations that these terms may carry in other contexts (a pitfall we also succumb to once in a while).

Use of Interview Reports. Members of the interview team were asked to submit written reports for each yearly interview. This they did, by and large, with exemplary thoroughness, but there is considerable variability in scope and richness of the interview reports that would make any systematic content analysis difficult. Nonetheless, the interview materials (especially those reports written with vividness and perspicacity) have made a tremendous contribution to our understanding of the students.

The questionnaire data constitute objective (quantifiable) indicators of subjective responses. The interview reports are subjective judgments by interviewers of observable student behavior. But the interview reports also add a measure of independent objectivity that cannot be found in the questionnaire responses. A student may claim to be interested in liberal education but the interviewer is in a position to accept or reject this contention on the basis of collaborative evidence—such as the kinds of courses the student has taken or what the student says about the professors in his or her courses.

The interview materials add flesh to the statistical skeletons fashioned from the questionnaire data. They provide a human texture to disembodied responses and make the data come alive. We rely heavily on the interview reports in subsequent chapters to illustrate and document student perceptions on a wide range of issues. And we provide biographical profiles to exemplify each of the four categories of students.

Although we have not used the interview data to second-guess the questionnaire-based classification of our students, the interview reports have helped to refine and expand our understanding of the typology. This has been particularly important with respect to the variance within each group and estimates of the prevalence of each type.

Changes Among Categories of the Typology. As we have noted, the typology is based on responses to the freshman and sophomore questionnaires combined. As such, it represents a one-time classification of the students that we cannot duplicate with responses from the junior- or senior-year questionnaires. Hence, directly studying changes among the typology categories is not feasible. This is not accidental; we combined the responses from the two questionnaires in order to include a large number of variables to ensure that we had reliable measurements. This approach necessarily sacrificed the possibility of studying change.

However, we can study change more approximately by using secondary scales that are based on the responses for individual years. Here we will use two sets of careerism and intellectualism scales, the first made up of freshman questionnaire items and the second made up of junior questionnaire items. The senior questionnaire cannot be used because it does not have two of the three sections used in the scales (reasons for going to college and characteristics desired in a major). Nonetheless, we think the junior-year responses are adequate for this comparison because students are very unlikely to change their basic attitudes significantly between the junior and senior years.

We find that the freshman intellectualism score is correlated .60 with the junior intellectualism score, and the freshman careerism score is correlated .58 with the junior careerism score. These figures indicate a strong relationship between freshman and junior attitudes, but they also show that there is considerable change—less than 40 percent of the variance in junior-year scores is accounted for by freshman-year scores.

A closer look shows such change to be more limited within the core groups: Seventy-five percent of the students in the core groups fall into the same type in the freshman and junior years, while only 25 percent move from one type to another. The amount of change for each category is roughly constant—about one fifth to one quarter of the students in each type change to another type by the junior year. But none of these shifts are between groups that are polar opposites: No Careerists become Intellectuals, none of the Unconnected become Strivers, and vice versa. Instead the shifts involve Careerists becoming Strivers, or the Unconnected becoming Intellectuals, and so on. This means that either the careerism or the intellectualism variable is shifting for a given student, but not both.

When the careerism and intellectualism scales are split at the median and all available students are classified, there is still little movement between polar groups. Students do shift categories in less extreme ways in about half of the cases, but because this version of the typology does not differentiate students as sharply as the core groups, we cannot separate true change from simple misclassification in one or both years.

Prevalence and Intensity. As soon as one becomes acquainted with our typology, the inevitable question arises: What is the proportion of the four types within the study population? The issue of prevalence is both interesting and important. After all, would it not make a tremendous difference if we found Careerists to be 90 percent instead of 10 percent of the student population?

Unfortunately, our present research cannot answer that question with any accuracy; the derivation of our typology does not allow it. Recall that we obtained the four groups by splitting the careerism and intellectualism scales at their median. In principle, this approach yields four groups with equal numbers of students in each. Splitting the scales elsewhere would produce a different set of numbers. In neither case would the proportions have any bearing on the proportions of the four types in the sample population.

The fact that each of the four core groups happens to have unequal numbers of students (ranging from nineteen to thirty-two) does not reveal anything about their true prevalence. Rather, it is purely a statistical artifact due to the relationship between the careerism and intellectualism scales and the particular cutting points used to divide them.

The interview reports allow us to remedy this problem to some extent. Having established a general profile for each of the four types and worked with them in many statistical analyses, we went back to the interview reports and read them "blind"—without knowing what category each student belonged to in the typology. This more intuitive approach is subject to numerous methodological perils that we need not spell out. But within these limitations, our best estimate is that the Intellectuals comprise the smallest portion of students, 15 to 20 percent of the total, while the Strivers are the most numerous, accounting for 30 percent to one third of the total. The Careerists and the Unconnected account for about 25 percent each, with Careerists perhaps being slightly more numerous than the Unconnected. Hence we find that students are most likely to combine strong intellectual interests with strong career interests, while they are least likely to have strong intellectual interests that are not accompanied by strong career interests.

To obtain a more reliable picture of the prevalence of our four types, we would need to do another study that would apply predetermined criteria for each category to a fresh sample of students. We have no illusions, however, that even the most rigorous methodology will yield crisp and clear figures since we are not dealing here with discrete and mutually exclusive entities. People are not pigeons; they do not fit in holes.

The scattergram makes it amply clear that although there may be some "pure" types in the corners, the majority of students are to be found in the amorphous center. The circle superimposed on the four-cell grid in Figure 6 reflects this reality whereby students within it constitute the marginal members of the types in which they are classified. The interview reports reinforce this view. Within each category there is a spectrum of intensity with which the characteristics of each type are manifested; at their low ends, students in the four groups can hardly be differentiated. Furthermore, the reports reveal that in at least some of the categories there are fairly distinctive subtypes, which we shall describe in subsequent chapters.

Other Typologies in Higher Education

Our cautioning remarks about typologies are not meant to discredit them but to place them in proper perspective. As we hope our own study demonstrates, they can be very illuminating if properly used. Since our typology of academic orientation is by no means the first or the only such attempt in higher education, it may be useful to compare our scheme with those of others.

Perhaps the most widely known typology in research on American higher education is that of Clark and Trow (1960, 1966). Working primarily with Berkeley students, they identified four student subcultures, labeled the Vocational, Academic, Collegiate, and Nonconformist. These authors maintained that the subcultures do not directly correspond to types of students since students move in and out of a variety of subcultural environments; this was a distinction often missed by others. Clark and Trow's typology has been widely employed and critiqued by other researchers (see, for example, Gottlieb and Hodgkins, 1963; Peterson, 1965; Warren, 1968; Ellis, Parelius, and Parelius, 1971).

Feldman and Newcomb (1969) present a chart comparing the Clark and Trow typology to a number of others, including Newcomb's own scheme (Scholar, Creative Individualist, Wild One, Political Activist, Social Group, and Leader types; see Newcomb, Koenig, Flacks, and Warwick, 1967; Flacks, 1963), Keniston's (1966) more impressionistic groupings (Professionalist, Activist, Disaffiliate, Big Man on Campus, Apprentice, Underachiever, and Gentleman-in-Waiting types), and several typologies that derive more directly from Clark and Trow's work, including those by Warren (1966, 1968) and Pemberton (1963). Correspondences between these typologies and the Clark-Trow subcultures are fairly easy to draw, except that a number of the types in the later typologies are outside the scope of Clark and Trow's conceptual scheme—for instance, Keniston's Underachiever type, Warren's Undirected orientation, and Pemberton's Social-Service orientation have no place in the Clark and Trow categories.

As shown in Table 2, there is fair correspondence between two of our categories and those of a number of others. Clark and Trow's Vocational subculture corresponds quite closely to our concept of careerism; our Careerists are very similar to Keniston's Apprentice type. Similarly, Clark and Trow's Academic subculture can be directly related to our concept of intellectualism, and our Intellectuals are roughly equivalent to Newcomb's Scholars and Keniston's Professionalists. Note, however, that two of our student types cut across these subcultures: Strivers are involved in both the Vocational and Academic subcultures, while the Unconnected are notable for their lack of involvement with either. Furthermore, Clark and Trow's other two types of subculture, the Collegiate and the Nonconformist, reflect dimensions of the college experience that have no counterpart in our typology. The Collegiate subculture is clearly not intellectual in orientation but stresses instead a strong commitment to campus life and student organizations (the "Joe College" style), while the Nonconformist subculture is largely intellectual in orientation but alienated from organized activity; neither of these subcultures speaks directly to the issue of careerism, and they only indirectly address the issue of intellectualism.

Other research that has produced important typologies is based on personality characteristics. The best-known personality typology is that of Holland and his associates (Holland, 1966, 1973; Osipow, Ashby, and Wall, 1966; Folsom, 1969), which investigates the determinants of occupational choice. Holland's typology identifies six distinct personality types, described as Realistic, Intellectual (Investigative), Social, Conventional, Enterprising, and Artistic, and then relates these types to a classification of corresponding model environments (similar to the subculture idea) to produce his theory of vocational choice. For Holland the typology describes both students and subcultures (environments), and the theory predicts that students of a given type will choose an occupation located in an environment matching that type.

Holland's Investigative personality corresponds rather well to our Intellectuals, though his Artistic personality contains

Table 2. Typologies in Comparison.

	Careerist	Intellectual	Striver	Unconnected	Other
Clark and Trow (1966)	Vocational subculture	Academic subculture	—	—	Collegiate subculture (Nonconformist subculture)
Warren (1966, 1968)	Vocational, Uncommitted orientations	Academic, Intellectual orientations	—	(Undirected orientation)	Autonomous, Social Frotest, Traditional, Self-Centered, Conformist orientations
Pemberton (1963)	Technical-Vocational orientation	Academic-Theoretical orientation	—	—	Academic Conformity, Nonconformity, Social-Service orientations
Keniston (1966)	Apprentice	Professionalist	—	(Disaffiliate)	Activist, Big Man on Campus, Underachiever, Gentleman in Waiting
Newcomb, Koenig, Flacks, and Warwick (1967)	—	Scholar	(Leader)	—	Creative Individualist, Wild One, Political Activist, Social Group
Holland (1966, 1973)	(Enterprising personality)	(Investigative personality)	—	—	Realistic, Social, Conventional, Artistic personalities
Korn (1968)	Career group	Intellectual interests group	—	—	Grades group
Allport-Vernon-Lindzey (1960)	Economic type	Theoretical, Aesthetic types	—	—	Social, Political, Religious types

Note: Parentheses indicate partial correspondence of categories.

elements that we also associate with intellectual interests and commitment. The Enterprising personality fits our Careerists to a large extent—such a person is essentially business oriented and displays leadership qualities—but some aspects of the Social and Conventional types also fit the Careerists, and the Social type in fact corresponds most closely to Clark and Trow's Collegiate subculture. The Realistic type, on the other hand, has no correspondence in our typology, and the Social and Conventional types are also not easy to match.

Another line of personality research uses the Omnibus Personality Inventory scales (Heist and Yonge, 1968) to investigate how student personality characteristics change over time (Korn, 1968; Elton, 1967; Clark and others, 1972). These scales include such dimensions as estheticism, social maturity, masculinity-femininity, impulse expression (seeking instant gratification), and so on. Other personality scales have also been used, such as Adorno's ethnocentrism (E) and authoritarianism (F) scales (Adorno and others, 1950). Only rarely do researchers construct actual typologies from these personality measures; more typically, they measure the amount of change students display on the various scales over the four college years. But Korn (1968), for example, has used these scales to validate and explore the consequences of a typology of students that identifies three "function groups" among Berkeley and Stanford students in the 1960s: those interested primarily in getting good grades, those concerned mostly about preparing for careers, and those interested mostly in intellectual issues and pursuits. The latter two types match our Careerists and Intellectuals rather well, but the grades-oriented students do not fit in our scheme.

Finally, Allport and Vernon's pioneering work in their Study of Values (see Allport and Vernon, 1931) has led to a large body of research on college students (see Allport, Vernon, and Lindzey, 1960). The Allport-Vernon-Lindzey approach measures the importance of six different value dimensions: Theoretical, Economic, Aesthetic, Social, Political, and Religious. They equate these dimensions with different student types, where a student is classified by the value area to which he or she attaches the most importance. Clearly enough, the Theoretical type is similar to our

Intellectual (with some of the Aesthetic thrown in), while the Economic type matches our Careerist.

There is a common methodological thread that runs through most of these typologies. Although the student types and subcultures they describe may be quite true to life, it is often unclear what their common denominators are. In most instances, these typologies mix and combine several dimensions so that one type is defined by one set of factors and another type by a different set of factors. For instance, in the case of Clark and Trow, the ingredients that make up the Vocational subculture are not the same as those that characterize the Collegiate subculture. The categories are not mutually exclusive nor even directly comparable to one another.

The approach that other researchers have taken is to describe the student population or environment phenomenologically; they show how academic and social life appears to be organized by institutions or the students themselves. Our approach, on the other hand, is more analytical: Our interest lies in understanding careerism and intellectualism, so our typology explicitly categorizes students on these two dimensions. All four of our types are based on the interplay of the careerism and intellectualism variables and nothing else; our categories are exhaustive and, within limits, mutually exclusive.

We see the use of typologies more as a vehicle than as an end in itself. The identification of student types is interesting and useful primarily insofar as the types help elucidate the processes underlying these academic orientations. Each of these academic orientations carries its own assets and liabilities, as we shall have occasion to spell out in succeeding chapters.

3

---···∽···---

Challenges and Changes
in the Undergraduate
Years

"Registration was not as bad as I feared. The worst part was handing over my lifetime savings, all in one shot. It was the first check I had ever written and it was devastating to say the least." Thus began life at Stanford University for one young woman. Over the next four years there would be many more of the best of times and the worst of times for her as she lay the foundations for her future life and career.

The college years constitute an important developmental period during which late teenagers are transformed into young adults. Whether or not this period is seen as a discrete developmental phase of life ("youth"), it is clearly marked by changes in physical appearance, personality characteristics, and social interactions. Within this larger matrix, college students fashion their educational and career choices that they must live with the rest of their lives.

What is the academic setting within which these choices are made? Is college one continuous process or is it marked by nodal points and distinctive transitions? Do students follow predictable paths or does everyone blaze a new trail? Does each of the four undergraduate years have its high and low points? Are notions like the sophomore slump myth or reality? These are the sorts of questions that we shall address in this chapter.

Common Themes in College Years

The official demarcations between the four years of college are not always congruent with students' class rank as perceived socially. Since units of credits acquired determine when a student attains a given academic status, students cross class boundary lines at different chronological points. A student with many units of advanced placement credit may technically finish the freshman year at the end of the first quarter while others who lag in accumulating units may still be "freshmen" well into their second year of college. Nonetheless, one can speak with fair confidence about the *freshman, sophomore, junior,* and *senior* years as meaningful entities with their own characteristic goals, challenges, and high and low points.

The progression of these four years constitutes the life cycle of the undergraduate experience. As with the major stages of life in general, they have their commonalities and differences. No two persons ever have precisely the same experiences over time, yet everyone shares some things with others. Thus, one may usefully compare the freshman year to the "childhood" phase of college life; the sophomore year to an academic form of "adolescence"; the junior year to "adulthood"; and the senior year to an undergraduate form of "old age."

Every student goes through each of these phases in a pattern influenced by a host of considerations. In Chapters Four to Seven we will deal with the distinctive pathways of Careerists, Intellectuals, Strivers, and the Unconnected. But in this chapter we shall be concerned with the commonalities of student experiences irrespective of academic orientation. We do this for two reasons. First, the natural rhythms of the four years are important to know about, in and of themselves. Second, the similarities among our four types of students are as important as the differences. By learning about them as a group first, we will have a backdrop against which to discuss their differences when we consider each type individually.

The standard pattern for Stanford students is to enter as freshmen and to graduate in four years (a pattern by no means shared by students in all other institutions). Our discussion of the four years will therefore be primarily based on this expectation.

There are two smaller groups, however, who deviate from this and should not be neglected. Some seventy students are admitted each of the sophomore and junior years as transfer students (joining some sixteen hundred incoming freshmen). A much smaller number leaves Stanford each year to study elsewhere or drop out of college altogether. Since these groups add an important dimension to the main body of the Cohort subjects, we shall discuss them briefly at the end of this chapter.

The material presented in this section is based on three sources of data: the interview reports, student responses on the yearly questionnaires to a number of specific items, and student responses in the senior year to a set of questionnaire items asking them to give retrospective descriptions of each of the four years.

Freshman Year

The most significant aspect of the freshman year is the challenge of adjusting to a new academic environment. The initial reaction on entering college is one of euphoria. The dream of coming to college is fulfilled; the pride of being selected by an elite institution is highly gratifying. But the giddiness subsides soon enough and is replaced by a sense of being overwhelmed.

Students who got straight A's in high school now must struggle to keep up with their work. The results of the first test may come as a splash of cold water. Student body presidents, accomplished musicians, star athletes, science contest winners, charming personalities, the owners of fancy cars—all now find themselves among innumerable others with similar and other claims to fame. High school celebrities sink into campus anonymities. A student whose dorm was studded with musical talent once asked the Dean of Admissions if she had been selected to act as the audience. Other comments by freshmen about their fellow students:

"Everyone is so bright and full of energy."

"Unbelievably wonderful, talented, fantastic!"

"Oh my God, I am so inadequate. There are all these talents around me and I have none."

"There are some pretty amazing people at Stanford. There was one guy with forty-five units of advanced placement credit. My roommate was a gymnast on her way to the Olympics, I think, until she had a hernia. She does flips down the hall. And there is another one in my dorm who is an outstanding violinist."

"They never cease to amaze me. They are all so talented. I am still finding little things out about them. For example, I just found out during a guitar sing-out in our dorm that my roommate has the most beautiful voice. I sometimes wonder how I got into Stanford, when I compare myself to others. They are all very well-rounded individuals, honest and open. They are good friends to be around. I am going to find it very hard in the summer to be without them."

The pull of social relationships, extracurricular activities, and the prospect of having a good time make enormous demands. The need to work to earn money adds an extra burden. Time becomes a scarce commodity, and its effective management a vital skill. Homesickness for some and parental intrusiveness for others cause problems. The exposure at close range to people of different ethnic and social backgrounds may have disconcerting effects.

Insecurity and a drop in confidence are common reactions to the onslaught of these new experiences. As the year progresses, however, most students learn to cope and feel less anxious about keeping their heads above water as they learn the ins and outs of college life. The following excerpts from the interview reports illustrate these points.

During the first month at Stanford, Heather was delighted with everything: "This is the place for me!"

Margaret ran around "like a chicken with its head cut off" for several weeks and lost ten pounds. She "loved it."

"My initial Stanford experience was the fact that I had to grow up fast! There was a lot to do and no one to tell me when to do it. I had to assume the responsibility of settling into my room. I had to take the

initiative to make new friends and deal with them as individuals who are not like me but just as individualistic and imaginative. I had to somehow form a plan for my next four years, using my adviser's help and the experience of upperclassmen."

As a freshman, George was baffled by the diversity and heterogeneity of Stanford. Not only was there no discernible focus to the various plans, programs, and pursuits taken by students, but there seemed to be a distinct barrier to establishing a personal sense of purpose. There were so many attractions and so many opportunities and possibilities that the place was positively overwhelming. He was also surprised by how much time, money, and energy people spent on issues and activities that were not purely academic.

"There is an automatic increase in maturity as soon as you arrive here. Perhaps subtle, but the change to college freshman, age eighteen, from high school senior, age eighteen, is definite . . . I am wondering when the shiny-newness, Christmas-present feeling will wear off—it's been three weeks and the excitement is still there. I have been told by the 'experienced' that things will soon become a bit humdrum, but look, I have met an alternate for the Olympic sailing team, somebody who loves hot air ballooning, and quite a few others like that. I know there are many, many more fantastic people all over this place and as long as I keep meeting them, it will take me a lot longer than even four years— the excitement will remain."

Some of the reactions shown by freshmen are obviously a function of suddenly being on their own in a place where the opportunities for fun seem boundless. David thought he "might just as well be in Disneyland . . . You could do anything you want—stay up late, get high, what have you." The lack of supervision made him feel "weird." One student was reported to have smoked pot every night during the first quarter until he finally settled down. This newly found sense of independence makes some self-confident ("I enjoyed the shock of being responsible for myself"), and even the excesses are relished ("it's great to be with a bunch of crazy freshmen"; "I like to get rowdy . . . maturity is a sham"; "I will be doing serious stuff all my life so I might as well do these other things while I can"). Such exuberance is counterbalanced by the tremendous seriousness with which others get into academics, a point we shall discuss shortly. Above all, there is a sense of growing up fast: "I have grown up more in eight months here than I have in four years of high school."

Emancipation from home is a mixed blessing. Some freshmen get desperately homesick (one student observed that the frenetic activity in the freshman year is an antidote to such feelings). They miss their parents and they miss their friends. Those who have been catered to at home now yearn for lost services. Others who have carried heavy burdens at home feel relieved. Carol lived on a farm and had to help look after the animals, as well as her infirm grandfather, so she luxuriated in the feeling that she now had only herself to look after. Dana, who had been overly attached to her mother, enjoyed her independence ("it makes you feel so much better to do what you want to do"). Freshmen deal with these issues of separation by simultaneously keeping in touch with their families and becoming more self-reliant. In an ingenious improvisation, a group of friends in a freshman dorm started a game known as The Family whereby everyone took on some family role to play, such as being mother, father, brother, sister, cousin, uncle, and so on.

Students are aware that their perception of parents changes significantly as a result of coming to college. There is often a greater feeling of closeness to and appreciation of parents as individuals. Ralph had left home in a state of full rebellion because his parents were "controlling his life." After finding the freedom he sought at college, he began to rethink and revalue his relationships with his family and came to see them not as people who are "parents over him" but rather as friends whose advice and opinions he valued. His exposure to the "crudeness, rudeness, and indifference" of dorm life led him to appreciate his family's values more than he had ever done before. Jonathan's mother was such a dedicated lover of classical music that he got rather tired of listening to it over the years. Yet when he returned home for Christmas, he realized on hearing it again how much he loved it; it felt so good to be home, and home felt like such a different place from what he remembered.

Parents also change their perceptions of their children and their ways of dealing with them. Mary noted that her mother now respected her choices and did not argue over them (as a consequence, Mary felt more willing to tell her what was going on in her life). Another student's mother became "less of a mother and more of a friend." When parents behave as they always have, there is a sense of disappointment ("I have changed . . . I've grown up a lot, but my parents are still treating me the same").

No less significant are the consequences of freshmen discovering each other. In some of the excerpts earlier in this chapter, college students sound far more fascinated by their peers than by their courses and those who teach them. One student said that she thought socializing was important because others "have their own wisdom from which you might be able to gain." Other comments from interview reports on the subject of fellow students:

> The most memorable thing about the first year is "getting involved with people. Not just meeting people but talking with them about their lives; meeting people from different backgrounds and seeing how people make decisions and choices." All of this leads to the understanding that "your way is not the only way."

> "I can always pick up information, but I will never have the same opportunity to be with such a group of people again."

Getting acculturated into the college social structure is no less a task than becoming part of the academic side of college. Freshmen are very preoccupied with dorm life and interpersonal relationships more generally. This is understandable, given that most of the students are living on their own for the first time and suddenly have sole responsibility for their relationships. Most friendships are dorm based, and interaction with both dorm-mates and residence staff is intense. It is therefore not surprising that other students are considered to be one of the "best things" about college life.

Freshman dormitories reveal a strong sense of solidarity among their residents. Four-class dorms make up for lack of solidarity by the support and mentoring provided to freshmen by older students. Roommates are obviously crucial to the students' residential experiences. They can be a source of great joy ("my roommate is great") as well as tribulation: "We just try to exist . . . I have finally given up on him. Even when I say good morning, he replies, 'What's good about it?'" Generally, students are enormously tolerant and accommodating, which makes life easier for those who generate the noise but harder for those who have to bear with it: "People who have the worst taste in music want others to know about it."

There is a great deal of easy camaraderie among freshmen, but developing more intimate relationships is not easy. Women are either more reticent or have less need to complain about this aspect, but for many young men, getting close to the more "sought-after girls" is not easy. As one put it, the typical encounter at a party is "spotting a pretty girl at a distance, surrounded by five or six males." So there is loneliness even in the midst of social plenty, while others are highly adept at snaring friends. Some relationships turn out to be more puzzling and complicated than others.

Philip's roommate spent "a few weeks trying out different girls" and then settled on one of the freshmen women. The girlfriend now does his roommate's washing and ironing, corrects his papers, reviews and checks his problem sets, and writes drafts, or even finished products, of his various assignments. When Philip asked her why she put up with all this, her reply was that she "wouldn't do it for just a friend, but a boyfriend is different." What puzzles Philip is that this young woman is interesting, well read, and one of the few people that he likes to talk to. Hence, he has become a good friend of hers while she remains the girlfriend of his roommate.

Where do academics fit in all this? In the interview setting freshmen talk more spontaneously about social interactions than they do about academic interactions. Is it because they consider the latter less important, or is its importance taken for granted? A certain measure of conflict between the two is quite common. Diana called it her "split personality—Dr. Jekyll (studious) and Ms. Hyde (social)."

Far from neglecting their classes, freshmen generally tackle them with great determination, and for good reason. A year's worth of high school chemistry is covered in a week; the amount of reading in history is hard to believe. One fairly typical response is to try to keep up by working harder, only to discover that this does not always work:

"In the first three weeks of class I was running myself into the ground. I wanted desperately to get everything done and always stay on top of things. Unfortunately, I was staying up until 3:00 A.M. every night to do it. I knew I was in sad shape when I slept through my class at 11:00 A.M.! However, a friend who is a sophomore helped devise a study schedule for me so I am in bed by 12:30 A.M. at the latest."

The realization that how well you manage your time and how effectively you study is as important as how hard you study is one of the major discoveries of the freshman year. Another important task is adjusting one's expectations and recognizing one's limitations. Some students are crushed by their first B grade; others are more resilient. Chris had been preceded at Stanford by two high-achieving brothers. When he got a B in chemistry, he became a social recluse. Jessica came with high hopes of becoming a "Renaissance woman," but her "college dream" ran full tilt into "college reality." She recovered nicely nonetheless by reorienting herself into subjects she liked and could do well in: "I've come to terms with the fact that it is not morally wrong not to be able to do a chemistry problem set or to enjoy the humanities."

Not everyone faces the music; some do not care to and others already know the score. Many a course is dropped; others are squeaked by. It is not uncommon to hear that a student "blew" part or most of the year, but many other students do not miss a beat. Melissa took every tough course in sight, from advanced physics (where she was one of three women in a class of fifty) to philosophy. She was also highly active socially and played coed football, women's soccer, Ping-Pong, volleyball, softball, and inner tube water polo. Gerald had already decided to double-major in chemistry (where he had a full scholarship) and philosophy, then go to law school. He got all A's. The interviewer wrote:

He is a fellow who does very well on minimum commitment and effort. He seems remote from what goes on, but I want to be very tentative in that judgment. He's so sharp and so flip that he may just want to convey the style of an intellectual James Bond—able to accomplish any assignment but able to keep his distance from people and events (while never missing a trick).

Some measure of uncertainty is the order of the day in the freshman year. Only about 15 percent have concrete career plans. At best, about the same proportion have clear educational objectives. While many come to college being less than certain as to what they want, others lose their certainty after they get there: "I had everything set out for my four years here but when I got to Stanford I saw different options and my decisions became more fuzzy." But there are also those who come with very clear and sophisticated academic objectives. Alan wanted a "Robert Hutchins education"; Charlene put together her own "personal distribution requirements."

Early career decisions may be based on long-standing choices. Some students are already fairly advanced in their fields when they come to Stanford. More often students know what they do not want and work their way to a decision through a process of elimination. Introductory courses serve the important function of turning some students on and some other students away from a subject.

Students are quite adept, albeit somewhat uncomfortable, at living with uncertainty. A substantial number actually manage to remain unconnected through their entire undergraduate career (Chapter Seven). Yet some have a great need to have clear and concrete goals even into the distant future. Ingrid carried this so far as to fret over how she would handle the death of her husband in her old age!

As noted previously, we have obtained systematic data on student views of each of the undergraduate years through a section of the senior questionnaire. We asked students to describe each of the four years by pointing out the high and low points, the key issues they faced, and the major events that influenced their academic lives. They were also asked to list the four or five adjectives that best described each year. The more salient responses are presented in Table 3, where we have separated the items into three groups: qualities that most distinguish the freshman year from later years, qualities that distinguish the sophomore and junior years from other years, and qualities that distinguish the senior year from earlier years. Because this section used open-ended items, the percentage of students mentioning any given quality is

Table 3. Characterizations of the Undergraduate Years in Retrospect, Senior Questionnaire.

	Freshman (N = 237)	Sophomore (N = 233)	Junior (N = 232)	Senior (N = 230)
A. Qualities most pertinent to the freshman year				
Problems of adjustment	30%	4%	7%	2%
Exploration	21	6	3	4
Meeting new people	17	4	4	3
Learning about oneself	17	10	10	13
Hectic, crazy, frantic, wild	25	5	5	9
Afraid	5	0	a	1
Lack of motivation	a	4	3	6
Relaxed, low-key	2	6	3	9
Academics focal aspect	5	13	14	11
Bad experiences w/ classes, grades	14	12	9	3
Good experiences w/ classes, grades	11	15	21	19
(Ratio of good to bad experiences with classes, grades)	(0.8)	(1.2)	(2.3)	(6.3)
B. Qualities most pertinent to the sophomore and junior years				
Overseas experience	a	12	22	3
Discovered (declared) major	3	17	17	9
Difficult year academically, worked hard	7	11	12	7
No academic direction	15	14	5	3
Content with school	5	5	12	15
C. Qualities most pertinent to the senior year				
Concern for the future	4	6	17	50
Ready to leave	a	0	1	15
Not ready to leave, time is short	a	0	a	6
Happy, fun, rewarding	12	10	8	19
Depressed	8	12	9	1
Busy	3	3	4	8
Good living situation	11	19	13	10
Bad living situation	11	14	9	3
(Ratio of good to bad living situation)	(1.0)	(1.4)	(1.4)	(3.3)

[a]Less than 0.5%.

generally low. Hence the table is best understood by considering sets of items and the amount of change that occurs over time. These findings largely confirm what the more impressionistic interview reports reveal.

The freshman year is described in terms of adjustment problems, exploration, meeting new people, and learning about oneself. The emotional tone of the year is captured in such words as *hectic* and *crazy*, and although only 5 percent of the students mention fear as an aspect of the freshman experience, this is far more than in later years. Additional items suggest that overall the year is a comparatively tense one. Words such as *fun* and *rewarding* are not absent, but they occur in the context of an almost frenetic level of activity.

Only a few students describe the freshman year as relaxed, and lack of motivation is an extremely rare problem. The academic side of life is apparently less the focal point in the freshman year than in subsequent years, and academic experiences are mentioned in negative terms more often than positive ones. In later years the good outweighs the bad by a substantial margin. This pattern also holds, although less dramatically, for such other areas of life as residential experiences and romantic relationships.

Fortunately for the sanity of freshmen, the year is experienced in more positive terms at the time than the retrospective descriptions in the senior year suggest. The expectation that one should be happy about being at Stanford, the need to deny reality if the contrary is the case, the solidarity of life in freshman dorms, and the social opportunities available for blowing off steam, all contribute to a self-sustaining sense of contentment. It is only with the benefit of hindsight, and in light of the more mature positive experiences of subsequent years, that the more negative aspects of the freshman experience are acknowledged.

Although academic life is not considered central to the freshman year by many, academic concerns nonetheless abound. More often than other students, freshmen describe their course work as demanding and say they need help with reading, writing, and mathematical skills. As Table 4 reveals, freshmen identify problems with course work as having many sources, the most prominent of which is the difficulty of the subject matter. Only in the area of

**Table 4. Perceived Sources of Difficulty in Courses
(means, based on a 1-5 scale).**

	Freshman (N = 268)	Sophomore (N = 289)	Junior (N = 258)	Senior (N = 239)
Amount of work	3.5	3.7	3.7	3.4
Subject matter	3.6	3.3	3.1	2.9
Faculty teaching	3.2	3.1	3.0	2.7
Competition	2.8	2.8	2.7	2.1
Inadequate background	2.8	2.7	2.7	2.3
Personal motivation	2.7	3.3	3.2	3.1

personal motivation are students less troubled as freshmen than in later years.

Another component of academic concerns is the sense that the university is academically less ideal than had been imagined. The overall level of academic satisfaction is high but there are numerous criticisms of courses and professors, many more than appear in subsequent years. Some find the going too rough, while others complain that the intellectual environment is less challenging than they had expected. Students are initially awed by their professors but soon recognize that their teaching ability is not always commensurate with their scholarly stature. They are flattered by being able to attend lectures by a world authority but disappointed at the lack of closer interaction. Students are quite conscious (and the parents of some students never cease reminding them) of the tuition they pay, and they talk frequently about the need to be sure they "get their money's worth" out of their education.

Educational and vocational goals are still uncertain for most freshman students, and for many this is cause for concern. Incoming freshmen are asked for their preliminary academic interest before they arrive because it is on that basis that they are assigned to advisers. Declaring such preliminary interest in no way binds a student, yet this practice encourages the belief that students need to settle quickly on a major. The result is that some students try to reach a decision prematurely. Similarly, while wishing to avoid enrolling in classes that they will later regret taking, students simultaneously flock to supposedly essential courses that they believe they need for gaining admittance to graduate or professional schools later on.

Sophomore Year

Students go home at the end of the freshman year with a sense of accomplishment: They have survived college, they have had good times, they have met great people. But they also carry with them a tinge of disappointment and some anxiety over the future. These feelings simmer over the summer and students return to college in a mood different from that of the year before. Their reentry is marked by a new ambivalence. Going to college is not a novel experience anymore—it strikes no fear in their hearts but neither does it generate much excitement. They are glad to find their way now, but they miss the welcoming embrace of freshman orientation. The intense freshman dorm experience is over and they are now dispersed and more on their own.

The greater sense of autonomy of sophomores is reflected in the feeling that they can no longer say, "My parents did it that way; therefore, I should do it that way." There is a subtle challenge from other students who ask indirectly or directly, "Why are you like that?" By the same token, what courses one takes and how one behaves become more meaningful ("what I am taking makes more sense . . . there is more purpose to what I'm doing").

Sophomores are conscious that a quarter of their college time is already used up. There is less excuse now for searching about, less leisure for trying things out. Courses cannot just be taken at random; there should be a reason for taking them. Yet there is also more opportunity since some of the required course sequences have been completed. The greater freedom of choice is valued by some but is more of a problem for those who are unclear about their directions.

"In my freshman year I was just taking classes that I wanted to take. In my sophomore year I am now asking, 'What should I do with these classes?' I'm not sure I even know which direction I am going. I wonder what is ever going to be useful. I'm getting a little nervous about what

to do with my life. I would like to go to school for the rest of my life, but I know that's not possible."

Even if their goals are set, the means of reaching them may be more arduous than they imagined. Premedical students bruised by the chemistry sequence may have already begun to wonder about their prospects. The hard work necessary to get good grades seems endless.

In this context, the sophomore year is characterized by many as one of "coping and groping," of maintaining a "holding pattern." These students are now more hard-nosed about the institution and less likely to entertain illusions about their lives. For example:

Though as a freshman Margaret had been highly enthusiastic about the prospect of living in a particular dorm, in the spring of her sophomore year she said, "It was all a facade . . . which was forced on me. I was kidding myself. I had had reservations about it from the start. I thought enthusiasm on the outside would change things but it didn't work out. It was a hassle."

Choosing and declaring a major is the bane and the blessing of the sophomore year. For many this event is accompanied by feelings of relief rather than excitement or pleasant anticipation. The pressure to select a major is widely felt. Some decide for the sake of deciding. Others choose a major more by a process of elimination than through attraction to a particular field of study.

Not everyone suffers such agonies. Those who know what they want eagerly move into their chosen field. University policy being flexible, many declare majors only to change them, sometimes more than once. When students view their decisions as less than binding, they get less anxious but then their period of uncertainty lingers as a result.

Declaring a major gives one a sense of belonging, "a place" in the university, and greater certainty of direction. As a freshman, one has a social base in the dorm; as a sophomore, one has an academic base in a department. The sense of purpose imparted by the discovery of the right major is exemplified by Sheila's comment:

"It was almost like finding the perfect gift for someone. You know it when you see it." The effects on her were also quite visible to the interviewer:

Sheila was happy last year but in a rather vague and unconvincing way. It was almost as though she expected to be content, and so she was. This year her satisfaction is not only a good bit higher, it is also better defined. It all ties in with new certainty about where she is headed with her education.

Sheila's emerging sense of academic identity and independence in the sophomore year is also illustrated in further comments by her interviewer:

She developed a close, almost "girlfriendish" relationship with her mother that totally superseded the more remote mother/daughter relationship she had left behind as a freshman. Sheila discovered for the first time that her parents are interested in what she is interested in and want her to do what she really wants for herself even if that means pursuing goals and interests that would keep her away from home in the future. This seems to have represented a symbolic release for Sheila. She indicated that for the first time she felt she was expected to seek out an education for her own sake, not merely to fulfill the expectations of family or anyone else. Discovering that her parents shared, understood, and respected her ambitions made Sheila value her growing independence. As a result, she now sees herself moving ahead on her own, rather than being "simply away from home" on a temporary basis.

One of the more persistent images of college is that of the *sophomore slump,* characterized by boredom, frustration, discouragement, and lack of motivation. Our questionnaire data do not reveal definitive evidence for its existence. Although sophomores are most likely to mention depression as a feature of the year's experiences, the differences from the years before and after are not great (see Table 3). There is something of a slump with regard to long-term educational aspirations whereby the proportion of students planning to obtain doctoral-level degrees drops from 49 percent among freshmen to 36 percent among sophomores and then rebounds to 46 percent in the junior year, but the significance of this isolated finding should not be exaggerated.

There is clearly something to the idea of a sophomore slump, yet it is neither a universal nor consistent experience. Not everyone experiences it, and among those who do, its timing and manifestations vary. The students themselves see this phenomenon as common but not unavoidable. It is also hard to reach a consensus about this issue among the interviewers, as shown in the following excerpts from interviews of sophomores.

Although Monika herself escaped the sophomore slump, all her friends suffered from it. Courses seemed to drag, the year stretched ahead, everything seemed boring and depressing—"the pits."

Brenda's year began not terribly well because the excitement of the freshman year was over and the academic routine had set in. The future appeared to be one long stretch of term after term of course work and heavy-duty studying with the end so far away as to make it difficult to keep up motivation. "Lots of students feel this way," Brenda says. In her case, going to the Vienna campus obviated her sinking into this morass.

Although John did not suffer from it, he recognizes the existence of a sophomore slump among his friends: They get preoccupied with "why you are here and where you'll go from here." Lots of people are worried about not knowing where they are going, what they are going to do "the next sixty years of their lives." Selection of a major is another source of concern. There is loss of cohesiveness and the unity of the freshman year. The primary cause of this syndrome is a lack of confidence in what one is doing.

Though we have emphasized differences, in many respects the sophomore year represents only a gradual transition from the freshman to later years. Courses are seen as more rigorous and more specialized but also more interesting. Satisfaction with classes is higher, owing partly to lowered expectations and partly to increased selection skills. Time management is more effective. Friendships are less extensive but closer. Identification with the university is more complete, and the campus has begun to feel more like home.

Junior Year

The junior year is the linchpin of the academic experience. By this time, most students know what they want and how to get it. They have settled on a major and have begun to concentrate on in-depth learning in a given field. There is a sense of mastery, intellectual excitement, and academic purpose. The more gifted and enterprising students are involved in individual projects and research, relating to their professors more like junior colleagues than pupils. Those who have settled down later or switched majors must scramble to fulfill requirements. One way or another, it is a time of heavy but satisfying work.

Juniors are also beginning to think more concretely about the future. They see themselves as having turned a corner and entered the downward (or outward bound) side of their college experience. This is a primary reason for viewing the junior year as the "big one," the "last chance to get it right." The following quotes from juniors capture some of these points:

"The freshman year was a lot of boundless and undirected energy. Sophomore year was more introspective energy. The junior year is wholehearted organizational energy."

"Junior year is a time when you find out where your talents lie and then you focus on that area. The longer I am here, the more I like it and the more I get out of it."

"This is when things start counting. If you don't take a class now, you can never take it. If you don't qualify for something now, you never will. If you don't get an experience now, you never will. This isn't exactly the senior-year fear of the real world, but it is probably the start of it."

Another important characteristic of the junior year is the off-campus experience. About a third of Stanford undergraduates attend one of the overseas campus programs; many others take an off-campus internship or work for one or more quarters. For many who go, the overseas experience is often the high point of the year, if not all four years. One consequence is the necessity of readjusting to life on campus upon return. Students who have been inspired and challenged by their new experiences feel they have grown dramatically as a result. Even those who have simply had a relaxing break from the routines of the home campus find it difficult to make the transition back to ordinary college life. They feel older and wiser than their classmates who stayed on campus, and they lack patience with the mundane aspects of daily activities.

Students are generally more satisfied with the junior year than either the freshman or sophomore years. They have a new sense of purpose derived from focusing on a particular field of study. There is a sense of direction, of things "falling into place." Juniors are more mature and have a stronger sense of self. They feel more in control of their own lives and less controlled by the institution or their parents.

There is little that stands out in the quantitative results regarding differences between the sophomore and junior years (Tables 3 and 4). The most notable but predictable exception is that 22 percent of the students mention their overseas experience as a significant aspect of the junior year. In some ways, therefore, these two years can be bracketed as a unit, forming the academic core of college between the entry and exit periods of the freshman and senior years.

The junior year does not seem to have any distinctive problems. Instead its difficulties are either carried over from previous years or arise in anticipation of the senior year. For students who have not yet settled down in their academic or career goals, there is cause for anxiety since time is running out. A student who had had a rather chaotic time with his studies said, "I see in front of me some very directed confusion," a phrase that conveys a good sense of his uncertainty.

Others suffer prematurely from the normative crises and problems of the senior year. They speak of "getting old," being "ready to get out," feeling "burned out," "senior panic," and trying "to figure out how I'll know what I'm going to do."

Most students by the junior year are fully integrated into one or another niche of the college subculture, socially as well as academically. They have fallen in and out of love, made and lost friends. Typically, there is by this time a significant restructuring of personal values marked by greater tolerance and understanding.

However sheltered a student's background, he or she has been inevitably exposed to issues and controversies revolving around gender roles, ethnicity, sex, drugs, alcohol, sexual orientation, and broader political issues. Yet some manage to remain quite insulated. As one interviewer wrote:

> Frank seems to be out of touch with himself and much of his environment. Even after being at Stanford for nearly three years, he still refers to blacks as "Negroes." His use of the word is totally ingenuous, thus suggesting his isolation from the rest of the university community. Even though he said his overseas experience had created many opportunities for him to reflect and reexamine his life, he seems at best inept in introspection and naive in the extreme.

Other social deficiencies are often more benign and more readily corrected. Jimmy had been something of a social recluse in high school and remained so the first two years in college. He worked hard and played little. In his junior year he began to come out of his shell and bought a stereo mostly with his own earnings. That and his having a room all to himself made it possible to project the image of a "sophisticated upperclassman"; that made it easier for him to get a girlfriend. In time, Jimmy was able to dispense with his stereo and other props and relate freely to women and men as a self-confident and relaxed person. This transformation was a key feature of Jimmy's college experience. He was ever so grateful to Stanford not only for educating him but also for helping him not to be such a "stick-in-the-mud" as he was in high school.

Senior Year

"I love it here, but I don't want to stay any longer." That parting statement pretty much sums up the prevailing sentiment among seniors. The dominant theme of the year is leaving the university. Half of all the students describe this as an important aspect of the year on the senior questionnaire. An additional 21 percent mention some other concern related to leaving the university (Table 3).

Academically, the senior year is most rewarding for students who are engaged in a culminating experience such as working on an honor's project. For those who have fulfilled their major and distribution requirements, the year provides a relaxed occasion to take a variety of courses for interest, to round off one's education, or to mark time. But there are also those who are trying frantically to complete their requirements so as to graduate and others who want to "drain every last bit of experience out of the final year."

Another major task is completing applications and interviews for graduate school or jobs, a time-consuming and oftentimes anxiety-ridden task. Most students fare well in this process, gathering the rewards of their success in a select institution. But pigeons also come home to roost for those who have not played their career cards well through negligence or because of the nature of their field ("the senior year liberal arts panic"). Separation anxiety and concerns about the future are primary ingredients of "senioritis."

The quantitative data show that the senior year is overall the most satisfying. Mentions of depression are notably absent and, more than any other year, the senior year is described as happy, fun, rewarding, and relaxed. Being busy and lacking motivation are also mentioned, but the context suggests that these are not perceived as problems. Academic experiences are much more often described in positive than negative terms ("I have learned to enjoy my serious time") as are the students' living situations. Social and romantic relationships are likewise seen as positive. There is a feeling of "heightened appreciation of the world around me."

Academic concerns are less in evidence than in any previous year. Courses are seen as less demanding, the perceived need for academic assistance is minimal, and such sources of academic difficulty as competition and the lack of adequate background dwindle in importance (Table 4). Interestingly, personal motivation, rated by freshmen as the least troublesome of all the causes of problems with course work, is among the most significant for seniors. Freshmen squander their time through disorganization and lack of direction; seniors fritter it away. In each case, a quarter of a student's college education is at stake.

Overall, the senior pattern is one of disengaging not only from academic life but also from extracurricular activities. Students follow through on commitments made in previous years but do not become involved in new activities. On the other hand, informal social life with small groups of close friends becomes very important. Students who live off campus enjoy entertaining one another for dinner. A few are already married and settled down. Many express the wish that they had paid more attention to friendships in earlier years instead of being so preoccupied with their studies. Feelings of nostalgia are quite pervasive among seniors; their reluctance to leave is quite palpable ("I feel like I'm being evicted"). Many express a deep sense of gratitude to the institution ("it has been such a privilege"), to their families ("they have done everything for me, and everything they have done is in my best interest"), and friends ("I have grown up with them . . . they have challenged me and I, in turn, have given myself to them").

Seniors are not only more likely to develop a social life that is not based on the campus but they also are more likely to engage in paid employment: Seventy-one percent of the students have jobs at least part of the senior year, compared to 47 percent to 58 percent in prior years. Furthermore, students who have jobs work more hours in them (an average of fourteen hours per week, compared to eleven hours in prior years), and they are more likely to say that their job is related to their anticipated future career.

The forward-looking quality of the year ("looking to the future is everyone's obsession") means that various aspects of campus life become less significant in determining overall satisfaction. Grades, housing, and the quality of instruction, all of which loomed large in student comments in earlier years, now recede in importance. Because of the focus on transition, the senior year is felt to be quite distinct from the two previous years and in some respects comparable to the freshman year. In both cases students experience the excitement of passing an important milestone in their lives and moving into a new and different mode of existence. The key question in the freshman year is, What am I going to do *in* college? In the senior year it is, What am I going to do *after* college? In the freshman year one asks, Where are you from? In the senior year the question is, Where are you going next year?

In sum, the freshman and senior years appear to be much more distinctive than the sophomore and junior years. They are characterized by more intense emotional involvements and concerns, largely of a positive sort: the excitement of entering a new educational world in the freshman year, the challenge of entering the adult world in the senior year.

Students develop and mature over the four years of college along a number of dimensions, in addition to their academic and career orientations. The overall effect of college on student attitudes is one of progressive liberalization. Although they mostly retain the political, religious, and ideological orientations they came with, undergraduates show a greater openness to and tolerance of other viewpoints, values, and life-styles by the time they leave. A few become radicalized while others embrace a more conservative stance. Some lose their religious moorings or become less dogmatic "liberated Christians." Others are "born again."

Interactions with those from other backgrounds leave few students untouched. Gender roles are reconsidered, ethnic roots are explored. The world of ideas expands their intellectual horizons. Experiences outside college—as they work, perform voluntary services, and travel—expose them to the adult world.

Variations in the Four-Year Pattern

The four-year sequence of undergraduate study that we have described is the standard pattern for most Stanford undergraduates. But this sequence is interrupted for many students by a "stop-out" period of one or more quarters during which they work, travel, or simply take a break from school. The prevalence of this practice, and the length of time taken off, vary significantly among the four groups in the typology. Because many students come with advanced placement units and can take heavy course loads when they need to, stopping out does not ordinarily delay graduation.

A small proportion of students graduate early (2 percent in the Cohort sample); a much larger proportion (15 percent) take an additional one to three quarters to graduate. To get complete information on as many students as possible, we extended our study period to the end of the fall quarter of 1982–83. By then almost 90 percent of the original sample had either graduated or left the institution with no intention of returning.

The most important variants on the usual sequence of study are students who transfer to Stanford from another institution in the sophomore or junior year and students who leave Stanford to study elsewhere or pursue some other activity. It is with these two groups that we shall deal briefly here.

Transfer Students. Since none of the transfer students completed the freshman questionnaire and only some completed the sophomore questionnaire, they are not classified in the typology. They are thus excluded from the discussion in the next four chapters, even though much of what is said is quite applicable to them as well.

Each year some 150 to 200 students are admitted to the university from other schools. Many of these students had applied to Stanford as high school seniors but were not admitted. We randomly sampled 50 sophomore transfer students entering in 1978 and 50 junior transfer students entering in 1979 (both groups thus graduating in 1981, along with the other students in the study) and added them to the study population, giving them the same questionnaires and interviews as the original students. At the end of their first year of Stanford they also completed a special transfer addendum questionnaire that asked about their reasons for transferring, evaluations of their prior school, views on Stanford, and the like.

As compared to the original cohort, transfer students are more likely to be female (48 percent to 42 percent), Caucasian (90 percent to 83 percent), and from affluent families (24 percent from families with incomes over $100,000, compared to 18 percent of the original cohort). In other dimensions, the transfer students closely resemble students entering as freshmen.

Most transfer students come from private colleges (60 percent), and their adjustment to the university proceeds easily and rapidly. They tend to complain about a reduction in faculty-student contact compared to their previous school (the faculty are less accessible, classes are larger, and advisers are less interested, they say), but they feel that their overall academic and, especially, nonacademic opportunities are enhanced. They appreciate the variety of academic programs, the overseas study programs, the quality of the libraries, opportunities for career preparation, athletic programs, cultural resources, and the climate.

Some 23 percent of the transfer students come from public four-year colleges and universities; most of them applied for admission to Stanford as freshmen and were not accepted. They are very favorably disposed toward the university and they give glowing evaluations of almost all aspects of their Stanford education, including the quality of their interactions with faculty. Their only complaints center on the high tuition and problems with off-campus housing.

The remaining transfers (17 percent) come from community colleges and usually enter as juniors. Most of them have not applied to the university before. They experience greater adjustment problems, with 60 percent of them saying that it takes them longer than one academic quarter to feel comfortable at the university (compared to only 40 percent of the students from public four-year schools and 26 percent of the students from private schools). They also are only marginally more satisfied with Stanford than with their previous schools, tending to complain about reduced faculty access, high tuition, and off-campus housing. Their positive evaluations are confined to the libraries, overseas study programs, and the academic strengths of the university. They nonetheless agree overwhelmingly that their decision to transfer was a good one (87 percent, which is similar to the percentages for the other two groups).

The Cohort questionnaires completed by all students reveal few differences between transfer students and the original cohort once the former have passed beyond the initial period of adjustment. Their levels of careerism and intellectualism are not appreciably different from those of the freshman cohort as measured by the junior-year scales alone. Their distinctiveness is mainly a function of their having come to Stanford at a different entry point. In their first year at the university, as either sophomores or juniors, the transfer students tend to respond more like freshmen in such matters as relying more on their families for advice, expressing concern about their academic abilities, and so on. They are also quite likely to develop initial friendships with freshmen rather than their fellow sophomores or juniors.

By the senior year, however, all transfer students—whether they entered as sophomores or juniors—have become almost indistinguishable from those who entered as freshmen. They experience the senior year in the same terms: The issues are the future and having a good time before going on to the "real world," they are very rarely depressed or admittedly unhappy, and they feel that their positive academic experiences far outweigh the negative ones. They feel satisfied about the same aspects of the undergraduate experience as other students and dissatisfied with the same areas, and both their academic performance and nonacademic involvements are very similar to those of the original cohort sample. Thus, whether by virtue of their similar family backgrounds and prior school experiences or the acculturative power of the university once they arrive, the transfer students very rapidly become like standard Stanford undergraduates, having the same views, outlook, and evaluations by the time of graduation as students who spend all four years there.

Students Who Left Stanford. Identifying students who have permanently left is not easy because university policy does not impose time limits for graduation, as long as the individual has made satisfactory academic progress during the quarters for which he or she has been enrolled. Thus a student may disappear for years without foregoing the privilege of eventually returning and completing a degree.

From the original sample we identified twenty individuals (about 6 percent) who left Stanford with no expectation of returning. Half of these students transferred directly to another college or university; an additional four eventually enrolled elsewhere. In most cases the institutions they went to were state universities, in or near the student's hometown. Of the total of fourteen students in college only four had graduated by the summer of 1982 (20 percent, as against 85 percent of those who stayed at Stanford). Four more appeared likely to graduate within a year or two; the others who were attending classes did so irregularly and their prospects were more uncertain. Four students did not reenter college. They expressed hope of eventually completing an undergraduate degree, but none had specific plans for returning to school. The following discussion is based on telephone interviews with sixteen of these students and conversations with the parents of two more. We also had statements from several of these students explaining their decisions to leave the university.

The modal length of time these students were at Stanford was one year, the median four quarters, and the range one to eight quarters. Some of them stopped out one or more times before leaving for the last time.

Seventy-five percent of this group was male (compared to 56 percent in the total sample) and 73 percent from out of state (versus 55 percent). They are not distinctive in their ethnicity or socioeconomic backgrounds, though the numbers involved are so small that it is difficult to draw conclusions about such variables. But they are distinctive in their academic backgrounds: Their SAT scores, particularly the verbal scores, are higher than those of other students, and they placed higher in their high school classes. Their questionnaire responses show further that they did not find their freshman-year work especially difficult—only 41 percent of them rated their classes as "very demanding," compared to 52 percent for other students. They report spending fewer hours attending class and studying, but they do not report more problems with their classes than others. They do complain more of lack of motivation and lack of time due to other commitments.

With regard to their intended majors (identified in the freshman year), those who left are especially likely to be interested in the humanities (23 percent, versus 14 percent of all students) and uninterested in the natural sciences (8 percent, versus 24 percent). They are also less interested in the standard professions, tending to prefer areas like the arts, teaching, and journalism. They are low on careerism (using the scale for the freshman year only) but do not score higher than their classmates in intellectualism. They are much more likely than other students to say that they are attending college because it is "the best available alternative."

By the end of the freshman year these students give clear evidence in both interviews and questionnaire responses that they may leave the university (indeed, some have already done so). In our telephone interviews we found that the reasons they had for leaving could be grouped into several categories: personal or academic problems, dissatisfaction with academic programs, and financial difficulty.

The first of these categories includes a variety of reasons: "I was tired of studying and had just broken up with my girlfriend; without any sense of direction, I couldn't see staying on"; "I wasn't doing well academically; I had no motivation." A sense of alienation is expressed by some (including several minority group students, one homosexual, and a student who was "not wealthy"), but this was always in conjunction with other feelings, such as lack of direction, personal problems, intimidation by the high-powered atmosphere, and so on. Six students could be subsumed in this group, all of them male.

Dissatisfaction with academic life was expressed by seven students, including four of the five women. They ranged from a general unhappiness with the intellectual climate to complaints about the specific programs they had hoped to major in (philosophy, mathematics, film, women's studies) or the wish to study a subject that was not available (architecture). Several of these students also said they wanted more of a "real world" atmosphere than what was available at Stanford, meaning a more urban setting and diverse student body.

Financial difficulties were the chief reason for leaving for only three students. The remaining four students had reasons that were more idiosyncratic: One was recruited by the Unification Church, another had to take care of his seriously ill mother, a third went to work as a musician in New York, and the fourth left to pursue a romantic interest.

Generally speaking, these students regarded Stanford in a positive light yet expressed no regrets for having left. Many offered variations on one theme: "Stanford is a fine school, but I lacked motivation"; "I needed a different environment"; "I didn't have the money." Only a few were openly critical, most commonly complaining of Stanford's "narrowness," its being "too white, too upper middle class," "too conformist." "It's like a greenhouse," said one, "which is not a healthy place for a roadside weed like myself to grow up."

Choice and Change: Basic Patterns

As one freshman put it, "Being a student is a matter of constant decision making." Out of the shelter of home and high school, making decisions becomes a daily imperative of college life. Having looked at the landmarks and hallmarks of the four undergraduate years, we shall now examine the patterns of student choices during their college careers. We mainly focus on the choice and change of careers and majors and what the significant influences are on those choices.

Choice of Career. Figure 7 presents the career choices of students over four years. (The full data are in Appendix III, Table 1.) In the freshman year 18 percent said they were uncertain of their career plans. Later questionnaires pressed students to indicate some choice of career path, even if they were very uncertain. Some measure of uncertainty is thus concealed in the patterns shown.

The most dominant feature of Figure 7 is the steep climb in the choice of business from 17 percent of all careers in the freshman year to 29 percent in the senior year. By contrast, the sharpest drop is in medicine, which falls from 21 percent to 15 percent. There is also a drop in engineering, from 10 percent to 7 percent, and in law, from 20 percent to 17 percent. Those four "standard professions" account for 67 percent of all career choices in both the freshman and senior years. These changes are reflected in the shifts in plans for postbaccalaureate study. As freshmen, 21 percent plan to stop their education at the bachelor's level, 30 percent expect to earn a master's degree, and 49 percent a doctoral degree (Ph.D., M.D., or J.D.). By the senior year, the proportion expecting no more than a bachelor's degree has dropped substantially, to 8 percent, and the figure for the doctoral degree has declined slightly, to 45 percent. Those expecting to earn a master's level degree (mainly M.B.A.s) have increased to 47 percent.

Among the other professions, the percentage of those going into teaching goes up from 6 percent to 10 percent, while careers in the natural sciences and health professions (exclusive of medicine) drop from 8 percent to 4 percent. Careers within the humanities such as writing, journalism, and the arts account for about 12

Percent

Figure 7. Career Choice by Year in School (*N* = 212).

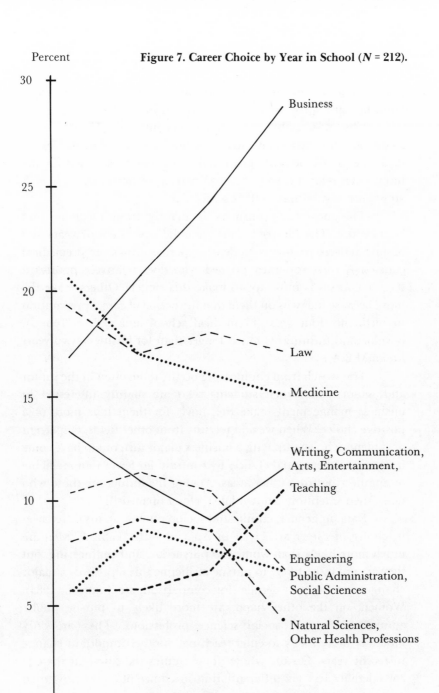

Note: Figure includes only those students with information for all four years.

percent of all choices in both the freshman and senior years. These "nonstandard" professions account for a third of all careers.

The most stable career choice is business; 77 percent of freshmen who express an interest in business stay with it. Next is medicine, at 66 percent. Least stable are the choices within the humanities-related careers; only 35 percent of freshmen with such an interest stay with it to their senior year.

The move into business is mainly from medicine and engineering. The former is fairly gradual over the four years and mainly reflects problems students experience in their premedical courses. A career-oriented premed who does relatively poorly in science courses is most apt to make this switch. Others make the move because it dawns on them that the period of career preparation in medicine (four years in medical school and at least four in postdoctoral training) is much longer than for business (two years for an M.B.A.).

The switch from engineering occurs more often in the junior and senior years when students who are mainly interested in business management make the move; for them it is more of a positive choice. When we add recruits from other fields, 66 percent of students who end up with a business major turn out to have come from some other initial choice. By contrast, far fewer join medicine or engineering from other areas. Among the former are those who make their intentions known late ("closet premeds").

Data on gender, ethnic, and socioeconomic status differences in choice of career are given in Appendix III, Table 3. Men are much more likely than women to pursue law and engineering, but they are not more likely to pursue medicine; this represents a major change over the past decade (for comparison, see Johnson, 1983). Women, on the other hand, are more likely to pursue public administration and social science professions. They are only modestly more likely to enter teaching, another important change in recent years. On the whole, these figures indicate that there is considerably less sex differentiation in choice of career now than there was even just ten years ago. Over the four years there are only very minor sex differences among our students in their patterns of change of career choice.

Ethnic differences are especially marked for Asian Americans, who chose engineering or medicine in much higher proportions than all other students: Thirty-six percent are interested in medicine as against 15 percent for Caucasians and 8 percent for Blacks and Chicanos combined; 20 percent chose engineering as against 5 percent Caucasians and 8 percent Blacks and Chicanos.

With respect to socioeconomic status, the lower-status group is strongly overrepresented in both engineering and teaching, while the higher group is overrepresented in medicine. Those in the middle group tend more toward law and careers in writing, communication, and the arts.

The interview reports provide fascinating glimpses into the dynamics of how students choose careers. The reasons are always multidimensional and the students themselves are far from aware of them all. What may seem like a straightforward choice, a capricious move, or a serendipitous stumble onto a career path conceals many more complex reasons than meet the eye. Some students are quite methodical in their decision making, while others take a more meandering path, as described by their interviewers:

Samantha was prompted by one of her high school teachers to think about her career talents and the best ways of using them. Though nobody in Samantha's family is in law (they are in the oil business), she somehow felt attracted to it. She read books and attended trials (and as a budding actress was fascinated by their more dramatic elements). She discussed with attorney friends of her father what it is like to be a lawyer and through those contacts she obtained further introductions to young women lawyers who work in prestigious law firms. To gain further exposure, she's hoping to work in one of these law firms the summer following her freshman year.

Tom was simultaneously interested in medicine and English. After he completed the premedical requirements, he decided that he did not "like what doctors do for a living" given the pressure of their work and the lack of time for family life and personal interests. So in his junior year he decided to "go with the English major and worry about the future later." After considering law and business, he settled on the former because law school offers "three good years of academics . . . there's an applicable objective body of knowledge that can be studied. . . . Law provides a context for reasonable and civilized negotiating of competing self-interests." By contrast, business struck him as "pseudoscientific."

Choice of Major. The natural and social sciences each account for about one fourth of freshman intentions regarding majors (though very few have actually declared majors at this point). The humanities and interdepartmental programs account for 15 percent each, engineering and earth sciences for close to 20 percent (Appendix III, Table 2).

As shown in Figure 8, the natural sciences have lost a third of their majors by the senior year (down to 17 percent from 24 percent). The humanities have increased from 14 percent to 18 percent, indepartmental programs from 16 percent to 21 percent, while engineering and earth sciences have hardly changed. Students are least likely to leave engineering (75 percent of freshman engineers stay with their initial choice) and most likely to leave the natural sciences (only 59 percent stay with their initial choice; see Appendix III, Table 4).

Sex differences in major choice at graduation are surprisingly small—women are only modestly less likely than men to major in the natural sciences and engineering, and they are only slightly more likely to choose the humanities and social sciences (Appendix III, Table 5). This indicates a substantial change in recent years, for women rarely majored in the technical disciplines even just ten years ago. Though there is greater sex parity in choice of major at Stanford (Boli, Katchadourian, and Mahoney, 1983) than in the country as a whole, the sex ratio at comparable institutions is probably not much different. Furthermore, women are still relatively rare in certain fields like chemistry and physics, even though they are very well represented in biology (which is the major gateway into medicine).

A higher proportion of women than men express an initial interest in the natural sciences (25 percent to 21 percent), but more women than men drop out so that more men complete majors in this area. For engineering the opposite finding applies: Men more often indicate an initial interest (22 percent to 14 percent), but there is a net loss of men by graduation while there is a net gain of

Figure 8. Major Choice by Year in School (*N* = 216).

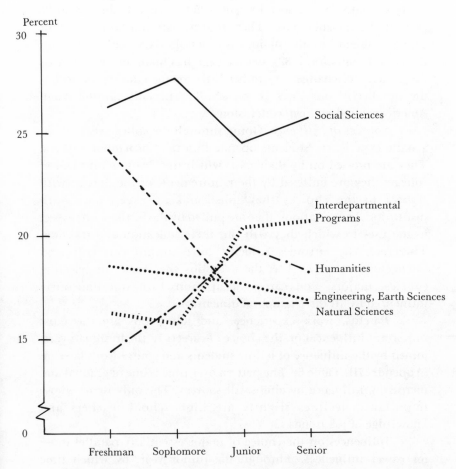

Note: Figure includes only those students with information for all four years.

women, yielding only a small sex difference in the senior year. And women do not concentrate solely in the less rigorous engineering disciplines, such as industrial engineering; they are well represented in chemical and electrical engineering as well.

Ethnic differences in choice of major are enormous. Asian Americans are heavily concentrated in the natural sciences and engineering (62 percent), about twice the proportion of Caucasians and Blacks/Chicanos. Blacks and Chicanos, in turn, are especially likely to major in the social sciences (50 percent, compared to 25 percent of the Caucasians). These findings are similar to those for college students in the nation as a whole (National Center for Education Statistics, 1982). Between the freshman and senior years the patterns of change vary rather little for the ethnic groups, but the number of our cases is too small (especially for the Asian Americans) to draw firm conclusions.

Sources of Influence. Going through the college years is not a static experience. Students operate in a field of temporal forces. They are pressed on by their past, which they bring with them to college; they are buffeted by the requirements of the present with respect to the choices they must make to keep pace with institutional expectations; they are pulled by the future with respect to the uses to which they will put their education and training. Therefore, the attitudes students have toward careerism and intellectualism, as well as the decisions they make in selecting courses, majors, and career occupations, are simultaneously influenced by all three temporal dimensions.

Parents, work experience, and job trends are the most important influences on the choice of careers in the freshman year, joined by the influence of fellow students and course work later on (Appendix III, Table 6). The pattern over time is one of gradual and increasing influence by almost all sources. The only items whose importance declines slightly are high school teachers and knowledge of job trends.

Influences on the choice of major essentially parallel those for career influences. Through the junior year, by which time virtually all students have chosen their majors, the degree of influence of the various factors increases almost across the board.

With respect to student patterns in seeking advice about various topics, the general finding is a decrease over the four years (Appendix III, Table 7). Students' propensity to seek advice from advisers and other faculty shows little change over the years regarding courses and career planning but significant declines in advice sought for personal problems and academic difficulty. Parental advice is sought less over time but even in the senior year a very substantial proportion of students continue to consult their parents with respect to career plans and personal problems. Fellow students are the most common source of advice overall, and there is little change over the years in the propensity of students to consult one another; hence student advice becomes relatively more important as time goes on.

In terms of helpfulness of the advice received, there is little meaningful variation except in the area of career planning. Here there is an increase in perceived helpfulness over time of all sources except advisers. Although not related to changes over time, it is interesting to observe that parents are seen as more helpful about career decisions than any other source, including the university Career Planning and Placement Center.

The increase in perceived helpfulness of career advice parallels the increases in influences on career decision making just described. Although seniors apparently do not seek career guidance with greater frequency than other students, they do appear to be more receptive to advice and influence in this area. It may also be that seniors feel that they are more influenced by others simply because they are more acutely aware of the pressure to make decisions about their future careers. The same reasoning can be applied to the increase in influence on choice of major through the junior year: As students come face to face with actually committing themselves to a particular course of action, they feel more pushed and pulled by parents, faculty, and peers.

The interview reports abound with examples showing the interplay of parental influences on the career and academic choices of students. As we shall discuss in the next four chapters, the four types vary significantly in this regard. Looking at these issues more generally, one can see parental influences that are direct or subtle, beneficial or detrimental. There are parents who exert direct pressure by making their financial support contingent on their children doing their bidding. More often there are unstated (but no less real) expectations that students feel obligated to live up to. Other parents will stand by the decisions of their sons and daughters, whatever those may be. In some instances, students are basically left to their own fate. After Joanna's father died in her freshman year, her mother remarried and moved to Australia, leaving Joanna essentially on her own (she managed very well).

The closeness between some students and their parents is remarkable ("we idolize each other"). Jeremy and his father (a physician) had a long tradition of talking things over every summer. In this relaxed and friendly setting, Jeremy formed many of his long-term plans with the full confidence that ultimately all of his choices would be his own. Several students were launched on their business careers in partnerships with their fathers. Sometimes there is a belated discovery that the parents "are not so dumb after all" and that "I should have been following my dad's advice for years. He's incredibly wise, and that way I'd have been a lot better off."

Parental influence can also be quite problematic. Some have a feeling of being "programmed" by parents. Some discover this early on and manage to extricate themselves from it; others struggle longer. Randy said, "I came with a strong interest in medicine because of my father, but I would have been unhappy if I had continued in it." His advice to freshmen: "If you have any doubts about your preconceived career choice, get out of it; there are many other things to interest you." Terry's father (in real estate) pushed her into engineering, which she did not like and did not do well in. She continued to work for him as a surveyor during the summer while backing off from engineering. He retaliated by cutting off her support and taking away her car. Terry planned to work overseas and eventually go into international business, hoping that her father would acquiesce to her decisions. Parental models can also be instrumental in turning students away from the professions of their parents. Having observed the impact of her father's career on the family, Sherryl was certain she was not going into medicine; she was just as certain she would not become a housewife like her mother.

Peers are often less directly involved in each other's career choices, yet in cases when couples decide to build a joint life together, their career paths have to be dovetailed. In a number of instances, this was accomplished by couples going on to the same graduate school or neighboring institutions; sometimes one planned to work while the other went on with graduate study. In the following instances, matters got more complicated.

Jill and Tom fell in love as freshmen and decided to get married in their junior year. To ensure that their futures would mesh nicely, their basic strategy was for Jill to pick a graduate school in an area where Tom could get a job. Though Jill was "really into a career," her visions of family life were fairly traditional—Tom would be the primary breadwinner and she would do the kind of work she enjoyed, adapting it to the needs of her family.

The couple happily settled down in their senior year ("I have a good roommate"). Although Jill felt somewhat "removed and independent," she managed to maintain her old friendships in her sorority and was actively engaged in completing her honor's thesis in human biology. Halfway into her senior year, however, Jill became pregnant unexpectedly. Her moods began to swing between depression and elation while she and Tom reworked their plans for the future. With a good deal of support from the families on both sides (who were quite delighted at the prospect of their first grandchild), Jill once again became confident and excited about the future.

Following graduation the couple planned to move to a town where Tom had a job. The baby was due in October, so Jill planned to take a year off. The following fall she should enter a master's program in community health at the local university. After getting her degree, she planned to have a second baby, then look for a job. She could not imagine not having a career, although she did not feel she needed to devote full time to it. In ten years Jill imagined living in a big house with lots of land, two kids in school, a dog, and a station wagon for going skiing on weekends: "your basic little family."

Candice had maintained a straight 4.0 average throughout high school and had SAT scores in the 700s. Intelligent, attractive, gentle, and gracious, she was also shy and somewhat withdrawn. She buried herself in her studies until she met Jeremy, who became the dominant influence in her life. Her general educational interests and career aspirations began to revolve on the expectation that they would get married following graduation. When Jeremy abruptly broke up with her and prepared to go on to graduate school, Candice found herself not knowing what to do next. Yet she was a resilient and gifted woman and her interviewer felt that Candice would find her own direction in due time.

Teresa was already engaged to a man in her hometown when she came to Stanford. He then got a job in the area and they lived together, planning to get married following her graduation. Called a "bright, motivated, and admirable person getting a great deal out of life" by her interviewer, Teresa's life as an undergraduate was quite atypical. Much of what preoccupied her undergraduate peers was irrelevant to her.

Teresa majored in electrical engineering and planned to work in that field. Yet she had already settled down to a life in her junior year that was more like being the spouse of a local engineer than a Stanford undergraduate.

We have gone into the lives of these three women in some detail to show the extent to which academics are embedded within the larger framework of a student's life. Their cases are unusual but the principle they illustrate is not: It is not possible to understand the academic experience of students in isolation; one aspect of life cannot be dissected from the rest for our convenience.

This principle must be kept in mind when we turn to examine in more detail the characteristics of the four categories of students in our typology. While we focus on their academic and career choices, these students are also growing and maturing as individuals. It is no wonder that they say at the end of the senior year, "I have changed . . . I have grown up . . . These have been four great years."

4

Students as Careerists: Training for the Professions

In his welcoming address on October 1, 1891, Governor Leland Stanford told the first incoming students to Stanford, "Remember that life is, above all, practical; you are here to fit yourselves for a useful career" (Mirrielees, 1959). The founder of Stanford University would not have been disappointed in the career attitudes of the students we discuss in this chapter.

Careerists view the college experience primarily as an opportunity to prepare for a vocation. They are not particularly concerned about education for its own sake, and they have relatively few intellectual and social interests that are unrelated to their careers. In deciding to attend Stanford, they are motivated more by the advantages a degree from the institution will bring them after graduation than by the quality of the educational experience as such. They exaggerate the value of Stanford credentials in the outside world (see Meyer, 1971). Whatever liberal learning they derive is largely incidental for most, though a number of them are stimulated enough by their undergraduate experience to develop a heightened interest in intellectual issues.

These men and women are not the only students interested in careers. All students are concerned, at one level or another, with acquiring the skills and knowledge that will make them competent professionals. However, the Careerists and, to a lesser extent, the

Strivers are more determined in their pursuit of career aims than are the Intellectuals and Unconnected; the Careerists are furthermore more willing to sacrifice their liberal education to those ends than are the Strivers. The Careerists thus occupy the extreme end of the continuum of interest in vocational purpose and emphasis.

Within the Careerist group itself the intensity of students' careerism is quite variable. At one extreme are students like Greg, who was characterized by his interviewer as "the worst example of the stereotypical, grade-grubbing, preprofessional student." Greg worked hard and did well in a narrow range of courses, even though he had no particular interest in them. He realized that he was merely going through the motions of getting an education but admitted frankly, "I don't care." Furthermore, he saw the coming years as a medical student as being more of the same. It was only when looking ahead ten years to the time he would be practicing medicine that he thought, "I'll finally be doing what I like." Others, like Christopher, were quite interested in what they were studying and made a qualifiedly more positive impression on their interviewers: "This student is bright, comes from a strong educational background, is clean-cut, clean-living, knows what he wants, works hard, and gets results. On the other hand, there is a certain narrowness, self-centeredness, and blandness about him."

Greg and Christopher were Careerists by deliberate choice. By contrast, Emily represents a more passive form of careerism by default. The daughter of an engineer, she followed his example to please him. Though she had academic interests outside of engineering, the requirements of her major were so demanding that she ended up learning little else. Biographical profiles 4.1 through 4.4 exemplify further the various Careerist types.

Profile 4.1: Bradley—Future Businessman

"Let's face it, if you are the be-all and end-all of youth in your community, you are in a very secure position." From this position of unassailable self-confidence, Bradley proceeded to lambast one or another aspect of Stanford during his freshman interview. The objects of his ire were mainly the residential system, his roommate, and his adviser. Having gotten straight A's in high school with minimal work, Brad still found it possible to do reasonably well at Stanford without exerting

himself. He would not, however, discuss the details of his curricular choices and expressed his general disappointment for not having been "electrified" by what he had been exposed to so far.

Bradley had made his academic decisions by "gut feeling," looking for courses that fulfilled the distribution requirements as well as classes in his major areas of interest. If that left room for other courses, he took them because "you are paying for it, so why not?" There was less ambiguity with respect to his career plans, which involved going to law school after majoring in either economics or political science. When asked if he would someday like to hold political office, he responded, "Sure, I would like to be president. Who wouldn't?"

In his sophomore year Bradley generally found his classes and the level of teaching more satisfactory. However, he was very dissatisfied with the prospect of majoring in economics, a subject he now found dull and boring, taught by professors who "don't care" and "can't teach worth a damn." Brad's political conservatism became increasingly more assertive. He was highly critical of the university administration for putting up with "radical" students. He characterized his own position by saying, "People like to call me reactionary, but I call myself a progressive conservative." He claimed that his political views did not affect his friendships and that in fact one of his closest friends was "nearly a communist." Nonetheless, his social contacts were primarily with his fraternity brothers and he showed little tolerance for those whose life-styles and values differed markedly from his own.

By his junior year Brad had decided to double-major in American studies and petroleum engineering. This meant that virtually all of his course selections thereafter would have to be for the purpose of fulfilling the requirements of these two majors. American studies appealed to him intellectually because of its combination of political science and history. His interest in petroleum engineering was in part linked to the family having oil property. But this meant taking physics, chemistry, and other science prerequisites that he found "brutal."

Another important determinant in his choice of majors was Bradley's continuing interest in law school. As he saw it, American studies provided him with a safe and respectable avenue to law school; the addition of petroleum engineering made him a more distinctive, even unique, candidate.

To gain practical experience Brad spent his summers working for an oil company near his hometown. He began by doing "manual labor," then moved up to a "definitely white-collar job" with a "big office and a secretary." He remained tight-lipped about his personal and family life.

Reflecting on his undergraduate years, Brad expressed satisfaction with his overall Stanford experience. He characterized as his major gain the changes that he had undergone personally. "I have become more polished and mellow. That's what Stanford really does for a person. I could have done the academic work anywhere. I learned by osmosis from the people and faculty that this place attracts." While other students had a hard time trying to define Stanford, the true purpose of the university was quite self-evident as far as he was concerned: "It's an elite finishing school."

After graduation Bradley planned to relax for several months and then go to work for an accounting firm or oil company. In two years he would head for law school: "I like to argue and I can put things over on people better than most. It would be fun, and I think that it's best suited to my personality." In five years he would like to work for a law firm specializing in tax law: "The government doesn't need any more money than it already has. I can argue with the IRS." Ultimately he would like to have his own business and settle down to a comfortable life in a house "with room to spread out—no obtrusive neighbors." When asked how he would describe his guiding philosophy, Bradley thought a while and replied, "Mercenary." He refused to elaborate.

Profile 4.2: Martin—Premed

Polite and reserved in manner, Martin comes from a small town on the West Coast. His father is a general practitioner; an uncle and several of his cousins are also physicians. Martin came to Stanford with the firm conviction of becoming a doctor, a hope that he has nurtured since the fourth grade. He is very close to his father, who is a "great guy" and has been a role model for him since childhood. Yet he intends to become a physician not simply to please his father but rather because he sees medicine as an excellent opportunity to practice an exciting profession and help people.

In his freshman year Martin plunged into the required premedical sequences. He had come to Stanford with a 4.0 average, but now he had to struggle hard to keep his head above water. His objective was simple: He knew he had to take certain courses and therefore applied himself to them single-mindedly, irrespective of whether or not he had an interest in their substance.

Martin came from a socially conservative background. He had no difficulty adapting to Stanford, although he found himself irritated by the views and activities of the politically more liberal students. He was also distressed at the amount of drinking that went on (he never touched a drop).

Martin declared human biology as his major and the sophomore year was taken up mainly with fulfilling major requirements as well as completing his premedical sequences. He took a course in Shakespeare that he very much enjoyed. He became actively involved with the

Campus Crusade for Christ. The death of Martin's paternal grandmother (a "great lady") stirred in him much reflection on old age and led to his interest in geriatrics as a possible future specialty. While he remained set on medicine, he began to express increasing concern over the problems he was having in obtaining a broader liberal education.

By his junior year Martin was openly complaining about the "premed atmosphere." He characterized some of the classes as a "depersonalized, disjointed mess." He continued to complain that the premedical curriculum allowed him too little time for courses of interest beyond his professional concerns, and he kept talking about the one Shakespeare class he had taken earlier.

The senior year was a time of greater freedom. He became a teaching assistant as well as a resident associate in a dorm, which he characterized as "the best experience of my time here." He took part in a musical production for the first time since coming to Stanford. Though Martin retained his conservative values, his role as a resident associate had a broadening impact on his perspective. He called it "a lesson in tolerance," an exercise "in looking for the good in people" and having to be "a mandatory friend." Martin could also more freely venture now into elective courses in Chinese culture and drama. But these were isolated experiences and could not, at this late date, come together in a coherent pattern. The preoccupation with the process of getting into medical school and the uncertainty of being accepted were sources of concern all though the spring, compounded by several rejections he received from the more competitive institutions.

Despite the narrowness of his educational scope, Martin remained quite positive about his Stanford experience. Nonetheless, if he could do it over, he would "first of all, get a clear idea" of what he wanted of his education apart from vocational concerns and then "find somebody to help him." Though Martin had not complained about his advisers during previous years, now with the help of hindsight he realized that the advising system had not done well by him. He also wished that he had not played the game "too safe" and had made bolder choices, such as taking courses in philosophy and literature rather than being satisfied with introductory-level offerings in psychology and sociology. And he fervently wished that the world of premeds had been different from what it was.

Profile 4.3: Cynthia—Future Financier

Cheerful, charming, bright, and enthusiastic, Cynthia came to Stanford from an affluent community in Southern California. Her high school is not known for its academic excellence and Cynthia had not really expected to get into Stanford. But once in, she loved it ("a very special place").

An accomplished tennis player, Cynthia wholeheartedly threw herself into athletics. She joined the sailing club, the track program, and later on the crew. She also joined a sorority and became socially quite active.

Academics took a backseat in Cynthia's life. She did not study very hard and did not do terribly well. She had a latent interest in science but was fearful of the fierce competitiveness and competence of her peers. She received little guidance from her adviser.

Cynthia tried several majors, but none of them really engaged her interest despite her initial enthusiasm for each. Her electives failed to reveal any serious concern for a liberal education. Her interviewer noted, "She probably will not be an intellectual. To her, being an intellectual is being one-sided, which is clearly something she wishes to avoid."

Although Cynthia did not show the grim vocational determination of the more extreme Careerists, she always assumed that her education would lead to promising career prospects. However she got there, her plan was to go to business school after a few years of working. Though quite happy at Stanford, she was itching to get going by the end of her junior year ("a mild case of senioritis").

Cynthia spent her summers gaining work experience. In the spring of her senior year, unlike most of her classmates who were hustling around desperately to find summer jobs, she simply picked up the telephone and called the president of E. F. Hutton in San Francisco. She introduced herself as a Stanford student interested in finance and asked if there was any possibility that she could have a summer job that offered experience and a little money. She was invited for an interview that afternoon and returned to campus with a summer job.

At the time of her graduation Cynthia had interviews lined up with three investment firms in New York City. If all went well ("and I cannot imagine that it would not," noted the interviewer), she planned to live and work in New York for several years and then pursue a career in finance, with or without an M.B.A.

Profile 4.4: Edward—Engineer

Reticent and self-contained, with speech short and to the point, Edward came from the East to study engineering. He had always loved to work with his hands and had spent his high school summers on construction jobs.

Edward had clear and compelling career objectives. He was in college to make the most of it—to have his education lead to the sort of job he wanted. He was determined to get as much competitive edge out

*of being at Stanford as he could. Exposure to the humanities was not part
of this scheme nor was dawdling in the "softer" social sciences. He took
one anthropology course and was dismayed at the belaboring of the
"utterly trivial and worthless." After a few false starts, he settled on
mechanical engineering.*

*The single-minded determination with which Edward went about
his business led the interviewer to comment: "It seems that virtually
everything he does is instrumental to his final purposes and goals; Edward
is committed to making every last course and every last experience count
directly toward his career goals. I have never met a person quite so intent
in taking care of himself. He is strongly committed and fully determined
to do just exactly what he has set out to do. Meanwhile, he is blithely
ignoring a great deal of the intellectual baggage that makes the university
such an exciting place."*

*Though Edward bent everything to his career interests, his career
aims were themselves not subservient to some ulterior motive, such as
making money (although he definitely wanted to make a good living).
Edward was truly dedicated to his vocation, which evolved more and
more in the direction of applying basic scientific research to socially
useful purposes, such as the harnessing of solar energy and protecting the
environment.*

*Edward had a girlfriend back home when he came to Stanford; he
kept his commitment to her throughout his stay and went back to marry
her after he graduated ("that's pretty good," he said, when announcing
the news). He was barely involved socially with his peers. He practically
lived alone and spent much of his time on his classes and research. He
abhorred politics. "Having a good time" was not part of his vocabulary.
Steady as a rock, enigmatic as a sphinx, Edward headed back home to his
bride and his job with IBM in Vermont. His eventual plan—starting his
own company. His one special ambition—learning to play the violin.*

We need to emphasize the considerable variance within each
group at the outset so that the more extreme exemplars do not
monopolize our discussion of the group as a whole. The relatively
"pure" types more effectively delineate the essence of a given
orientation (and their stories make more interesting reading). They
are the most typical examples in the sense that they embody the
most salient features of careerism but not in the sense of
representing the average Careerist.

The goals and attitudes of Careerists are more readily
discernible than those of the other groups. Their dominant interest
in careers sets them in the center of the issues we are concerned with

in this book. Therefore, these students set a useful baseline from which to launch our discussion.

The Careerists are the most discrete and homogeneous of all the groups. The patterns that emerge from the questionnaire data and the interview materials from the core group of Careerists are quite consistent; only in a few instances are the assessments of the interview reports at odds with the classification assigned to them on the basis of the questionnaire data.

The relative consistency of this group does not mean uniformity. Going beyond just the intensity of their career orientations, one can discern significant differences in the interview reports among three subgroups: social scientists (mainly economics majors) interested in business careers, engineers (many of whom are also interested in business management), and premedical students. Students in these major areas are, of course, also represented in the other three categories but not in the same proportions. Especially striking is the paucity among Careerists of students majoring in the humanities. In the following discussion we shall dwell mainly on the features common to all Careerist students, but we do not wish to gloss over the intragroup and individual differences that further distinguish them.

Interviewer Impressions of Careerists

The Careerists elicited mixed feelings in their interviewers. The more positive responses were generated by their determination, high aspirations, willingness to work hard, and the more adult features of their personalities. The negative responses were elicited by their narrowness, utilitarian approach to education, and materialistic attitudes.

On the whole, Careerist students come across as being independent, self-sufficient, sure of what they want, and single-minded in the pursuit of their goals. Their strong vocational orientation contributes to their image as mature and worldly young men and women. But they also reveal elements of insecurity, excessive anxiety about the future, and a certain sense of being driven. The quotations from interviewer reports that follow convey the impressions they make on others.

Kevin is a bright, thoughtful, high-achieving son of a top-level executive. Confident to the point of aggressiveness . . . a glib customer.

In a sense our whole office participated in this interview because Eileen's perfume permeated the entire Old Union. It seems that she was having lunch with her adviser at the Faculty Club and was duly dressed and scented for the occasion.

A thoughtful but quiet young man. If I were ever in a tight spot, I would like him to be with me. I think he is probably one of the more able and independent young men to go through this university. An inner-directed person if I have ever met one.

Ted is a lively, charming boy. I liked him immensely in spite of the fact that his first reaction to me was, "Are you somebody's secretary?"

A rather superficial, undeveloped student who has done all the right things but hasn't really wrestled with commitment or depth of understanding or feeling. His performance has been quite perfunctory. Everything seems to be in order on the surface, but I doubt if he has really found meaning or reason behind his educational experience. I have no reason to believe that he will not meet his educational goals. I just hope that he develops a better understanding of the whys behind where he's going.

Steven impresses me as an excellent example of the sort of student who comes to Stanford with well-formed aims and moves through the institution like a duck in water without being particularly influenced by what goes on around him.

He is so "good" that I find him irritating and I find myself being irritated with myself for being irritated with him.

The interview reports on Careerists often do not make particularly exciting reading because so much of their academic lives is predictable. Once one gets the general drift of their curricular and career choices, the reading of subsequent reports becomes repetitive and monotonous. The interviewer reports about other students also have their dull moments (just as some Careerist reports have flashes of excitement) but, generally, their flavor is much more varied. On the other hand, Careerists convey a soothing image as a serious and solid group of young men and women who will do the work of the world and effectively look after themselves. If one needed a doctor, engineer, banker, or lawyer, one would be glad to have them around.

Background Characteristics of Careerists

The careerist orientation of these students is largely formed by the time they come to college. The decision to go to college and the choice of the particular institution to attend are heavily influenced by that orientation. It is no wonder that the attraction for Careerists of elite institutions like Stanford is largely based on the premise of future vocational success.

Gender. The dominance of men in the professions is reflected in the anticipatory phase of college preparation. Men are almost twice as likely as women to be Careerists: Twenty-nine percent of the men but only 16 percent of the women fall into this category (tables giving the full results for this and all other variables used in Chapters Four through Seven are given in Appendix IV). Put another way, over 69 percent of the Careerists are men, far above the proportion of men (55 percent) in the total sample. While there has been a very significant increase in the past two decades in the proportion of women who plan on having careers after college (Theodore, 1971; Astin, 1982), it remains very much the case that women are less likely than men to view higher education primarily as a vehicle for professional preparation.

Ethnicity. There are no differences among ethnic groups (Caucasians, Asian Americans, Blacks, and Chicanos) in the tendency to be a Careerist. It is not ethnicity, as such, but other dimensions of social differentiation that are relevant here.

Socioeconomic Status. Socioeconomic status (SES) is an important influence, with students in the highest SES group less likely to be Careerists: Only 20 percent of the top third of our SES Index (see Appendix II) are Careerists, as against 28 percent of the middle third and 29 percent of the lower third. Since the index is skewed upwards relative to the general population, students in our lowest group actually come largely from the middle class in national terms. Hence, it is upper- and near-upper-class students who are less likely to be Careerists than students from the middle classes.

There are two factors that explain this difference. First, students of higher socioeconomic status are less likely to be careerist because they have less reason to be so, given the security provided by family assets. Second, there is a positive social value in obtaining a liberal education for students of higher-status families because of the social gloss and polish that such education has been traditionally expected to provide to privileged individuals. In earlier periods the education of gentlemen was a noncareerist endeavor provided by select private colleges. In more recent times, affluent women often went to college to acquire social graces rather than professional training. Some residue of these traditions is still present. Finally, beyond social utility, affluent students are more likely to come from families that cherish cultural and intellectual traditions as ends in themselves.

Either on their own or as the result of family pressure, students from middle-class and lower socioeconomic backgrounds choose careerist paths for purposes of upward mobility. "I am guided by the importance of upward mobility," said Debby, a Black woman from a middle-class background. Leon came from a Chicano family where neither parent had been to college. He did well academically while helping to support himself by working on construction jobs during the summer. His fraternity helped him to become socialized into a higher socioeconomic milieu, and he was admitted to Harvard Law School.

In their striving for economic security and affluence, the Careerists are either carrying on a pattern, still incomplete, established by their parents or helping to sustain what has been already achieved. In this process the requirements of liberal education are seen at best as secondary and at worst as being in conflict with career goals. Even though intellectual aims may be valued by these students in principle, they lose out to careerism in practice.

The tendency to be a Careerist does not have a simple inverse relationship with family income. While the most well-off are least likely to be Careerists, the least well-off are not the most likely to be Careerists. The proportion of Careerist students from families with less than $40,000 yearly income is 23 percent, which is almost identical to the percentage of Careerists from the $75,000 or higher annual income groups. In the case of the lowest income group, it appears that a concern for liberal education often accompanies the emphasis on careers, for such students are especially likely to be Strivers. Students in the middle of the social ladder, however, are most apt to push for upward mobility through career success without much regard for liberal education.

When we look at the specific occupations of fathers, we find that the children of corporate executives are especially likely to be Careerists (34 percent of such students), while only 12 percent of the children of physicians fall in this group. Since corporate executives are among those with the highest incomes, the pattern based on father's occupation appears to contradict that based on family income. We noted earlier that children from the wealthiest families are less likely to be Careerists; now we find that the children of corporate executives are most likely to profess this orientation.

This apparent discrepancy is due to the fact that corporate executives are not a uniform group. The father whose son is more likely to be a Careerist is typically a vice-president or somewhat lower-level manager. By contrast, the top-of-the-social-ladder students who are less likely to be Careerists have fathers who are the most senior executives or are men of independent means whose status or income is not based on executive rank.

The educational level of the father sheds further light on the family background of Careerist students. They are especially likely to have fathers who hold master's-level degrees (40 percent), while students whose fathers hold doctoral-level degrees (Ph.D., M.D., J.D.) are much less likely to be in this group (10 percent). Additional information from the interview reports makes it reasonable to infer that the fathers of Careerists, typically businessmen, may be Careerists themselves.

We find no correlation between the educational level of mothers (two thirds of whom are college graduates) and the likelihood of being a Careerist. Similarly, although about half of the mothers of students in our sample work outside the home, there is no significant correlation between outside employment by mothers, or the nature of the work they do, and the chances that their children will be Careerists. (This lack of influence of maternal employment and education also holds for students in the other three categories.)

Academic Background. There is no difference between private high school graduates and public high school graduates in their tendency to be Careerists. But SAT scores do seem to matter. Splitting students at the median into groups of high and low SAT scores, we find that 27 percent of students having higher mathematics scores (601–800) are Careerists, while only 19 percent having lower math SAT scores (600 and below) are Careerists. A weaker complementary trend is revealed with respect to verbal scores: Twenty-one percent of students having high (611–800) verbal SAT scores are Careerists, compared to 26 percent of low-verbal students (610 and below). Hence, typically, the high-math–low-verbal students are more likely to be Careerists than the rest of the sample. This partly explains the choice of academic majors by this group (as will be discussed later). Note, however, that this finding is accounted for entirely by the men in our sample. High-math–low-verbal women are more likely to be Strivers than Careerists; this suggests that even when women have strong career inclinations and the academic backgrounds sufficient to support this drive, they usually retain strong interests in liberal education and intellectualism.

Sources of Influence on Careerists

Parents. That Careerists tend to have fathers who also appear to be Careerists suggests that the families of students in this group may have considerable influence on their decision making in college. This is indeed the case: Students who feel that their families have strong influence on their academic and career decisions are more than twice as likely to be Careerists as students who indicate weak family influence (34 percent to 15 percent). In fact, where the family has strong influence students are more likely to fall into this type than any other; fully 73 percent of the Careerists indicate strong family influence on their decisions. As we shall see in the next chapter, the opposite finding characterizes Intellectuals, of whom only 40 percent indicate strong family influence.

The interview reports reinforce the impression that the parents of Careerists are the most influential and intrusive of all the four groups. Such parental pressure is generally in favor of promoting career ends. These parents do not appear as eager to encourage their children to get a broad liberal education; several students were quite explicitly discouraged from doing so. There is a clear sense that the parents expect their children to "get their money's worth" out of their education, and the return on their investment is measured in terms of financial success. The following excerpts from the interview reports illustrate these points.

Ted is under considerable pressure from his father; though quite wealthy, the father is very conscious of where the money is going.

Gertrude is particularly influenced by her mother in terms of choosing a career. She feels pressure from her mother "to succeed in a male-dominated profession." Her mother was working in a job in education that she was quite dissatisfied with; she is now attending law school and thinks Gertrude too should find something challenging in which she can excel.

Jonathan's father is a business executive and apparently gave his children quite a bit of pressure in the past. Jonathan feels that the constant pressure destroys enthusiasm and prevents spontaneity.

George and his father have agreed that George should avoid a liberal arts education . . . such as being an English major or anything where you "end up not having a job."

Her parents control the purse strings, so she feels she has no choice but to accommodate their wishes.

Henry's parents are willing to pay the Stanford tuition if he will major in biology and go to medical school; otherwise, if he plans to major in English, he might just as well go to the state university. He is in touch with his parents frequently, talking to them and trying to justify what he is doing—"how I am putting their money to good use."

Paul's family seems anxious for him to finish school and get to work.

Randy was more under the influence of his father than practically any other student I have seen—his father has always pounded into Randy that he should be the best, he should orient his life toward something that makes lots of money, he should avoid the "fuzzy" studies that are quite useless occupationally.

Parental influence operates in this group in favor of a career orientation even when there is no overt pressure applied. In several instances these students were already involved in family businesses before coming to Stanford and continued to work in those settings during vacations. One woman Careerist worked as an accountant in her father's store one summer and became the manager the following year. This experience helped her appreciate the advantages of being independent and "her own boss." Similarly, the children of doctors work in hospitals, those in the oil business on drilling rigs, and so on.

With or without parental help, some Careerist students show remarkable entrepreneurial aptitude. Quite a few start their own small businesses (and many more talk about it). The career-oriented friend of a Careerist student reportedy parlayed a $2,000 investment into $30,000 between his junior and senior years; whether fact or fantasy, the story says something about the Careerist vision.

Careerist students and their parents often have the same views on career objectives, but there are instances where students are pushed by parents into career paths against the students' own wishes and better judgment. Parental attempts at such pressure are not restricted to this group. Careerist students, however, are either under greater pressure or more likely to pay heed to parental expectations. Students in the other groups more often stand their ground and choose the directions that they wish to take; most parents acquiesce to their desires.

Faculty. It is no wonder that neither faculty nor academic advisers appear to have much impact on Careerists. Though they show far more concern for educational and intellectual issues than parents, the faculty are not a very effective counterinfluence against

personal and parental pressure for career success because they do not
interact much with Careerists. This is exemplified by the case of
Rodney:

> *He feels that neither faculty nor the nature of their courses has had
> any impact on his undergraduate experience because his direction
> (economics) has been clearly set all along. He's assembled a set of goals
> and values that haven't been and probably will not be vulnerable to the
> influence of new thoughts or credos. Rodney retains his concrete and
> straight-arrow sense of what he wants out of his college education . . .
> to get a technical training that will serve as "another stepping-stone for
> my future."*

There are some important differences, however, in this
respect. Those majoring in engineering and earth sciences more
often have close working relationships with faculty members. These
schools are primarily engaged in career training; though they offer
undergraduate majors, they are more like professional schools and
their students share the career interests of their teachers. The School
of Earth Sciences, in particular, is small enough that every
undergraduate has the opportunity to carry out collaborative
research with the faculty. These and other factors generate a
commonality of interest that brings faculty and students together.

Careerists in the School of Humanities and Sciences are
another story. Careerist premedical students ordinarily have little
intrinsic interest in the courses that biologists and chemists teach
them; the latter, in turn, have little interest in having their
departments cluttered by students whose vision is already aimed at
the exit gate. Those who flock to economics courses on their way
to business school fare only somewhat better. Mismatched
educational objectives and sheer numbers thus tend to operate
against closer associations between these Careerists and faculty. But
there is also something more about Careerists that fosters such
alienation: Intellectuals and Strivers who are also interested in
medicine and business manage to form closer ties to faculty, despite
the handicaps in their way, as we discuss in the next two chapters.

Some Careerists fare perfectly well without the help of
advisers so far as their vocational objectives are concerned. But

broader educational purposes clearly suffer from the lack of a guiding hand, as illustrated in the following interviewer comments:

Jeremy says his undergraduate experience has lacked direction, unity, and a sense of completion. His freshman year was a "hodgepodge" and he sorely needed direction, but his adviser was rarely in the dorm and when he did come he did not know very much outside of his own field. As a result, he got no advice about structuring his courses nor on how heavy a course load to take and how to make coherent sense out of the year.

Fred had essentially nothing to say about the impact of faculty and their classes . . . since he hasn't become close to any faculty. Despite immense academic confusion, Fred doesn't think an advising relationship would have helped him much and cites his confusion as the reason why an adviser couldn't have helped him . . . unless he had a set academic focus and an adviser in that same field, there is little they could have done for each other.

Rebecca has had few faculty contacts, and she can think of only one person to ask for a recommendation. She says she wishes that in her freshman year someone had taken her by the hand and told her exactly what to do. But I don't think it ever occurred to Rebecca to ask for help, and I'm not sure she would have taken advantage of it if it were offered to her. She's very passive—an obvious disadvantage at a school where importance is placed upon student initiative.

Other Influences. Fellow students have no net impact on the likelihood of being a Careerist; as we shall see, student peers tend to reinforce both careerist and intellectual concerns. On the other hand, students who are strongly influenced by knowledge of the job market in choosing their majors and careers are much more likely to be Careerists (33 percent, compared to 17 percent of students who are weakly influenced). This works both ways. Careerists have a keen interest in the job market because of their strong vocational orientation. But the nature of the job market influences their choices as well. Careerists, more than others, choose fields that are more likely to provide job opportunities following graduation.

Major and Career Choices of Careerists

For Careerists, the choice of academic major largely turns on one question: Which major will best prepare me for my chosen career? There are two forms this concern can take. The first is to choose a major that equips one for immediate employment upon graduation, without the necessity of further schooling. Engineering is a good example: Careerists choose engineering majors more than any other group (24 percent of Careerists are engineers, compared to 16 percent of all students).

The alternative route is to use the major as a stepping-stone to one of the professions. This is why Careerists favor particular social sciences (economics but not anthropology) and natural sciences (biology but not physics). By contrast, they avoid the humanities—only 6 percent of Careerists major in the humanities, compared to 19 percent of all students, because such majors are perceived as poor bets for entry into the professions. They are also somewhat less likely than other students to major in interdepartmental programs (18 percent versus 22 percent) because of the fear that such programs, less sharply defined than departmental majors, might be seen as suspect by graduate schools.

The major is often selected by Careerist students for pragmatic considerations. For example, premeds choose the biological sciences ("the path of least resistance") because of the overlap between the requirements for the major and the requirements of medical schools. Even where there are no requirements set up in the professional schools, as is the case for business and law, these students generate their own constraints based on what will "look good" on their transcripts. These tactics sometimes misfire. A number of industrial engineering majors among Careerists came to regret their choice because not only did they have no particular interest in the subject matter but their expectations of how such a major would enhance their careers turned out, on hindsight, to be a miscalculation.

As a further manifestation of this lack of true interest in the major, these students generally do not get as involved in their major departments as other students, whether it is with the faculty, student organizations, or their peers majoring in the same field. These observations are less likely to apply to Careerists majoring in engineering departments and in earth sciences, for the reasons discussed earlier.

In the general student population, students with higher verbal SAT scores choose majors in the humanities more than do students of lower verbal scores. But this is not the case for the Careerists. Splitting the Careerists into two groups, we find that none of the high-verbal group (above 610 SAT score) choose the humanities. This finding suggests that vocational pressures among Careerists tend to overwhelm considerations of academic interest and aptitude; students who on the basis of SAT verbal scores would normally be expected to major in the humanities opt for other majors instead if they are Careerists. The small number of Careerists who do choose majors in the humanities constitute 10 percent of the Careerists with low SAT verbal scores. These students are caught in a double mismatch: Academic majors in the humanities are poor prospects for Careerists, just as Careerists with low verbal scores are poor prospects as humanities majors.

The choice of majors by Careerists is not always governed by ulterior motives. Some Careerists choose biology both because they are interested in it and because biology is an excellent preparation for medicine, just as economics is suitable for business and political science for law. There are academically legitimate reasons for making these choices, as well as understandable concessions to be made for enhancing one's attractiveness as an applicant to professional schools. Hence for some Careerists their choice of major is a happy combination of academic interest, aptitude, and career serviceability. However, what we want to highlight here is the greater tendency on the part of Careerists to let practical and tactical considerations determine their choice of major and career considerations overwhelm broader educational purposes.

A large proportion of Careerists plan to pursue graduate-level study: Fifty percent of Careerists plan to obtain a doctoral-level degree, compared to 42 percent of all students. This finding would be ironic were it not for the fact that the pursuit of advanced degrees by Careerists is usually not for the purpose of getting better educated but to receive advanced technical training in a profession like medicine. In principle, a student could pursue any subject, be it English, anthropology, or philosophy, for Careerist ends, but we have few such students in our sample. This is hardly surprising since such vocations are typically not the best means to attain Careerist objectives (such as making money or gaining prestige.)

The choice of a career itself is largely an instrumental decision for Careerists. Typically they do not ask themselves, What kind of work will I find intrinsically interesting and rewarding? but rather, What will offer me the greatest income, security, and status in the future? This is not to say that they are not prepared to work hard for the rewards they seek, but they are more likely to emphasize external rewards over intellectual interests and other sources of personal satisfaction. Thus, when a particular career plan does not pan out, the shift is usually to another lucrative profession; if not medicine, then business; if not business, then law. But here again there are exceptions, as illustrated by the biographical profile of Edward (Profile 4.4).

The majority of Careerists plan careers in business, medicine, and engineering. About 40 percent of Careerists plan to enter business (against 30 percent of all students), while 22 percent go into medicine (13 percent of all students) and 12 percent head for engineering (8 percent of all students). The overall result is that 92 percent of the Careerists plan to pursue careers in one of the four professions that have become the standard fields for students in the selective universities—business, law, medicine, and engineering. Only 8 percent plan to venture into other occupations. This far outstrips the 68 percent of all students pursuing the standard professions and the 50 percent of Intellectuals planning to do so.

The dominant value orientation among hard-core Careerists is to make money: a lot of it, and fast. Sometimes making money appears to be an end in itself, but more often it is presented as the means to a life of financial security and leisure; for some this means a settled experience, for others one of ongoing excitement. Most of these students make no secret of their "mercenary" aims in life. Unlike some students from wealthy families in other groups, Careerists show no self-consciousness or embarrassment over having money or the prospect of earning a lot of it. Some Careerists have perfect role models in their fathers. In other cases where students come from financially deprived backgrounds, their fathers represent the very antithesis of what they themselves want to become. The women in this group also tend to be very ambitious, although in their case aspirations to have a family tend to temper their Careerist zeal. The following interview excerpts illustrate some of the more exaggerated vocational attitudes of Careerists.

Peter's immediate goal is money. Money is a substitute for happiness in the sense that it will "make comfortable the search for love and happiness." He isn't too concerned about his occupation—it can be anything that makes money and it seems that he wants to be in an occupation that has to do with handling money. He's also very interested in gaining power (he's really "into power") and will do this by making money.

What Clint wants out of his education may be rather cut and dried, perhaps even a tad mercenary, but it's also as clear as a bell and solid as a rock at this point. His very clarity of purpose means a matching narrowness of scope. Clint is disappointed with his major (economics), which he finds not practically oriented enough. His ultimate goal is to be an entrepreneur to avoid paying excessive taxes. His father is a business executive whom taxes "rake clean." An entrepreneur can put money back into the business instead of giving it to Uncle Sam.

Clint had no trouble imagining his life in ten years. He'll be a vice-president of a firm in Southern California, driving a blue Mercedes and living in a nice house with a view of the ocean. He'll be financially secure, love his job, and have all the things he wants. He'll be raising a small family of one or two children, with high spiritual standards; in short, he'll "be your stereotypical executive."

Coleen declared engineering as a major because "she felt a need to get started in engineering before I changed my mind." She's having a hard time with her choice since her interests are elsewhere, but she will stick with it because "there are jobs out there for engineers."

Eventually, making money is his ultimate aim—whether he achieves that as a businessman or as a rock musician, which is what he would like to be if he really had his druthers ("a successful rock musician with a very strong investment portfolio").

Bill selected law school because he wants a profession but isn't interested in being a doctor or an accountant. He wants a job that has some intellectual content and high prestige. Besides, he has never met a lawyer who didn't like his job. Although he imagines his working situation to be fairly conventional, he hopes his life-style won't be. He likes adventure and a bit of lunacy in his life, and hopes this will continue.

Fred wants to be a lawyer and will do whatever it takes to make the grade. He sees the rat race for the game it is and he is going to play it. His motivation is to get rich and to get rich fast—he wants to be able to retire at thirty-five and do what he wants from then on. He is a "capitalist at heart" whose ten-year vision is to own his own company and probably be married but without children. He says that he hates the little brats but could see having one at most if he could be sure it was a boy to "carry on the family name."

The tendency of Careerists to choose engineering and economics majors more than other students is already present to some extent in the freshman year, where Careerists are slightly over-represented in engineering (26 percent, compared to 21 percent of all students) and the social sciences (30 compared to 25 percent) as their initial choice of major. But these differences increase considerably by the time they leave the university. Similarly, in comparing final career choice with initial choice we find that the college years intensify the vocational tendencies of the Careerists. While 83 percent of them choose one of the four standard fields during the freshman year, 92 percent are heading in these directions by graduation. Though they are very slightly overrepresented among premeds in the freshman year (23 percent compared to 21 percent of all students), a higher proportion of them are premeds by the senior year (22 percent, as against 13 percent of all students). These findings suggest that family influence and the other forces that push students toward narrow career choices are further aided and abetted during the college years, while countervailing influences are unable to deflect these students toward more diversified interests.

The 8 percent of Careerists who do not enter one of the standard professions differ significantly from the majority in several respects. Making money is less often a major motive for these students, although job security is important. Their choices of major and career are not merely instrumental. On the contrary, these students have an intense involvement in their chosen subject. For example, Alan was so interested in biology that he did most of his work in that area and went on to seek a Ph.D., hoping to teach at the college level. Susan lived and breathed journalism for four years and was already an accomplished reporter by the time she graduated. This type of Careerist is also present among those choosing the standard professions; some engineers and premeds would choose these fields even if they were not lucrative. Finally, there are "milder" Careerists who are mainly interested in making a decent living and are not obsessed by a relentless careerist urge. They are not much concerned about liberal education, but they are unlikely to discount its value to the same extent as more extreme Careerists.

Since Careerists are generally less open to experimentation and the exploration of new academic interests, we would expect to find that they change their major and career plans less than other students. In fact, they are not less likely to change majors than others, but they are less likely to change career plans: They average only .6 changes in career choice per student, compared to a mean of .9 changes for all students. Put another way, 62 percent of the Careerists stay with their initial career choice, while 51 percent of all students (and only 34 percent of the Unconnected) do likewise.

If we consider business, law, medicine, and engineering as a group, we find that virtually all of the Careerists (97 percent) who indicate an initial career choice in these four standard fields stay within them, compared to 82 percent of all students and 67 percent of the Unconnected. The general attrition suffered by premeds over the four years does not affect the Careerists to the same extent. On the other hand, Careerists are not more likely to stay in engineering than others because a large proportion of Careerist engineers see their long-term prospects in business management, and some of them switch out of engineering to take a more direct route to their goals through business.

Careerists are also more likely than others when leaving other occupational fields to join one of the four standard fields (57 percent of those starting in nonstandard fields join one of the standard fields by graduation, compared to 41 percent of all students). Finally, they are much less likely than other types not to have made at least a tentative career choice in the freshman year (10 percent, compared to 17 percent of all students and 23 percent of Intellectuals). In sum, the Careerists come fairly fixed in their interests—they know what they want to do when they begin college and are unlikely to change their minds.

Pursuing a Liberal Education

It is quite clear from the questionnaire data and interview reports that most students in this group by and large fail to get as broad a liberal education as they could, should, and sometimes want to. In quite a few instances, they come to college with a conscious decision (often endorsed by their parents) to avoid courses and subjects that do not have pragmatic value or will not enhance their careers. Such rejection is typically aimed at the "soft" subjects in the humanities and the social sciences, but in some cases it is more diffuse. Others choose their elective courses haphazardly ("there is no rhyme or reason to my course selection outside my major") or with an eye to pleasing admissions committees in professional schools ("I have taken courses from about every field—business schools like that rather than a single focus"). But there are also many in this group who express genuine interest in exposure to liberal learning but are either prevented from doing so because of the constraints imposed by their majors (particularly engineering) or through miscalculation, bad advice, and inertia.

The premeds are more likely to admit to an interest in a liberal education but then excuse themselves for failing to pursue it because of the pressures of premedical and major requirements. The engineers generally seem least concerned, either because they have less interest in outside subjects or they have resigned themselves to the fact that the many and rigorous requirements of engineering education severely limit exposure to a liberal education. The social science majors, by virtue of the broader nature of their own majors, manage to get a more rounded education.

Careerist students have their liberal educational opportunities more seriously compromised than even the Unconnected, the other group that is low on the intellectualism scale. At least some of the students in the latter group manage to get exposure to a wide variety of fields by meandering through various courses and majors.

A single-minded dedication to career combined with the rejection of all else that would not contribute to it proves to be a worse obstacle than the seeming uncertainties that hinder commitment to the institutionally endorsed goals of education. The following excerpts from interview reports show some of the more marked attitudes of Careerists toward liberal education.

Anthony senses a "big tension in purpose" between the desire to explore and acquire a broadly liberal education against the needs of preprofessional training. He sees most students as being career oriented, and though he decries this tendency, his family expects him to follow suit and he, too, is quite clearly keen on pursuing a professional career.

Jeanne selected biology as the best bet for a premed even though she hates her biology courses—they have no relevance or value for her and are only a means to an end. She plays the piano, the viola, and dances but has had to drop all of them because they take too much time. She would like to take classes in economics and psychology, but she cannot because she doesn't have time.

Bill asserts that political science courses have heightened his social and political awareness. "I can make much better conversation at cocktail parties now, although for $40,000 I'd better be able to."

She has been able to take few courses outside of her major, but those she has taken have proven to be the highlight of the term: "It keeps me sane."

He feels that undergraduate education is basically incoherent or at least not very well organized. One chooses courses and the major because of one's professional and career aspirations.

He did very little reading other than for his courses—he has no time for it . . . He feels that his education was not up to his expectations, especially in that it was not as broad as he expected, but he saw that there were time constraints that operated and it may have been as good as one could hope for.

Overseas Study. One of the important educational opportunities offered by Stanford is its overseas studies program, whereby students can spend one or two quarters in Stanford programs in several foreign countries. Since the overseas campuses primarily serve broad educational and cultural enrichment purposes and are generally not linked to vocational enhancement, participation in overseas programs may be an index of liberal educational interest and involvement.

Between 35 percent and 40 percent of all undergraduates attend an overseas campus, and in this respect the Careerists are quite typical—36 percent go overseas. Yet, the quality of the overseas experience of Careerists seems somewhat different from that of other groups, particularly the Intellectuals. The satisfaction of Careerists is more often expressed in terms of the "unbelievable amount of fun" they had or the relief they experienced in getting away from the home campus. Like everyone else, these students travel extensively and find their way into cathedrals and museums, but they are less likely to show the exuberance and exhilaration manifested by other students for whom the overseas experience is an enormous source of cultural enrichment.

Not all of the Careerists who do not go overseas fail to do so because they are not interested. Quite a few of the premeds and engineers express much regret at being unable to avail themselves of this opportunity. Yet the engineering schedule makes it difficult for them to go and the Careerist premeds are too panicked to leave the scene. Others will not allow themselves to be diverted from their career goals, which press on them so urgently. The following quotes from the interview reports illustrate these points.

He would have a hard time justifying going overseas to his parents. If he were a humanities major, it would make sense, but for a bio major, it is an expensive way to spend time in Europe.

His motivation for going overseas included the opportunity to prepare him for a possible international business focus. "Fun" was another motive.

He took a few courses in German studies to prepare for going to Vienna and considered adding it for a double major because it would "look impressive." It turned out to be a mixed experience.

"Overseas? Not as an engineer."

Following his overseas experience, he expanded his European horizons even further: He saw Rome and Sardinia by motor scooter, viewed the French Grand Prix in Monoco, came close to having his car bombed in Belfast, and camped on Crete. During his stay in Europe, he skied at seventeen different resorts.

Stopping Out. Another fairly common practice for under-graduates is stopping out for one or more quarters. In this respect Careerists are atypical: Only 13 percent of Careerists take time off from school, as against 24 percent of all students. This is the lowest percentage of all groups, and it indicates once again that the Careerists pursue their degrees with uncommon single-mindedness of purpose. But is that good for them? There were a number of students in this group who were quite confused and ambivalent with respect to their educational and career objectives. They could well have used a period off to think matters through and sort out their purposes and priorities. Other Careerists operated under tremendous pressure and were quite unhappy; they could certainly have used a period of reprieve and recuperation. Yet very few of them took time off, either because they were set so rigidly on their career paths they did not want to be distracted, or because they felt so anxious and insecure over their career prospects that they could not let go even for a short period of time.

Social Life and Extracurricular Activities

Single-minded dedication to career preparation does not preclude involvement in campus social life. The extracurricular activities of Careerists are only slightly less numerous than those of other groups, as shown by the Involvement Index (Appendix II). The mean number of activities is 3.7 for the Careerists, 4.0 for all students.

A more detailed look shows Careerists to be significantly less likely than other students to engage in activities that are cultural or service oriented. They are more likely than other students to engage in athletics and student organizations, especially fraternities and sororities, but less likely to get into areas that are primarily intellectual, artistic, or altruistic. There is a distinct strain of political conservatism running through this group. Quite a few students were active in the Young Republicans and in evangelical Christian groups.

Our indicators of social and political involvement show Careerists to be less active than other groups. For example, in the sophomore year they report spending about one hour a month on volunteer or community service activities, while the average for all students is about three hours a month. Similarly, in response to items in the junior and senior years asking how often they discuss social or political issues with other students, the Careerists indicate that they do so less frequently than any other group. Further insights into the social attitudes of Careerists can be gleaned from the following quotes from interview reports:

No cultural commitments to speak of (blank look on face when asked this question).

So far as social and political concerns go, he neither has the time to be bothered nor does he care.

John is a Puritan. His mood is self-righteous, highly moral, and subtly indignant. He hates politics and has not wanted to have anything to do with it—he sees it as only empty rhetoric and rather disgusting. But he has also come to see that political involvement is inevitable for him because of his personal concerns and career plans.

Cliff's philosophy of life is that "everyone is out for himself. Every useful person has something valuable about himself that he should trade rather than give away." Nonetheless, Cliff's one organizational involvement is with a group that provides adult companionship to boys who have been in trouble. His assignment is with a fifteen-year-old with whom he spends five to six hours a week. The boy is a "pain in the ass," but Cliff enjoys his company—"I can see a lot of myself in him; when I was fifteen, I was all for immediate gratification too."

Social and political issues have not interested Jimmy. He says he and many others like him are not involved because they're interested in their careers, the preparation for which is "what we are paying for."

The interview reports reveal the peer relationships of these students to follow distinctive patterns. In the more typical form, relationships tend to be superficial, even where there is a great deal of socializing with many people. As one student put it, the people he feels close to are interested in going out for pizza, playing Frisbee and sports, partying, and having a good time. There is less willingness to make serious commitments ("I can't think of myself as anything but a bachelor; it upsets me to see my friends getting picked off one by one").

A high proportion of all our students, including Careerists, expect to be married or in a committed relationship in ten years, and to have children. However, a higher percentage of Careerists say they will not be in a stable relationship (6 percent, as against 2 percent for Strivers, the lowest type). This difference is entirely due to men: Ten percent of Careerist men but none of these women make this claim. With respect to having children, Careerist men and women show the highest percentages for not expecting to become parents. Among Careerist men 84 percent say they will have children, as against 93 percent for Intellectuals and the Unconnected and 100 percent of Strivers. Careerist women have the lowest percentage of either sex in all four groups: Only 79 percent anticipate ever having children, against 95 percent for women in each of the other three groups.

Concomitantly, there is a distinct core of individuals among Careerists who show the opposite tendency. Interviews reveal that they have very close and stable relationships that are likely to eventuate in early marriage. "He has a steady girlfriend and much of what they do together involves just the two of them"; "She is engaged to be married following graduation." In these cases, students are following the same pattern they manifest with respect to their careers—choose early and settle down. Careerism is thus compatible with both being more shallow and unwilling to make personal commitments as well as being precociously more adultlike in one's close personal relationships.

Academic Success and Satisfaction

Academic Performance. With respect to grades and academic honors, Careerists are just about average in all of the dimensions we have examined. Thus, while 8 percent of all students win election to Phi Beta Kappa, 6 percent of the Careerists receive this award. This minor difference could be easily explained by humanities majors being overrepresented among the recipients of this honor and underrepresented among Careerists. With respect to departmental honors and graduation with distinction, Careerists are very near the mean figures. They also have quite typical grades, in terms of both their overall grade point averages and their grades in different types of courses (humanities, natural sciences, social sciences, and so on). Though most of them are less motivated by intrinsic intellectual interest than students in other groups, the instrumental importance of their academic work for their careers clearly leads them to work hard to do as well as others.

Self-Assessments of Knowledge and Abilities. In general, self-assessments of academic skills elicited by the Senior Survey are closely related to academic major. Thus, engineering students rate themselves highly in subjects like the natural sciences and technology, while humanities majors rate themselves highly in understanding literature, the fine arts, and similar areas. Given that relatively high proportions of the Careerists major in the natural sciences and engineering, it is not surprising to find that their self-assessments in these areas are higher than those of other groups, while they tend to have lower self-ratings in areas such as foreign languages, understanding Western culture, and understanding literature and fine arts.

One surprising finding is that Careerists give the highest self-ratings for their ability to write English well (mean of 4.3 on a five-point scale, while the next highest type, the Intellectuals, are at 4.1). We have no independent evidence that the Careerists are actually more proficient in writing than the Intellectuals. Perhaps they interpret this question as a test of their proficiency in communication skills, which they recognize as an important asset to their future career, while Intellectuals may understand the ability to write well in a more literary sense, which is a more demanding concept to meet.

Satisfaction with the Undergraduate Experience. Our information on student satisfaction with the undergraduate experience comes from two major sources. One is a series of items on the senior-year questionnaire of the Cohort Study, which asks students to rate their satisfaction in the senior year only in such areas as interaction with instructors, level of interest in courses, and overall level of contentment. (A five-point scale is used, with 1 = not at all satisfied and five = very satisfied.) The second source is the Senior Survey questionnaire (Appendix II), distributed annually to all graduating seniors. This is a retrospective assessment of all four years that asks students to give an evaluation "on an absolute scale" (1 = very poor, 5 = excellent) of fourteen different items, such as "the overall quality of your undergraduate education," "the adequacy of your training for graduate/professional school," evaluations of the faculty as teachers, scholars, and advisers, and other such items.

The evaluations from the senior-year questionnaire reveal few exceptional responses by the Careerists; on almost every dimension they are quite typical. Their level of overall contentment (mean of 3.8) is almost identical to the overall mean of 4.0 and somewhat below the mean of the Strivers, which is 4.2. Whatever complaints the Careerists may have must be viewed within this context of an average level of general satisfaction.

The Senior Survey questionnaire shows somewhat more interesting and distinctive differences. The Careerists are especially satisfied with their training for graduate or professional school (mean of 4.1 compared to 3.9 for all students and 3.7 for the Intellectuals). On the other hand, they are considerably less satisfied than others with the quality of their major courses and the adequacy of their liberal education. This pattern is exactly what we would expect.

A stronger sense of dissatisfaction comes across in the interview reports of Careerists, some of whom express considerable anxiety over the future and regrets over the past.

Wears a facade of contentment but seems excessively discontented underneath.

He single-mindedly sacrificed everything to the aim of getting into medical school but since that does not seem to be happening, he is very dissatisfied with his undergraduate experience. His whole effort seems marred by a sense of futility.

Expresses repeated concerns about failure, about worry over success, and a great deal of anxiety generally.

During her senior year she plans to take the LSAT, the GMAT, and perhaps the GRE's. "I'm always scared I'll leave something out."

He has lost all enthusiasm and vigor for his studies and is suffering from a terrible state of ennui about school and schooling. Though he came to Stanford with forty-five units of advanced placement credit, he really has failed to challenge himself or work harder than he did in high school. He does not seem to blame anyone for this, but he does not credit anyone with trying to help either.

Has a good deal of ambivalence about his choice of future career. This is showing through the way he picked his major late, did not get an adviser in time, and is now having trouble getting letters of recommendation. His problems are being manifested by a sense of lack of meaning in his life and bouts of depression for which he is getting counseling.

She has seen an erosion of self-confidence take place over her four years here. What she will take from Stanford is "insecurity."

Some of the most disheartening tales in the interview reports are in the accounts of premedical students who have not done well. The sense of having failed their families is perhaps the most galling aspect of their undergraduate experience.

Scott found it difficult to explain to his parents that he had not been able to do well enough in the premedical curriculum. In high school he had gotten great pleasure out of seeing his parents' pride in his academic performance. His parents have always told him that if he worked hard, he would achieve whatever he set his mind to. Yet he has found that just making the effort is not sufficient. At the end of his sophomore year Scott seemed hurt by his perceived failure but was still trying to adjust to no longer being the best in everything as he once was. This he thinks was a maturing experience.

Scott shifted to chemical engineering (his father's profession) and remained strongly career oriented. He had no interest in taking courses outside of what was of vocational value to him. Courses in the humanities or the study of history, in particular, did not interest him. He could not understand how one could "get into a major without knowing that there is a job to follow it." His concerns about the future dominated his thinking and his approach to his education. As the interviewer put it, "He sees his education as a job which involves putting in a certain number of hours a day."

Diane was described in her freshman interview as a "very attractive, poised, young woman looking like a model gymnast, which she is." She had done very well in her small-town high school and had received the "Young Businesswoman of the Year Award." She was athletic, musical, socially popular, and academically outstanding.

On coming to Stanford she plunged into her premedical studies, dropping virtually everything else and sacrificing her desire to become liberally educated. She worked hard ("I didn't think it was possible to work so hard") and did very well for a while. But then she began to lose her motivation. She was too far away from home ("I have always felt responsible for my mother's happiness; she has done nothing but raise kids"). She "started to relax, be more social." By her senior year she had gained twenty pounds and became increasingly "depressed and obsessed" about food. It took three attempts to get her to the senior interview, which had to be cut short when she broke down and related her personal difficulties during the rest of the hour: "I haven't felt very good about myself for a long time. I was trying so hard to please my parents and I just couldn't do it anymore. I couldn't handle it. Last year was pretty nasty . . . I didn't have any personal goals or ambitions."

Her parents served her an ultimatum that there would be no further support after June 15. So her immediate plans were to work as a waitress as a stopgap measure while she looked for a better job. Her parting remarks in the senior interview were: "I don't really want to do anything. I'm not sure I still want to go to medical school. I may volunteer once a week in a hospital. I've thought of being a nurse but that would really throw my parents."

These comments emanate from the casualties of the Careerist orientation. They do not reflect the majority view. Yet even some of those who do not express much discontent seem fretful and inordinately worried about anything, however trivial, that may interfere with their career aspirations. One student, when asked if she had any educational concerns that had not been covered in the interview, said, "I used a number 2.5 lead pencil (instead of number 2) when I took the Medical College Admissions Test. Does it matter?"

At their most contented, the Careerists are a happy lot. This is particularly true for some of the engineers in this group. These are highly competent and successful students who are energetic, enterprising, and by all indications headed for exciting and successful careers. They exude self-confidence ("I don't need anything like grades to prove myself") and the ability to handle stress ("academic pressure is like atmospheric pressure—it's always there and one needs to learn to live with it"). These students have worked hard and played hard. If they have missed out on some things, they do not see their losses as serious; after all, one cannot have everything. What they have gotten is what they came for, and that is what matters to them. The following accounts illustrate these points.

Although what Joel is taking away from Stanford is primarily "a degree," he has been very satisfied with his experience: "I love it here"; "the greatest place"; "a paradise." Joel did not work terribly hard, had a very active social life, and did quite well. He had very little exposure to the humanities even though he had grown up in Mexico and was bilingual. He was less involved in social or political issues because "I'm an engineer, I don't get into discussions much." He was a delightful fellow ("so likable").

Julie followed her brother to Stanford, sustained by the thought that "if he could do it, so can I." Her expectation was that people come to Stanford to assure themselves of an interesting and lucrative life— objectives that matched her own precisely. She had come to Stanford with the clear intention of eventually going to business school. Her earlier expectation that she would major in economics now gave way to an interest in industrial engineering. But that did not deter her in her fast-paced social life, which was further enhanced by her joining a sorority. She continued to regard her academic education as a means to an end and seemed to find no real pleasure beyond a notion of its being a good "investment." Furthermore, Stanford's primary value remained its effectiveness in exposing her to fascinating and intelligent people.

By the end of her senior year Julie had obtained a job with a major corporation and had been admitted to the Stanford School of Business, which she planned to attend after working for a year. The interviewer *summed up her impressions of Julie as follows: "a very competent, hard-working, self-confident, and cheerful person ... although her educational outlook is very much a pragmatic one, there is no hint of manipulativeness or cynicism in her choices. Indeed, she seems unusally open and accepting. I couldn't help but think that had this been a job interview, I would have hired her in a minute." Julie's parting comment: "I have led a charmed life."*

Balance Sheet

Although our primary focus in this book is descriptive rather than prescriptive, there may be some value in an overview of each orientation in our typology with respect to its strengths and liabilities. This will facilitate the discussion in Chapter Eight of the implications of our findings. But whatever evaluations we make must be tempered by the following caveats. First, we are evaluating these students before their professional lives have begun to unfold. It may take a decade following graduation before meaningful statements can be made about issues like how successful they have been professionally.

Second, we evaluate these students in accordance with certain standards; namely, a successful college education must provide both broad liberal learning and effective career preparation. Stated in such general terms, few people are likely to quarrel with these standards; if pressed as to what we precisely mean by them, it will be hard to maintain agreement. The criteria of evaluation, therefore, will have to remain rather ambiguous.

Third, we will assume each orientation has assets and liabilities both as a whole and with respect to each individual. The four categories in the typology can be thought of as adaptive patterns to academic and life challenges. Hence, their merit is relative to those challenges. When the oldest child of a socially disadvantaged family pursues a lucrative profession to lift the family out of poverty, our evaluation will be more sympathetic than when the scion of a wealthy family blindly pursues a career to make yet more money.

The main asset of the Careerist orientation is self-evident: It is the safest ticket to job security. This is not a trivial consideration. When the expenses of an education at selective private institutions add up to well over $50,000, it is not unreasonable to expect one's job prospects at graduation to be very bright. Monetary considerations aside, a sought-after profession goes a long way in providing status, security, personal satisfaction, and potential for public service.

Careerism is most compatible with majors in engineering and earth sciences. Majors in these fields provide meaningful career training, professional certification, and immediate job opportunities following graduation. By contrast, undergraduate programs that are taken solely as preparation for careers in other professional schools impart far less useful career training. If the student is accepted into a graduate program, well and good. Otherwise, the baccalaureate degree in most of the arts and sciences has relatively little marketable utility. Most vulnerable in this respect are the premedical students; if they do not make it into medical school, they have the least to show for their pains.

The main liability incurred by Careerists is not in what they do but in what they do not do—in failing to obtain an adequate liberal education. To lose out on this prospect vitiates one of the main purposes of higher education. This loss is doubly sad because it is unnecessary. Many other students attain the same career goals without paying the same price. Ironically enough, Careerism may not even be the best path to truly spectacular career success. While we cannot be certain of this, there are good reasons to expect that the vocationally successful are more likely to emerge from among the Strivers and the Intellectuals. The more gifted among these latter students are not so desperate as to sacrifice everything in their quest for a successful career, nor do they forgo career interests altogether. Their greater intellectual orientation and broader educational aims help make them into more polished and sophisticated individuals, thereby endowing them with those personality and social characteristics that are just as important as technical competence, drive, and naked ambition for true professional success. If this message can be gotten through to Careerists, it will have the greatest chance of removing the vocational blinders that prevent them from seeing the full benefits of a college education.

5

Students as Intellectuals: Learning for the Joy of It

J. Wallace Sterling, late chancellor of Stanford University, characterized the educated person as someone who is able to entertain three things: an idea, a friend, and oneself. The Intellectuals we discuss in this chapter come closest to attaining this ideal.

Intellectuals are defined as the group scoring low on careerism and high on intellectualism, the opposite of Careerists. For them, college is primarily a place where they can broaden their established academic interests, develop their intellectual capacities, and seek out new interests and challenges. They are less concerned about preparing for professional careers. For some, this orientation is based on the self-confidence that comes from knowing that they have strong capabilities—they assume that the pursuit of their academic interests will lead naturally to a desirable occupation. For others the de-emphasis on career concerns is more explicitly ideological; they decry the excessive vocationalism of their peers and deliberately downplay their own career concerns. Their interest in Stanford is based more on its reputation for academic excellence rather than its function as a stepping-stone to lucrative careers. The value of college credentials on the job market is for them a desirable bonus but not a substitute for the intellectual opportunities offered by a strong liberal education.

It was harder to find a label for this group than for the Careerists. Career objectives tend to be concrete; the desire for learning for its own sake is more diffuse. The requirements of preprofessional education are spelled out more readily (rightly or wrongly) than those for liberal education. The label we have chosen makes good sense in terms of how our culture defines "intellectuals," but it is a bit grandiose and burdened with the implication that these students are somehow more intelligent than their peers. This label may also suggest the notion that these students are grade-grubbing "nerds" who grind away their lives in the library, missing out on all the fun of being in college. Actually, what sets them apart is neither the power of their intellect nor their social life-style but their attitude toward intellectual issues.

In principle, intellectualism is based not on the subject matter of a field of study but on its intellectual perspective, depth, and focus on "first principles" (Hutchins, 1936). Both intellectual and nonintellectual approaches are possible in any subject area. Yet conventional distinctions are commonly made among academic areas both with respect to academic rigor as well as degree of intellectualism. Such comparisons are easier (and less inflammatory) within a cognate area, like engineering or the social sciences, than across them. Thus, few people will disagree that electrical engineering is intellectually more demanding than industrial engineering, though not necessarily more intellectual. Likewise, literature is seen as more intellectual than journalism but not necessarily intellectually more demanding. The distinction between the "hard" and "soft" social sciences mainly is based on how "quantitative" (hence "scientific") a field is. The lack of the use of experimentation, on the other hand, tilts a field in the other direction; theorists may be seen as more intellectual than applied physicists. There are many ambiguities in such comparisons, and when poets are compared with petroleum engineers these confusions are compounded. Yet students must struggle with these judgments and will assimilate the disciplinary pride and prejudice of their teachers during the process of their academic socialization.

What we have said so far, and much of what we will say, applies primarily to the core group of Intellectuals who set the tone of this orientation. But as with Careerists, there is much variation in the intensity with which students within this group conform to intellectual ideals. Moreover, Intellectuals have far greater difficulty in putting their ideals into practice than do Careerists, an issue to which we shall return. Hence, the individuals we are dealing with in this group cover a considerable range. At one extreme are those who are highly focused on intellectual issues and remarkably broad in their educational aims; at the other, more attenuated end are students who minimally fulfill the requirements of liberal education and are barely distinguishable in this respect from the Unconnected. With respect to career attitudes there is a similar range whereby some Intellectuals are highly conscious of developing their vocational prospects (without sacrificing their broader educational goals) while others seem to give little thought to the matter until the senior year rolls around.

For example, Judith had an intensely intellectual and artistic orientation throughout college, being primarily interested in literature and drama, and went on to pursue a Ph.D. in English. Likewise, Kevin came to Stanford to get "the best liberal education he could get," which he saw as "an end in itself." At the time of graduation he planned to take the foreign service exam and work for the State Department. As an alternative, he would spend two years in the English countryside with books and music and then go to law school. By contrast, Gilbert took a happy mix of courses, made good money working during the summer as a house painter, but was quite vague about his career prospects. Similarly, Shirley explored a variety of subjects and had wonderful experiences at overseas campuses but was quite uncertain about her future at the time of graduation. Biographical profiles 5.1 through 5.4 present further examples of various types of Intellectuals.

Profile 5.1: Keith—Future Academic

"Keith was so engrossed in Mahler's Third," wrote the interviewer, *"that he completely forgot his appointment . . . it was well worth the wait and I could just as easily have spent the whole morning talking with him. It was refreshing for me to talk with someone who obviously enjoys using*

his mind, has found real meaning to his educational experiences, and knows where he is going."

Keith came to Stanford with the desire to obtain a strong liberal arts education. He had a wide range of interests, was an avid debater, and had played the cello for eight years. *"Everything about Keith points to an academic orientation. His father is a university professor in the humanities and the family places a great emphasis on education."*

An excellent niche for Keith's academic interests was provided by the freshman program in Structured Liberal Education, which offers a residentially based set of integrated courses. In his sophomore year he remained intent on taking as broad a liberal arts schedule as possible. Simultaneously, he had developed a keen interest in political science and declared it as his major. Keith's intellectual concerns were nonetheless by no means confined to the academic world. During his vacations he worked as an intern in the office of the state governor and then that of his state senator in Washington, D.C. One of the projects he worked on involved writing a background paper on student government, which was printed and distributed to high schools in his home state.

Keith's work experiences in the public sector led him to conclude that people working in those fields *"get burned out too quickly, and lack security."* Consequently, he shifted his career focus to university teaching, thinking he would be much more comfortable in intellectual surroundings.

Keith established excellent relationships with his academic advisers and several professors. His intellectual curiosity continued unabated (*"there is so much to learn, and I think I'm really learning for its own sake this year"*). He became a tutor in the Structured Liberal Education program and began to think of himself seriously as a future academic.

In his junior year Keith continued to maintain a straight-A average. He had a serious involvement with a young woman whom he planned to marry. His interviewer characterized him as someone who *"knows what he wants, recognizes his strengths and weaknesses, and knows how to go about meeting his educational goals . . . He's a serious student, and yet not without a light side. He certainly has one of the healthier attitudes about learning that I have witnessed . . ."*

In his senior year Keith wrote an honor's thesis in his major and was admitted to several outstanding programs in political science. He planned to get married following graduation. He chose to go to the University of Chicago (*"It is probably the best in political theory"*). Both he and his wife planned to spend the next four or five years in school and then look for jobs. Keith hoped eventually to teach at the university level and live in an academic setting. The parting comment of his interviewer: *"This is a caring, concerned, warm individual with lots to offer. I am very impressed with his maturity and depth of being. He can roll with the punches and make the most of whatever situation. I know he will be missed at the political science department, as he will be elsewhere on campus. He will make his mark at Chicago as he has here, no doubt."*

Profile 5.2: Kirsten—Cosmopolitan Life

Kirsten is the daughter of a physician on the staff of a well-known medical center; her mother is a nurse. Kirsten chose Stanford over a prestigious East Coast university because she thought she would obtain a more rounded education here. As a freshman she was somewhat undecided as to her course of study and career but full of self-confidence: "It's a matter of knowing what I want to do, not what I can do," she told the interviewer. When asked what she thought that "can do" included, her characteristic and remarkably honest response was, "Anything." There was no arrogance in her answer, even some embarrassment. It's just that she felt broadly prepared and capable.

In her Freshman Seminar, Kirsten was distressed at the hostility expressed by some of the students who resented the professor's extensive critique of their work and the fact that he was demanding far more of them than easy-A seminars. Her own reactions to the course were quite the opposite: She enjoyed the class work, valued the great wealth of knowledge the professor had to offer, and ended up feeling a great deal of sympathy for the way he was being treated. By the end of the quarter, he seemed hurt and lonely. Kirsten made a point of stopping by to visit him, and she gave her only strong show of emotion in providing this account.

Kirsten took a broad mix of classes including the introductory chemistry series for possibly going into medicine. But she became rapidly disenchanted with the "cutthroat fashion" in which her fellow premeds were approaching their education. Eventually she abandoned the idea of becoming a physician because medicine would be too confining for her needs. Instead, she chose to double-major in Spanish and international relations to prepare herself for a possible career either in international business or in the foreign service.

A major part of Kirsten's sophomore year was spent at the Salamanca campus. Fluent in Spanish, she made excellent use of local acquaintances and friends. Relationships with the members of the faculty were excellent, but Kirsten also spent a good deal of time following up on her own interests, checking out archives and cathedrals, reading voraciously, and expanding her cultural horizons.

To the very end of her undergraduate days Kirsten continued to pursue a wide variety of interests. Her one regret was that the requirements of the international relations degree made it difficult for her to incorporate as many of her own choices into her study schedule as she would have liked. In her senior year she branched further into economics and accounting courses; she took calculus "just for fun."

Concurrently with her varied and demanding academic life, Kirsten was very active in a variety of student organizations and was an accomplished athlete. She held a steady part-time job and put a lot of energy into her friendships.

To test her interest in a possible business career, Kirsten worked for an international company in Spain. Based on that experience, she then applied and was accepted into a prestigious business school and headed for a career in international business. The interviewer, impressed by her intelligence, sense of independence, and self-confidence, was moved to ask, "Can an undergraduate be this self-sufficient?"

Profile 5.3: Heather—Modest Expectations

Pleasant but rather bland and low-key, Heather came from a high school that is "not well known for anything." She had a strong science background but was also interested in music (played the piano and classical guitar) and athletics (swam, ran, and played rugby). Her parents wanted Heather to obtain a broad liberal education: "My mother doesn't really care if I finish here in four years. She wants me to take lots of art and humanities and become well rounded." They had always supported her in what she wanted to do.

In her sophomore year Heather's interests simultaneously moved toward geology and archeology. But her primary aim remained to obtain a liberal education rather than become trained in technical skills. She went to the Vienna campus in her sophomore year and found the experience culturally enriching, but it also made her "appreciate living here more than I did before." She learned German quickly and primarily focused on art and music, spending a lot of time at the opera, symphony, and concerts. She followed up her Vienna experience by obtaining a translator's certificate in German.

All through her junior year Heather remained undecided between the earth sciences and archeology. To help sort out her thinking, she spent her summers working on archeological digs and eventually decided in her senior year that archeology would not be the best career choice for her. This then left her free to focus her attention on an undergraduate degree in applied earth sciences, with a career along the same lines. She planned to work for a master's degree or get a job in city planning for a few years and then go for her graduate degree.

Heather's senior year was a time of much soul-searching: "I've been trying to rethink what I've gotten out of Stanford. It's been a hard year in questioning the purposes of being here . . . People I've talked to are going through the same, although some single-minded people don't even stop to question."

Looking into the future, she said in her parting interview, "I do not plan to have a hectic life-style. It will be something low-key. I can see myself working on and off as the need arises. I'll need enough to eat. I don't see a career as a major focus in my life. There is no one thing that I am so interested in that I want to devote my life to it. I want to travel, read, take things easy. I wouldn't mind a farm somewhere. I think education has been a good background, and I want to go on learning. Basically, I didn't come to Stanford to get a degree in order to work. Rather, the question is how much work do I have to do in order to live."

Profile 5.4: Kim—Social Activist

Kim is a relaxed, cheerful, and soft-spoken young woman from a Japanese-American family. Both parents are scientists on a university faculty. With the aid of an excellent young faculty adviser, Kim systematically went about establishing a curriculum that fulfilled her intellectual curiosity, while simultaneously satisfying her need to interject practicality and avoid wasting time ("there is too much goofing around to justify the extra cost"). Even in her freshman year she felt a gratifying intellectual overlap between her courses. Beyond academics, the experience of meeting new people of different backgrounds and ideas was an equally exciting "eye-opening" experience. "She always tried to see the best in people and the things they do," wrote Kim's interviewer; "a warm and uncomplicated young woman . . . an ever-affable achiever, who simply expects to be content, and thus tends to be so."

Kim chose economics as her major because she felt it provided the best opportunity for her to focus on policy-related issues. She selected it over political science because it offered a stronger analytical framework. Nonetheless, she found herself less than enthusiastic about some of the economics courses she had to take and compensated for this by continuing to select a wide variety of other interesting courses. These included diverse offerings in civil engineering, chemistry, Japanese history, acting, and dance. She impressed the interviewer with her "mature and serious attitude toward academic decision making."

Kim's conversion to Christianity in the sophomore year and her strongly liberal political convictions became instrumental in shaping her academic and career future ("my outlook on everything"). She became committed to a life in public service. Her choice of economics as a major and additional training in the social sciences were for Kim not a springboard to a successful business career but rather a practical vehicle to work for social change. To begin furthering these aims Kim served on the boards of a number of student organizations dedicated to social *concerns. Her sense that there is something "intrinsically wrong" in being "catered to" by working-class people led her to establishing a living arrangement with like-minded people committed to a cooperative ideology.*

· To tie together the various strands of her academic and social interests, as well as to have a culminating educational experience, Kim undertook an honor's thesis in the program on Values, Technology, and Society. She spent the summer following her junior year as an intern in a congressional office in Washington in order to evaluate the prospects of someday working for the government. Following graduation she returned to Washington to work as an intern with a national conservation organization. Her plan was to go back to school within a year—either law school or for graduate study in public policy. She was leaning toward law because she thought it would provide a broader career base. She was committed to working for social change, although she was as yet somewhat uncertain how to go about doing it. The future did not worry her—everything had fallen into place so well for her up to this point that she was confident things would work out in the future too. In ten years, she hoped to be doing environmental advocacy, either on the West Coast or possibly in Washington. She liked the idea of living in a cooperative community and expected to have children in a long-term relationship.

Interviewer Impressions of Intellectuals

The interviewers were generally quite impressed with the Intellectuals. These students come across as personable, thoughtful, intellectually curious, and academically serious. *Mature* and *articulate* were among the adjectives repeatedly used to describe them. The other common strand that impressed the interviewers was the high level of satisfaction expressed by Intellectuals with their educational and broader experiences in college.

While the interviewers were positively ecstatic over many of these students ("a delight to see"), there were also cases where interviewer reactions were more ambivalent. This was usually triggered by what came across as a tinge of intellectual arrogance and an alarming lack of career direction. Yet, even in these instances interviewers tended to downplay the negative elements in favor of the more generally positive image. The following interviewers' reactions to Intellectuals illustrate their sentiments:

Donna is a bright, independent, and genuinely self-confident young woman who is getting exactly the rounded experience that she considers her first priority in undergraduate education. She has a sensible, level-headed approach to academic decision making, a wish for a broad exposure to ideas combined with a reasonably focused program, and a high degree of confidence that college is the place where she can realize her goals.

Sarah is bright, articulate, thoughtful, personable, totally in charge of her life (or so it seems). The "wish for new experiences" really does seem to dominate her decision making. "The main influence in deciding whether to do something is whether I have never done it before." She wants to be broadly educated in all senses, a shift (in her view) from her freshman year when she was an intellectual snob. She seems able to extract from any experience all it has to offer. At times I wondered whether her quest for breadth of academic experience represented an excess of virtue, whether she might be out of necessity sacrificing depth. Only time will tell, but my tentative conclusion is that her approach is definitely not a superficial one.

I'm enchanted! What a pleasure to talk with Ingrid—she is so excited, alive, interested, and thoughtful that I enjoyed her interview more than any so far.

Laurie is confident without being cocky; open-minded without being empty-headed; committed without losing her objectivity or her independence; intellectual without being pretentious; modest without being overly so. She is articulate, thoughtful, and likely to take risks. . . . she can be critical without being negative. She doesn't just speak about social concerns, she does something about them.

Andrew is a very bright but troubled young man. Handsome, well groomed, well dressed, but restless, a bit cynical, and in my judgment, basically unhappy. He feels alienated from his affluent background and from much of life here at Stanford, and has been unable to find any philosophy, life-style, or commitment to which to give his energy and talents. "My mind was too well trained in prep school. I can always see both sides of an issue, and thus can't commit myself to either."

If I had to choose a roommate from among my cohort interviewees, I would probably pick Nina . . . she seems the most engaged in her college experience in both an intellectual and personal way. In addition, she is absolutely delightful to be with . . . extremely attractive, very articulate, bubbly, cheerful, as well as thoughtful and exceptionally mature.

Steve is one refreshing, independent, bright, and likable soul. In many ways he very much resembles the ideal everyone has in mind when they talk about getting a liberal arts education without worrying about a job . . . I find him an unusual combination of idealism and practicality. Probably comes as close to using college in the way I think it ought to be used as any student I have ever known. Kind of person I would like to know the rest of my life and one I wouldn't mind having as a next-door neighbor.

The interviewers not only thought highly of these students but clearly identified with them; no wonder that they felt they would be good roommates or neighbors. The last excerpt, in particular, is not just descriptive but prescriptive; this is the way college "ought to be" used. Though there may be good reasons for such bias, the reader should be aware of its possible presence in the perceptions of the interviewers and perhaps the authors as well.

Background Characteristics of Intellectuals

Gender. While men are overrepresented among Careerists, nearly two thirds of Intellectuals are women; Intellectuals account for 34 percent of women but only 15 percent of men. This is by far the largest share of women in any of the four categories.

Are women overrepresented among Intellectuals because they value liberal education more, or is it because they shun careers? The evidence is in favor of the former. Far from shunning professional careers, *all* of the women in the core group of Intellectuals planned on having careers, as did the majority of those in the more inclusive Intellectual category.

Ethnicity. Ethnic background strongly affects the likelihood of being an Intellectual. Minority students, be they Asian American, Black, or Chicano, are less likely to be classified as Intellectuals than whites: Only 14 percent of minority students fall in this category, compared to 27 percent of Caucasians. This is not because minority students are unconcerned with liberal education, but because they rarely combine such interest with a relatively low level of concern for professional training. This means that ethnic minority students who score high on the intellectualism variable tend to be Strivers, valuing both the intellectual and career dimension of college life. Our findings in this respect are consistent with the general thrust of the literature on minority group motivations for attending college (see, for instance, Thomas, 1980; Blackwell, 1981).

Socioeconomic Status. The SES Index also shows a powerful association—14 percent of the lowest third, 26 percent of the middle third, and 36 percent of the highest third in our ranking are Intellectuals. This is the strongest and most consistent effect of the index for any group. The most obvious explanation for this finding is that students lower in the social hierarchy are under greater economic and social pressure for upward economic mobility, while those at the top can take material success more for granted and have less need to be concerned about career building. Coming from homes with less highly educated parents, the lower group may also lack the models and traditions associated with the pursuit of liberal learning.

A more detailed look suggests that this interpretation is too simple. Considering family income, for example, we find that 27 percent of students from families above $75,000 a year are Intellectuals, as against 40 percent of students from families in the $50-75,000 bracket, and 12 percent of students from families of less than $50,000 per year. Hence it is not simply that the wealthiest students can "afford" to emphasize education over careers, while the poor cannot; rather, the strongest contingent of Intellectuals comes from upper-middle-class families that are affluent but not at the very top of the income scale.

Particularly significant are the occupational and educational levels of fathers. We noted in the previous chapter that the children of corporate executives are especially likely to be Careerists; interestingly enough, they are not rare among Intellectuals but are proportionately represented in this type. On the other hand, the children of professors (33 percent) and doctors (30 percent) are especially likely to be Intellectuals while the children of engineers (8 percent) and blue-collar workers (0 percent) are virtually absent in this group. These results are exactly the opposite of those for

Careerists, as is the finding that students whose fathers hold doctoral-level degrees are much more likely to be Intellectuals than students whose fathers hold master's degrees (34 percent compared to 16 percent). The consistency with which lower socioeconomic standing inhibits students from being Intellectuals is shown once again by the fact that only 9 percent of the students whose fathers have less than a college education are Intellectuals. We find no correlation between maternal education or career and the likelihood of being an Intellectual.

Taken together, these results suggest that the relationship between the SES Index and being an Intellectual is dependent more on paternal education and profession than on income as such. The families of Intellectuals have more status than wealth; the fathers are highly educated men in well-regarded occupations but they do not have the highest incomes. Students who are unlikely to be Intellectuals, on the other hand, may be of one of two types: Either they belong to ethnic minority groups and come from families with relatively low income and education, or they are from Caucasian families of very high income but only moderate levels of education (in which case they are likely to be Careerists).

Academic Background. We would expect academic background to be closely related to being an Intellectual, with students of stronger verbal than mathematical ability most likely to be of this type. This expectation can be best examined by considering men and women separately. For women, those who score above the median in both the verbal *and* math portions of the SAT (610 and 600 respectively) are most likely to be Intellectuals (44 percent, compared to 34 percent of all women). By contrast, the low-verbal–low-math male students are overrepresented among Intellectuals (21 percent, compared to 15 percent of all men). Even more surprisingly, high-verbal–low-math students of both sexes are *least* likely to be in this group. To the extent that SAT scores can be taken as indexes of academic ability, one could say that the most competent women and the least competent men are the ones most likely to value liberal education over career success, while the stereotypical view of the Intellectual as verbally competent but mathematically inept is refuted by these findings.

Sources of Influence on Intellectuals

Parents. While Careerists are strongly influenced by their families and weakly influenced by the faculty, the contrary is true for Intellectuals: Twenty-nine percent of students who say family influence on their decisions is weak are Intellectuals, compared to 15 percent of those saying family influence is strong. Conversely, 29 percent of those who are highly influenced by faculty are of this type, but only 13 percent of those indicating weaker faculty influence. Once again, it appears that families tend to push students toward careerism and away from intellectualism, while members of the faculty have the opposite effect.

There is no lack of affinity between the families of Intellectuals and their children. ("As a professor's child, it had always been part of life's game plan for Ray to go to college.") Just as the fathers of Careerists appear to be Careerists themselves, those of Intellectuals seem to have a more intellectual orientation. But while the Careerists' parents steer their children actively, the families of Intellectuals endorse a liberal educational ideal more indirectly and allow their children much leeway in their choices. ("The family puts no real pressure on her to pursue anything perceived as practical or anything that doesn't interest her.")

Faculty. The interaction of Intellectuals with the faculty shows far more closeness and empathy than is the case with Careerists. The following excerpts from interviews are illustrative:

Julia's contact with faculty outside her major was every bit as positive as it was within her major and contributed to her overall feeling that this year has been very good for her academically.

Ted talks about his involvement with the faculty as being one of the major highs in his four years here. He feels that many students miss the valuable contact with their teachers—because of too much "striving for professionalism."

Jeremy has become a part of the Computer Science Department where he knows a number of the faculty and graduate students. Since becoming a TA, he has been watching his teachers as pedagogues and using what he sees in his own teaching.

Susan has always wanted to be a writer. When she conveyed this wish to her literature professor, he told her "you already are a writer" and encouraged her to begin a novel . . . she has since completed about seventy pages of her first literary effort.

Intellectuals are more likely than other students to refer to the impact of the faculty on their thinking. Christina ascribed to her philosophy professor her ability "to question, to seek the basis for a statement, to uncover assumptions." Drue spoke of the influence of Rousseau and Goethe.

Closeness to the faculty is not shared by all Intellectuals. But where there is lack of such interaction, these students are more likely to miss it and there are reasons other than indifference to explain it. One interviewer reported that "he regrets the lack of interaction with professors . . . and admits that he's 'made no effort' of his own due to shyness and fear of appearing foolish." Another student said, "The biggest thing I have missed is having a mature adult person around."

Some two thirds of Intellectuals say the faculty strongly influence their decisions, far more than any other type (barely half of the Strivers indicate such influence, the next highest type). But is it faculty influence that leads to Intellectualism or do Intellectuals seek out the faculty more, get to know them better, and listen more to their advice and opinions in making decisions? The two factors probably reinforce each other. Faculty members are more likely to establish closer relationships with students who display greater intellectual curiosity and interest in their courses, while the naked concern for career success is less likely to foster close interaction.

A good illustration of how a bright and enterprising student can tap into the resources of the university, even as a freshman, is provided by Harold. His excellent performance in a psychology class led Harold to get actively involved in research that was being carried out by the professor. Harold said:

"It's like being right at the crest of a wave of discovery where you can begin to frame what are the root questions and you begin to understand what you really might be testing for. It isn't that I understand how to frame those questions, but they let me participate and every once in a while I could say something helpful and I learned a tremendous

*amount. I even have developed an idea that fits into the project that's
really my own and that is what I am working on with the data collection.
People get excited with me and they are respectful of the questions I am
trying to ask and of the answers and results I am getting. And the really
exciting thing is that I can do that almost any place in the university."*

In addition, the fact that there are more humanities majors
in this group is significant. Faculty members in the humanities are
consistently rated more favorably as teachers in the Senior Survey.
Though they are no less preoccupied with their scholarship than
are scientists and engineers with their research, their professional
lives generally seem less distracted by outside concerns such as
consultative and entrepreneurial activities. Even more compelling
are the time restrictions imposed by faculty-student ratios.
Professors in economics, biology, chemistry, and engineering must
deal with hordes of undergraduate majors and large enrollments,
while professors in other areas often do not.

The very nature of academic disciplines also colors the
interactions between faculty and students. Engineering course
sequences are clear and well coordinated; once a student gets on
track, there is relatively little need or occasion for "faculty
influence." The School of Earth Sciences provides more opportunities for individual research with faculty than any other school; yet
even there students are probably less likely to perceive "faculty
influence" than, for instance, in the field of literature, where faculty
are more likely to get involved in the more personal concerns of a
student's life.

Other Influences. Consistent with the influence of the
faculty, the Intellectuals also indicate much greater influence of
course work on their career decisions (a feature they share with the
Strivers, who are also high in intellectualism), while saying they are
influenced relatively little by their knowledge of the job market.
These findings are very much as expected: Intellectuals make
decisions less with an eye to finding a profession that is strongly in
demand than with a concern for a field that is intrinsically
interesting and rewarding, and they use their experience in courses
as a guide in their search.

Like Careerists, these students feel that their fellow students have an average level of influence on their academic and career decisions. Unlike the Careerists, however, their work experience is relatively influential in their decision-making processes: They are much more apt to take work experience into account in evaluating prospective occupations, again showing a concern for intrinsic properties rather than external rewards.

Major and Career Choices of Intellectuals

We would expect Intellectuals to select majors that are of intrinsic interest to them and relatively loosely linked to specific professions. The question of what fields are more intrinsically "intellectual" has no clear answer. But the humanities are conventionally defined as being more intellectual, and we find that 31 percent of Intellectuals choose humanities majors, compared to 19 percent of all students and only 6 percent of Careerists. Only 8 percent major in the natural sciences and 8 percent in engineering (compared to 15 percent and 16 percent of all students, respectively). In the social sciences and interdepartmental programs Intellectuals are proportionately represented, but only 25 percent of those in the social sciences major in economics (the most "careerist" major) compared to 47 percent of all social science majors and 67 percent of the Careerist social science majors.

Because women are such a large proportion of the Intellectuals, and women in general favor the humanities over more quantitatively oriented fields, it would be expected that the choice of majors by Intellectuals would be influenced by gender. Yet we find that, on the whole, the choices of women and men in this group are quite similar. The main difference between them is that these women are much more likely to major in engineering than the men (13 percent of Intellectual women, but none of the men). Intellectuals constitute the only group where women are more likely than men to choose engineering; men who are interested in engineering are more likely to be Careerists.

The distribution of major choices of the Intellectuals in the freshman year is almost indistinguishable from the distribution at graduation; the only difference is a decrease in the proportion majoring in engineering (from 14 percent in the freshman year to 8 percent at graduation). Hence the undergraduate experience does little to alter the tendency of Intellectuals to prefer the humanities and avoid the natural sciences and engineering; their academic tendencies, like Careerists', are fairly set at the outset of their college career.

A strong commitment to education might be expected to lead to graduate work culminating in a doctoral degree. But we already know that it is the Careerists, not the Intellectuals, who express the highest aspirations for graduate study. In fact, the Intellectuals have the *lowest* overall postbaccalaureate expectations: Only 35 percent plan to obtain a doctoral-level degree, compared to 50 percent of Careerists; 13 percent say they will go no further than a bachelor's degree, contrasted with 4 percent of the Careerists. How can this be?

The explanation is based in part on the enormous discrepancy between Intellectual men and women in this regard. Among men, the Intellectuals have the highest postbaccalaureate aspirations, with fully two thirds planning on obtaining a doctoral degree; among women the Intellectuals have the lowest aspirations by a wide margin. The other three groups do not show comparable sex differences: Why should the Intellectuals be different? And why is the difference so counterintuitive with respect to academic background, given that Intellectual women have the higher SAT scores while men have the lower scores on both the verbal and math portions?

To answer these questions, we need to examine the career choices of Intellectuals. Because these students are concerned about the intrinsic merits of prospective careers rather than making instrumental choices as a means to wealth and prestige, we would expect them to venture into humanistic and academic careers more than other types. That is, in fact, what they do: Intellectuals are less likely than other students to choose medicine (9 percent versus 13 percent), engineering (2 percent versus 8 percent), and law (11 percent versus 17 percent). The percentages of Intellectuals choosing law and engineering are the lowest of all groups. By contrast, they are most likely to choose careers in the humanities (23 percent choose writing, the arts, and entertainment, compared to 12 percent of all students) and teaching (14 percent versus 9 percent).

The net result is that only 50 percent of Intellectuals choose one of the four standard fields (business, law, medicine, engineering).

The fact that only half of the Intellectuals choose a standard field should be rephrased to say that as many as half do so. This is necessary to counteract the common perception that intellectualism is the domain of philosophers and writers rather than doctors and lawyers. While there may be some truth to that, we must emphasize that at the undergraduate level intellectual and career aims can be compatible and mutually reinforcing. The career interests of the core Intellectuals give tangible substance to their intellectualism and are in turn enriched by it.

Intellectuals can be extraordinarily multifaceted academically, vocationally, and socially. Consider Harold, whom we quoted previously:

Harold double-majored in philosophy and chemistry, completing honor's programs in each. His interest in chemistry was primarily intellectual: "It's kind of purely metaphysical. I like reading about a theory and working it out in lab or maybe just working it out with pencil and paper, and when it works, being able to say, 'Hey, that's neat!'" The course on medieval philosophy in his freshman year intrigued him because "every night it's a hundred pages of people who are dead and you can't ask them what they meant and that was kind of interesting." The main theme of his sophomore year: "I like to play with ideas, whatever comes along. If you've got broad basic tools, you can do that."

Harold's extracurricular activities were just as diverse and he was no less accomplished in them than in the classroom. He was a talented musician who played in the Stanford band and with his own group, an accomplished satirist who wrote for national publications and edited a student publication. During the summers he worked for IBM, did technical writing for a New York publisher, got himself invited to a conference for business executives, did serious biomedical research, and visited medical centers.

Harold sought out faculty members he respected, dropping in on them "to see what he's thinking about right now." He said, "What you get from a teacher is a kind of new life, his life, so you don't want to be taking courses from the living dead. That's what libraries are for." He had close contacts in half a dozen departments.

After considering a number of options, Harold became interested in medicine. He was no ordinary premed. He characterized his visit to the neurosurgical unit (his father's specialty) of the Massachusetts General Hospital as "one of those epiphany moments."

Though very fond of Stanford, Harold was not naively positive. He was sharply critical of some of his classes and faculty ("this course is just the most God-awful thing I have ever had to do"; "he taught me that a person can be respected in his field and still be a neurotic, horrible creature . . . I hate him"). More typically, he poked fun at most anything—including the Cohort Study. In response to the senior questionnaire query on participating in organized activities outside Stanford, he wrote: "I am now a member of the Central Carolina KKK and may get some sort of elected post in the fall, though going to school in California has hurt my chances." What changes would he make for financing his education? "Make my parents pay more . . . they got bread but they are stingy. Don't they realize I am their son?"

Intellectuals manifest a number of sex differences in their career choices: Only 45 percent of the women, but 60 percent of the men, choose one of the four standard fields, and the differences are especially great with respect to law and medicine, which 40 percent of the men but only 10 percent of the women plan to enter. Women in this group are much more likely to choose careers in business, the humanities, public administration, and the social sciences. Hence, the pattern of career choice in this group is set by the women, especially with respect to the choice of nonstandard fields.

The lower educational aspirations of Intellectuals can now be explained in the context of choices made by the women. Their choice of career typically includes fields that generally do not require doctoral-level education: business, the arts, entertainment, writing, journalism, and public administration. Their male counterparts, however, are more likely to aim for careers in law, medicine, and university teaching, all of which require doctoral-level degrees. For most students, be they Careerist or Intellectual, the pursuit of a graduate degree is primarily a career-related decision. Opportunities for a liberal education are confined mainly to the undergraduate experience.

A comparison of final career decisions with freshman-year expectations shows that the Intellectuals change their choices as other students do, with an increasing proportion choosing business and a decreasing proportion choosing medicine. They differ from other students in that a sizable proportion shift to humanistic careers, while for other students there is a shift away from humanistic careers. Thus, the proportion of Intellectuals in all nonstandard fields increases over the four years (from 42 percent to 50 percent) while for all other students this proportion decreases (from 31 percent to 26 percent). As with Careerists, the college experience does not deflect Intellectuals from their initial plans but reinforces them.

There is a greater tendency among Intellectuals to change career plans: They average 1.1 changes per student over the four years, compared to .6 changes for Careerists. This difference is also reflected in the fact that only 42 percent of Intellectuals have the same final choice of career as their freshman choice, compared to 62 percent of Careerists.

Intellectuals are also less likely than other students to stay with a career choice in one of the four standard fields (business, law, medicine, engineering) and more likely than other students to stay with a choice in a nonstandard field. The latter difference is especially striking, with 73 percent of Intellectuals staying within the nonstandard fields compared to 43 percent of the Careerists. They are also more likely not to have made a career choice by the end of the freshman year (23 percent, compared to 10 percent of the Careerists), and these initially uncertain students are especially likely to settle on a career in a nonstandard field.

This pattern may be seen as symptomatic of career uncertainty or as reflecting thoughtful exploration before making a choice; we believe there is an element of both. The Careerist has an easier time in this regard: The vocational choices are more standard, their purposes clearer. It is easier to determine, after all, what career will make a good living than what field of work is likely to be personally fulfilling in the future.

The Intellectuals are by no means uniform in their career attitudes. Not only do their career choices encompass a wide range, but their level of career ambition also varies a good deal. Some are as uncertain as the Unconnected, while others are almost as ambitious as Strivers ("I want to be Faulkner"). Nonetheless, even the more driven among them seek professional excellence rather than material success as such. They also are quite willing to compromise if necessary: One interview report stated that the student's "motto about career development is that you should think first what you are good at and try to do what you would like to do even though eventually you may have to do what you *have* to do." The following excerpts from interview reports give further insights into the career attitudes of Intellectuals.

She received four offers from retailing firms and two from insurance companies but turned them all down, saying: "I want to work around educated people." She turned down a job in Indiana because "I don't want to live and die diesel engines."

Joanne decided not to major in communications even though her primary professional interest is in journalism because she wanted tools for thinking about current events rather than learning the techniques of journalism that she felt she could acquire through experience. In five years Joanne would like to be on the staff of a major metropolitan newspaper and be a political analyst in Washington. She is confident she has the skills to report not just the "how" but the "why" of news.

Robert knows that he will never have trouble finding employment . . . but he wants to be able to concentrate on broader issues . . . and hopes he won't have to "settle down" for at least ten years.

The group with which he works in the Center for Integrated Systems is forming a company. They offered to let him "in on the ground floor." He declined. Getting rich is not on his list of things to do.

Megan sees for herself a rather low-paying yet personally rewarding career . . . possibly in an area of public service, but beyond that she hasn't given it much thought.

In ten years Laurie predicts that she will be a published author and a professional director, being determined to break into that "male profession." She might also be teaching, married, and have children. Meanwhile she says that she "wants to have some adventures for a while." This might include spending some time in Venice while working and writing.

Her decision was that medicine, while interesting, was not interesting enough for a life's work. She anticipates a career in either diplomacy or international business. To explore the latter possibility she will be returning to Europe next summer to work.

Law school is a possibility. He's concerned about social inequality and thinks law might be a route to promoting social change.

Overall, he isn't clear as to exactly what he wants to do with his life, and his experience of the last year demonstrates that planning doesn't do much good anyway. But he is confident that his abilities will allow him to do something that is worthwhile.

Pursuing a Liberal Education

Intellectuals typically come to college with clear expectations of obtaining a liberal education. They have broad intellectual interests and their choice of courses confirms their seriousness of purpose. One freshman said, "I would love to take every introductory class." Another claimed he would be happy sampling courses in different fields all through his undergraduate years. There is a concomitant recognition of the need for depth. One student who had had four years of high school French continued to take electives in French so as to read "existentialist authors in the original."

There is a keener interest among Intellectuals than others in the quality of the courses they take. There is less of a tendency to take what is merely popular, and more attention is paid to intellectual content. At a broader level, there is concern with the coherence of their programs of study ("she has experienced a gratifying intellectual overlap among almost all her courses, something she never dreamed of in high school"). There is less random shopping around or flitting from one area to another and more forethought and planning ("I want to get something cohesive out of my education; I want to do *something* and not have things *happen* to me"). This tendency is reflected not only in the choice of courses but also in longer-term decisions over when and where to go for study overseas.

Particularly compelling is the passion and exuberance expressed by the core Intellectuals over their academic life. One student said she felt "intellectually dead" when not taking literature courses; others did not know how to make room for all they wanted to learn. This hunger for learning was still present in the senior year. While some of the other students were having trouble filling up their schedules in their last quarters, one senior said, "There are still so many classes that I would like to take." And others: "I've never been happier. I'm on top of things. I hate to leave"; "I would be happy if college went on forever." Though these students came with as many advanced placement credits as others, they had no wish to parlay that into graduating early or taking lighter academic loads. Sandy would try cutting down on his academic load yet end up with a large number of units because he could not resist so many good courses.

In response to their varied interests, Intellectuals may spread themselves too thin or lack direction: "I don't have a clear purpose, I guess. I enjoy learning and ideas but see no clear path. Sometimes I feel a sort of helplessness." Though more eclectic than others, these students also still face a serious barrier when crossing over from humanities to science and technology. Humanities majors are in fact least likely to take courses completely unrelated to their majors; in this sense, it is not the engineers or natural scientists but the humanists who have the narrowest perspective. We have confirmed this trend not only among the subjects of the Cohort Study but in the overall student population, through the Curriculum Study (Boli, Katchadourian, and Mahoney, 1983). Thus, humanities students in the class of 1981 took 33 percent of their course units in their majors, an additional 26 percent in other humanities departments (for a total of 59 percent), 13 percent in the social sciences, and only 8 percent in the natural sciences. Natural science majors, by contrast, had only 26 percent of their units in their major departments, an additional 27 percent in other natural science departments (a total of 53 percent), 12 percent in the social sciences, and fully 20 percent in the humanities.

Even with the best of intentions there is a sense on the part of many Intellectuals that they "learned a bit about a lot of things" but did not receive the great "classical education" they were expecting. The requirements of some majors and professional schools interfere with the freedom to learn what one wishes. On a more philosophical plane, education does not seem to be effective enough in dealing with "life's helplessness and hopelessness," nor in resolving the social problems confronting society. One student keenly interested in art history felt trapped between her intellectual interests in the subject and her desire to help others: "I love it, but it seems trivial and the ultimate in luxury."

The educational perspective of the core Intellectuals sometimes brings them into conflict with other students and even the institution—they can feel like a beleaguered minority, as expressed in the following excerpts from interviews:

Kevin expected to be surrounded in college by philosophically oriented, intellectual repartee. Instead, the first conversations he heard concerned the chances of being admitted to grad school and the starting salaries that lay beyond. He thinks that too many of the students are success oriented at the expense of honesty and depth of spirit . . . The result is a superficiality, super-coolness, and avoidance of substantial, satisfying common concerns.

Eric thinks most students are concerned only about getting a good job and the amount of money they will make. They are unable to question the existing system and to ask interesting and important questions about the assumptions the professors are making.

In her journalism class she got the feeling that she was engaged in job training. To explore this idea she did a paper about preprofessional students at Stanford. She found that while some were pushed into a preprofessional direction, others actually like it. They were rewarded by noncreative work, which she would find hard to sympathize with.

Ted perceived himself to be an intellectual and had a difficult time finding other students who shared his enthusiasm for deep intellectual discussions.

Overseas Study. The rationale behind the overseas programs is that living and studying in a foreign country can lead to a broader understanding of the world, a better perspective on American society, and less parochial views on important problems of human society. Such expectations would suggest that attending an overseas campus should be of particular interest to students who value a liberal education, and this is indeed the case: The Intellectuals are far more likely than any other group to go overseas, with fully 55 percent availing themselves of this opportunity, compared to 38 percent of all students (and only 28 percent of the Unconnected).

There is, however, a confounding feature here in that the curricula of overseas programs are heavily slanted toward humanities courses, since these can be most readily linked to the cultural setting (such as studying the Renaissance in Florence). This makes it easier for humanities majors to integrate overseas programs into their courses of study and most difficult for engineers, who have the most structured programs and the largest number of required courses in their majors. Because there is a preponderance of humanities majors among Intellectuals, the effect of that variable is hard to separate from that of being an Intellectual with respect to study overseas.

Whichever of these tendencies motivates Intellectuals to go overseas, they view the experience as one of the most attractive opportunities available at Stanford, as manifested in the following excerpts from interview reports.

Florence was a very good experience for him. He was pretty tired of the home campus and felt alienated from the competitive career orientation exhibited by so many of his classmates. Although he had had four years of high school French, he chose the Florence campus over France because he wanted to learn a new language and he believed the Florence program to be better. He took three quarters of Italian, and while in Italy he really applied himself in order to learn as much of the language as possible. He was very successful in making contact with Italian people and culture. Roman and Etruscan Art was his favorite course.

She spoke very highly of the opportunities to go to plays and museums in London.

"Adored Florence"—cried for a week after she left.

The yearning for travel, apart from overseas study, is shared with other students. Yet Intellectuals are more likely to include a serious purpose in such travel. For example, from another interview:

Upon graduation, Sally and her boyfriend will buy one-way tickets to Europe and will keep traveling for as long as they can make a go of it, several years at least. They have saved quite a lot of money but also plan to work as necessary in order to finance their adventures. They'll spend the summer in Europe, then move on to Africa and/or India. Sally plans to do lots of still photography, partly because this medium is new to her and she feels she has lots to learn; in addition, it is good training for doing film (which she still believes to be her ultimate destiny). She also hopes to write for magazines and newspapers during her travels. But most importantly, she wants to "ride the crest of adventure, to challenge myself in ways other than the academic."

Stopping Out. Intellectuals are especially likely to stop out for one or more quarters: Some 36 percent do so, well above the average and far above the Careerists (13 percent). Because they are more open to experimentation and exploration of new interests, they feel the need to take time off from school in order to reflect on what they have done and where they are headed. Another motivation is to gain work experience so that their eventual career decisions will be better informed. We should point out that stopping out is not associated with failing to obtain a bachelor's degree, nor even with taking a longer time to obtain the degree. Students who stop out can easily make up for one or two quarters' absence, either in summer school or by taking extra units in other quarters.

Social Life and Extracurricular Activities

Intellectuals are involved in more extracurricular activities than any other group. They average 4.6 activities on the Involvement Index, well above the mean for Careerists (3.7) or the Unconnected (3.4).

Not surprisingly, Intellectuals are more likely than other students to become involved in academic projects outside the classroom (such as internships and independent study) and in artistic activities, like music, drama, and dance. They also take a more active part in volunteer service, spending over three times as many hours on volunteer work as the Careerists during the sophomore year. These involvements are further reflected in the fact that they discuss political and social issues considerably more often than other students; for example, on a scale from 1 = rarely to 5 = daily or almost daily, they have a mean response of 4.3 in the senior year, compared to 3.8 for the Careerists. Thus, throughout the college years the Intellectuals are not only highly engaged with culturally enriching activities but they demonstrate a strong level of social concern as well.

Intellectuals share many of the concerns of some of the more critical students among the Unconnected. But their outlook is more likely to be reformist rather than radical: "This year I have met lots of leftist radicals who are very negative about the status quo. Intellectually I can understand them, but as for myself I am not an activist person. I just can't dwell on things or I'll get depressed." This student found it hard to identify with people who come from conservative backgrounds and are protesting against their own parental values, even though she too comes from a similar cultural background and considers its values far from "ideal."

Intellectuals are not less likely than other students to engage in athletics or organized campus-based activities, and they are even somewhat more active than others in off-campus involvements. In sum, two thirds of them report significant involvement in every campus activity we have looked at and close to a third are significantly involved in off-campus activities as well. The following excerpts from interview reports illustrate some of these points:

Music and debate have been a big part of his extracurricular life.

His major commitment this year is being a resident assistant. He decided on this because it offers a way to meet and interact with people, and because he wants to be able to share his perspective with other students. He hopes he can influence them to consider the importance of a liberal education and to value their time here as an end in itself, rather than focusing exclusively on career concerns.

She is finding it difficult to reconcile her political and religious involvements, since many of the friends she has made through her political activities are antireligious and many of her Christian friends are politically conservative.

If you have a day off, what would you do? "I'd go to San Francisco and visit museums."

Most of the time outside the classroom and libraries is spent making new friends and taking in concerts, guest speakers, and drama productions on campus.

Is the more active social involvement of Intellectuals a function of their having more time because of less demanding academic schedules? There may be an element of that for some students in this group, but time alone is not a sufficient explanation. Their high degree of extracurricular activity is nearly matched by the Strivers, who are as pressed for time as the Careerists. The Unconnected are less involved (particularly in the arts and volunteer service) even though they have time to spare. It would therefore seem that students who are highly concerned about liberal education more often engage in social, artistic, and altruistic activities, while the students who do not share that concern are more likely to get involved in athletics and campus organizations or to remain detached from extracurricular activities altogether.

Intellectuals are generally quite "people oriented." But they are not overly gregarious party goers, nor do they seem as likely to form stable ties leading to early marriage as do Careerists. Intellectual men, in particular, see themselves as less likely to be married in ten years than men in other groups. The women, however, are no different from those in other categories—almost all expect to be married or be in a committed relationship in a decade.

The friendships that Intellectuals form appear to be quite close and their personal relationships tend to integrate with their broader academic orientation, as shown in the following excerpts from interview reports:

He is integrated in a community of friends having similar values— sincerity, appreciation for art and music, spontaneity, and no goal orientation in terms of their careers. He is concerned with making every moment important, rather than simply filling up his free time with meaningless activities.

The general exposure to people here has been the "highlight" of his first-year experience. One of the apparent pleasures of this year is finding more depth in what others want out of their social relationships at Stanford.

She definitely wants both family and career and is convinced she can find a way to combine them. She'll look for a man who can fit into her plans. She's prepared to do some compromising, but she wants a husband who'll do the same.

She describes herself as "intense about everything" and very "serious." When she exchanges confidences with friends, when she gives something of herself to them, she takes it very seriously and expects them to give to her in return. She is reflective almost to a fault . . . She is constantly evaluating herself, her life, her interests, her friendships, and her academic growth. When she is excited about something she has just read or studied, she wants to rush out and tell everyone else about it; not everyone is able to relate to someone like her.

Academic Success and Satisfaction

Academic Performance. Intellectuals garner more than their share of academic laurels in the most visible indicators of achievement, such as honors at graduation. They are more likely than any other group to win election to Phi Beta Kappa (14 percent, versus 8 percent for all students), to earn departmental honors through participation in an honor's program (14 percent versus 8 percent), and to graduate with distinction (29 percent versus 20 percent). These honors are in part based on grades; hence, it is not surprising that the grades of Intellectuals are somewhat higher, with a mean grade point average of 3.46, compared to the average of 3.35 for all students.

Particularly noteworthy is the higher proportion of Intellectuals participating in departmental honor's programs, about twice as high a percentage as any other type. The decision to enter an honor's program is rarely an instrumental one, for the demands of such programs are such that they attract only the students with a genuine interest in a subject.

Do these differences reflect true discrepancies in academic competence and performance among students, or are they a function of the field in which they work? To put it bluntly, are Intellectuals "better" students or do they do better because they major in "softer" fields with inflated course units and easier grades?

In Chapter Four we pointed out the problems in making comparative judgments with respect to the academic rigor and intellectual content of courses in various fields. These ambiguities notwithstanding, there are widely shared perceptions among students as to how demanding various fields are and how courses within those fields measure up against each other. For instance, engineering courses are thought to offer fewer units of credit for equivalent amounts of effort than courses in some of the humanities and social sciences. Similarly, it is assumed that it is tougher to get an A in chemistry or physics than in sociology or music.

We have extensive documentation from the Curriculum Study (Boli, Katchadourian, and Mahoney, 1983) that supports these perceptions. The highest mean grade is in humanities courses (3.51), the lowest in engineering (3.21). Within the humanities the mean grades range from 3.80 for music to 3.27 for history; within engineering they range from 3.35 for electrical engineering to 2.97 for chemical engineering.

Though the issue of rigor remains relevant, we find that class size is an important confounding variable in determining these differences. There is an inverse relationship between class size and mean grades: Students in smaller classes receive higher grades. Humanities courses generally have smaller classes, a fact that may account for much of the difference between humanities grades and those of other areas. When we recalculate the mean grades while controlling for class size, the difference between courses in engineering and the humanities shrinks from 0.24 to 0.12 points.

We do not know for certain what it is in the dynamics of small classes that leads to higher grades: Do students learn more and deserve better grades in smaller classes or do these settings breed a familiarity between instructor and student that softens the grading standards? Whatever the explanation, the fact remains that the higher grades obtained by Intellectuals may be at least partly explained by the fact that they take a higher proportion of smaller classes where mean grades are higher.

However, when we look at the grades of the Intellectuals in separate types of courses, they still do better than other types. They get higher grades than all other types in all areas except engineering courses, even in the natural sciences. Thus we can conclude that the Intellectuals truly are superior students, though we cannot say whether that is due to their choosing courses that interest them, working harder, or simply being better at academic work.

Departmental honor's programs, which entail writing honor's theses, are also more available to students in the humanities. In the engineering departments students are more likely to do individual research without the benefit of honor's programs. Although these considerations are noteworthy, they do not invalidate the fine academic records attained by Intellectuals.

Self-Assessments of Knowledge and Abilities. The Intellectuals, who are concentrated in the humanities and social sciences, rate themselves more highly in such domains as foreign languages and understanding Western culture, literature and the fine arts, social processes, and the workings of government. They see themselves as relatively weaker in mathematics, the natural sciences, technology, and computers. There are no surprises here.

Satisfaction with the Undergraduate Experience. The Intellectuals' assessment of the senior year are in line with everything else we have learned about them. They are significantly more satisfied than any other group with interaction with faculty, serious intellectual discussions with peers, and interest in courses. They also manage their time better, which suggests that they are more organized and feel less harried than other students.

On the other hand, Intellectuals express only average satisfaction with most other aspects of the senior year, including social interaction, getting the desired grades, their sense of belonging, and their overall sense of contentment. But it is noteworthy that they also express no less than average satisfaction with the development of their career plans. Without having put a great deal of emphasis on planning their careers, they nevertheless feel that their plans are shaping up well as they approach graduation. Of special significance here is the fact that the

Careerists are no more satisfied with their career plans than the Intellectuals, though it may well be that they have higher expectations that are harder to fulfill.

The Senior Survey confirms these findings. The Intellectuals are significantly more satisfied than other types with their major courses and the liberal education they have received. They also are happier about the faculty, as advisers and as teachers, and they feel most positive about the opportunities for individual work with faculty. They even rate teaching assistants higher than other types do. Thus, in every dimension related to the academic enterprise Intellectuals feel the most satisfied. Their overall evaluation of the undergraduate program, however, is not significantly higher than the mean (4.4 compared to 4.3, on a five-point scale).

The only dimension on the Senior Survey where Intellectuals express somewhat less satisfaction than Careerists is in their training for graduate or professional school (mean of 3.7, as against a mean of 4.1). But this is further mitigated by their attaching less importance to this item (a mean of 3.2 compared to 4.1 for Careerists). The Intellectuals thus recognize that they may have incurred some liability with respect to career preparation but they do not see this as a serious problem.

The Balance Sheet

No matter how even handed we try to be in our evaluation, we find it hard not to conclude that Intellectuals, at their best, come closer than any other group to fulfilling the aims of a college education. Their dedication to the ideals of liberal learning shines through their undergraduate years. If they did this at the risk of compromising their career prospects, one could fault them for being unrealistic and imprudent. But they do not. By all indications, the core group of Intellectuals seem just as likely as the most diehard Careerists to be vocationally successful; indeed, some of them are apt to beat the Careerists at their own game, for reasons we discussed in the previous chapter.

It is hard to find fault with an orientation that achieves these aims while simultaneously allowing enthusiastic engagement in the full range of worthwhile social and extracurricular activities.

That all of this is accomplished by students who also perform well academically and leave college highly satisfied is surely cause for celebration.

The debit side of the Intellectual orientation lies not in its ideals but in the difficulties in attaining those ideals. The questionnaire data that form the basis of our typology reflect primarily what students are aiming at, what they hope to accomplish; the interview reports are more objective accounts of how well these aims are attained. The degree of concordance between questionnaire data and interviewer impressions is therefore a good measure of the attainment of these aims. Based on the interview reports of the core groups (students representing the extreme ends of each category), we find a striking discrepancy between the actual experiences of Careerists and those of Intellectuals.

Among Careerists, there are very few cases where the interview reports are not congruent with the typological designation based on questionnaire data. In other words, the behavior of Careerists as manifested in the interview material is quite consistent with their stated educational aims. In the Intellectual category there is far more discordance between the two accounts. Only two thirds of the interview reports of the core students identified as Intellectuals show convincing evidence that they are in fact pursuing the sort of educational aims they say they are after.

When we go beyond the core group, the liberal learning of Intellectuals becomes further watered down. At the bottom end of the category, students merely show a greater inclination to take courses in a variety of fields (especially in the humanities); but there is no passion for learning, no drive to expand one's intellectual horizons, merely a tepid endorsement of liberal education at best.

Another shortcoming that compromises the Intellectual ideal is the tendency to favor the humanities and social sciences over the natural sciences and technology. This is most marked among humanities majors, whose idea of "breadth" is often restricted to their cognate fields. Many of these students recognize this in the same way that Careerists recognize the value of liberal education: It is the sort of recognition that does not get translated into action.

The obverse of this problem is that Intellectualism does not seem to be as readily compatible with some academic and career choices as others. In this case, the problem is more structural than personal. In other words, once a student gets on a professional track like engineering, or a preprofessional track like premedical studies, pursuing an Intellectual orientation becomes an uphill climb; some can do it quite well, many more cannot.

More ominously, Intellectualism may be at odds with the sentiments of the peer culture and even with the ethos of the institution. Intellectuals, more than others, find college a natural place to be; it is "home" for them. In many ways there is a good and comfortable fit between them and the institution. Yet it is also ironic that these students who embody so well the ideals of higher learning should also feel like a beleaguered minority in a distinguished center of higher learning. Whether this is a problem for which the Intellectual orientation itself is responsible or the fault lies elsewhere is an intriguing issue.

6

⟶⟵

Students as Strivers:
Trying to Have It
Both Ways

Aristotle asked, "Should the useful in life, or should virtue, or should the higher knowledge be the aim of our training?" Our Strivers would answer, in the words of one of them, "I want a good liberal education and a good job." That statement neatly sums up the orientation of students in this group. Like the Intellectuals, they value liberal education; like the Careerists, they are concerned about successful careers. But given the wide range of differences between Intellectuals and Careerists, can Strivers have it both ways? Some can. But as we shall see, the answer is that more often they cannot, if by "having it both ways" we mean combining all of the aspirations and accomplishments of Careerists and Intellectuals. Not only is there too much to combine, but some of the characteristics of these two groups are antithetical.

Strivers reveal strong, varied, and at times conflicting motivations. They are not as intense and determined about careers as the Careerists. Likewise, though these students are interested in a broad range of courses and academic values, most of them lack the intellectual depth and spark of the Intellectuals. What these students do have in abundance is enthusiasm, energy, and a positive attitude toward college. It is therefore useful to think of Strivers as a hybrid group, bred from Careerist and Intellectual stock but still a distinct species not reducible to its parent lineages. To some extent they resemble the Intellectuals more than the Careerists, in that their concern for liberal education keeps their careerism from getting out of hand; only rarely do we find nakedly materialistic attitudes among the Strivers, despite the strong commitment to career success evident among many of them.

The Strivers in the core group, like their counterparts among Intellectuals, are most impressive. These highly gifted students largely succeed in getting the best of both worlds. But they are only a minority. The others strive mightily but do not attain the same levels of accomplishment, nor do they integrate liberal education and career preparation as well. (As one student put it, "I'm a better juggler of little balls than a lifter of heavier ones.") Biographical profiles 6.1 through 6.4 provide examples of various types of Strivers.

Profile 6.1: Geraldine—Actress

Geraldine is articulate and engaging, striking looking and very poised. Her father is a scientist who has gone into business, and her mother has studied drama. The family is well-off and travels extensively. Geraldine had the pick of prestigious Eastern colleges but chose Stanford in part because her sister was already at Harvard. She wanted a "superior education," but beyond that her academic and career plans were a bit vague.

In her freshman year Geraldine enrolled in a wide variety of courses, combining the natural sciences and the humanities. She had thought of going into medical school and had already worked for two summers in a medical research institute. But she was also intensely drawn to acting and had had considerable experience both in the theater and singing. Her parents did not actively steer her in either direction.

In her sophomore year Geraldine lost some of her academic zeal. Her grades dropped as she shifted her energies from studying to social interactions. Pulled in different directions by her many talents and interests, she went through several choices of majors ranging from environmental science to literature and philosophy. She felt some attraction to a career in law. Meanwhile, most of her energies and time went into singing in musicals, acting in plays, attending concerts, participating in sports, and getting involved with people.

In her junior year Geraldine began to see more clearly the various academic and career choices facing her. She began to think more carefully about what she herself wanted to do as against what may have been subtle parental expectations of what she should do. She discovered geology and decided to major in it and then pursue a master's degree in acting. This rather disconcerting combination led the interviewer to remark, "Her career plans seem almost schizophrenic . . . it's as if she is clinging to geology for stability, but her heart isn't in it."

To resolve these contradictions Geraldine stopped out following the summer of her junior year. She went to an actor's training program, then took private lessons in acting and dance. She got a job and supported herself for the first time in her life. A lengthy series of candid discussions with her father ("we talked for five days straight") greatly helped to clear up matters between them.

On returning as a senior, Geraldine changed her major to drama. Her true academic and career aspirations finally came together. She felt settled and happy with her choice. Even though she had ranged widely over a lot of subjects (some by choice, some through indecision), there was still a "vast wealth of things here that I have left untapped." Though grateful that Stanford had allowed her to be free to seek her own way, she complained that "creative people die a slow death" in its academic setting "because it's such a homogenized environment."

Geraldine was accepted for graduate study in the theater at two first-rate programs. She had a standing job offer from a friend in Paris, as well as the prospect of working with the Royal Shakespeare Company. In ten years she would like to be involved in the theater in New York City, or in film and television. Geraldine's parting comments: "I'm guided by what makes me happy and doing things that I enjoy. It's important to me not to be locked in . . . I need to feel I am experiencing my potential. I need to test myself in all different capacities. It's important to keep myself alive and living."

Profile 6.2: Pierre—Renaissance Man

Pierre entered Stanford at age sixteen, with thirty units of advanced placement credits. He had accumulated a straight-A record, with a 97 percent average in his courses. When he was in the sixth grade his science teacher had predicted that Pierre would win a prestigious national science award while in high school; Pierre in fact won that award, of which there are only about forty recipients in the country. All told, he had seven years of extensive science work before coming to college.

Pierre's particular interest in science is biology, and he intended to pursue a career in medicine. So he began his freshman year by enrolling in the premedical required sequences. But he also sampled widely, taking courses in art, philosophy, international relations, and geology. He got all A's. Pierre had a special preference for small seminars that focused on specific topics as against large, introductory-level courses. He was especially fascinated by his philosophy seminar, although he would have liked to have a bit more reading than was required in the course. He chose his courses carefully and would not enroll in one unless he was fairly sure that he would continue with it through the quarter. Pierre also participated in research at the medical center. He worked for the student radio station as a reporter and newscaster, and became very involved with photography.

By his sophomore year, Pierre had seriously rethought and reevaluated his academic and career goals. His experience with the chemistry sequence had been disappointing because so little remained with him when he was done with the course (he compared it to "collecting snowflakes"). By contrast, he found that the material from his philosophy courses stayed with him longer and continued to be intellectually stimulating. He retained his interest in biology but then became concerned that perhaps he was "too programmed" into that subject, and it would be too confining to remain channeled in it. Pierre then began to have second thoughts about medicine. He had become so bogged down in its requirements that he had lost sight of his interest in it in the first place.

As Pierre thought through these various choices, he made careful distinctions between courses that were "stepping-stones" and what he considered to be "a valid course." A valid course would have intrinsic interest and remain useful for the rest of one's life, the others would not. At a more basic level, Pierre asked himself: "Is my aptitude really in a particular area like biology, or is it possible that I have aptitude in virtually any field that I choose to spend time with?" He thought the latter was the case and decided to pursue whatever interested him, without any further concerns. By the middle of his second year, Pierre had already obtained junior-year standing. He therefore had to decide to declare a major sooner than his peers. He settled on a double major consisting of art history and biology, while continuing to be very interested in geology and exploring courses in mechanical engineering (because they had to do with "visual thinking," and hence fitted well with Pierre's basic fascination with thought processes).

Rather than graduate early, Pierre decided to become a coterminal student in biology, aiming for a master's degree. His interests, however, had shifted to the more social aspects of biology and away from basic research. By this time he had abandoned all thought of medical school because "once you are a doctor, there is only one thing you can be." He felt by contrast that business school would allow him a greater variety of choices. Combined with his background in biology, he considered the possibility of going into environmental planning and eventually working for the government or perhaps a private agency.

Pierre's broadened social horizons led him to spend his summers working as a volunteer for the Sierra Club and serving in a camp for emotionally disturbed children. It became very important for him to learn how to relate to a variety of people and he sought different experiences to enhance his ability to do so.

In his senior year Pierre abandoned the plan of working for a master's degree in biology since he had now become firmly set on going to business school. Nonetheless, he continued to consolidate his knowledge on environmental issues, taking a wide range of courses in engineering, earth sciences, humanities, and the natural sciences. He expanded his social activities, serving as dorm president and coordinator of the escort service on campus.

Pierre got accepted at a leading business school on a prestigious scholarship. The interviewer suspected that despite Pierre's claims to the contrary, he had strong ambitions in business and aimed to be president of a company, a goal he would attain in a short time. But whatever Pierre did in his professional life, he was certain to retain his keen interest in the liberal arts. Building on his earlier interest in photography, Pierre had begun to do some painting. He also wrote poetry in his senior year. If there was one person in our sample who could be called a Renaissance man, Pierre would be among the likeliest candidates.

Profile 6.3: Daniel—Unfilfilled Ambitions

The second youngest of ten children of an Asian-American family of modest means, Daniel was deeply grateful for the chance to come to Stanford ("I have been dying to get out and see the world . . ."). He came with an abiding interest in gymnastics and academics ("that's not a rank order, just the two most important things"). He had also been very interested in drama and music.

Though full of enthusiasm and determination, Daniel was also fearful of Stanford. He thought the other students would be like "walking computers" and he was nagged by the feelings of self-doubt ("I feel insecure and unsure of myself at times . . . life feels like some huge net that I am tangled in").

Daniel plunged into a set of rigorous courses and arduous gymnastics training. It was hard going ("I cannot believe I put myself through so much agony"). Training twenty hours a week (and working for ten more) left little time for studying. His performance was not spectacular in either gymnastics or academics. He got some relief by getting small parts in musical productions.

Though Daniel was very serious about college, his academic and career goals were quite unclear. There are hints that his widowed mother expected him to fulfill the stereotypical role of the highly successful Asian-American premedical student. Dan entered the premedical courses but did not fare particularly well and had doubts about his chances ("I don't know if I am good enough").

He thought of declaring a psychology major but settled on human biology. He had little contact with faculty and did not seem engaged in intellectual issues; his interviewer reported that he "introspects a great deal but not about intellectual matters . . . he is very serious—earnest would be a better word; but he is not intellectually excited." He was also troubled by a keen sense of "physical aging" and wondered how long his body would hold up under the intense demands made on it.

By his junior year, Daniel's Stanford experience had soured. He had gone to the Berlin campus but had a mixed overseas experience. Getting acquainted with German gymnasts and their training methods was interesting but his courses at the local university were too burdensome ("more work than any Stanford course I've ever had"). Back home, he got into the core sequence of his major a year late and "hated the teachers." Lectures were either "without substance" or "over everyone's head."

Daniel's interest in gymnastics also began to wind down. Instead he became much more involved in student musical productions where his dancing and gymnastics talents served him well. He thought of dance-theater as a career but saw little future in it. Besides, "theater isn't what a good son does." So he began to think of medicine again.

Dan thought of stopping out but then came back for a much more satisfying senior year ("my academic high point"). It was deeply fulfilling since "I proved to myself that I could do it." His adjectives for the year— "happy," "acclimated," "exhausted." He planned to work following graduation and then reconsider becoming a dancer or a doctor.

Profile 6.4: Melanie—Preparing for a Life of Service

Melanie is a reserved and quiet Black woman with "a lot of presence." The daughter of an Army officer, Melanie was highly influenced by her father, who steered her to Stanford because of its reputation. The basic decisions in Melanie's life had always been made by her father; his plan for her was to complete a degree in a first-rate college with flying colors, go to medical school, and become a successful physician. Melanie's own preference was to work for a few years before

*going to college. Her father prevailed. But while he could make her go
to college, he could not make her work at it.*

Melanie's freshman year was largely squandered in a whirl of social
activity, with little attention paid to academics ("I pretty much messed
up"). She chose a light load of courses in the social sciences, but even
these she barely attended. Moreover, Melanie enraged her father by
keeping him completely in the dark about her studies. He threatened to
fly over and set her right. But then he thought better of it and instead
offered to buy her a car if she became more communicative about her
academic progress.

Having won the first round in her struggle for emancipation,
Melanie settled down in her sophomore year to an academic program
well designed to provide her with the kind of general education she
sought, laying the groundwork for her future career as a clinical
psychologist. Her change over these first two years was quite dramatic.

Melanie continued to make good progress in her junior year. Her
major in psychology turned out to fit her needs "exactly." She was happy
with her courses and her adviser. She moved off campus and learned how
to handle better the requirements of adult living. She had already been
quite involved socially in the Black ethnic theme house. Now she began
to focus more seriously on Afro-American studies, which became her
primary vehicle of obtaining a broader education; it fit nicely with her
intellectual interests, ethnic affinities, and professional aspirations.

During her interviews, Melanie spoke with much insight about the
experience of being a Black student at Stanford. She was frequently
troubled by the affluent, "unreal," and "resortlike" atmosphere of the
campus ("even the stray dogs are pedigreed"). Having been exposed to
a middle-class background (through her own family) and one less
advantaged (through her grandmother's family), she was particularly well
equipped to understand and to be dismayed by the class divisions within
the Black student community itself.

Melanie had decided by her junior year to spend her professional
life in an inner-city neighborhood. Her plan was to get a degree in clinical
psychology, then establish a halfway house for psychiatric patients and
disturbed adolescents. She had her own definite ideas for developing
special therapeutic strategies. To this end Melanie combined her study
of psychology with volunteer work at a mental rehabilitation center,
gaining firsthand experience in leading therapy groups and doing
individual counseling. Following graduation, Melanie planned to work
full-time at a halfway house in order to get further experience as well as
to take a breather before going on to graduate study in clinical
psychology at a state university.

Interviewer Impressions of Strivers

The Strivers make highly favorable personal impressions. Energetic, gregarious, ebullient, forthright, and friendly, they are fun to listen to and be with. Their personal charm is so compelling that the impression they made on the interviewers was often more positive than was justified by a more objective evaluation of their assets. Some of the interviewers did comment, however, on their relative lack of depth and direction, their tendency to spread themselves too thin. Following are some excerpts from interviewer comments on Strivers:

Mark is one of the most accomplished, energetic, personable, and able young men I have known at Stanford. It has been exciting to watch him grow and develop. He seems to live life to the fullest, and his contribution to this place will be a lasting one I am sure.

I'd be a rich man if I received a nickel every time Jaime used the word great. He is enthusiasm personified. He talked for almost two hours and I am sure he would have been willing to stay all day. As long as the subject was Stanford, he had plenty to rave about.

Nancy is not primarily an intellectual person but one respectful of intellect. She sets a nice balance between breadth and depth. She has taken charge of her life personally and academically. She will never be a great student but she has been able with effort to do good work in hard-for-her courses.

An interview with Yvette is a great way to start the day. This bouncy, almost giddy live wire is about as spirited and zestful a Stanford student as I've ever talked to. It's hard not to admire and respect someone like Yvette. She has an infectious enthusiasm and concern about this place . . . though there have been ups and downs in her college experience, she has built on her losses and been humble about her gains. I will really miss her presence on campus.

Greg is attractive, eager, and young. He is full of conflicting and confused feelings and beliefs, but he has intelligence and energy, and is an activist; he is also introspective when he allows himself the time so the confusions will probably sort themselves out.

Lisa does not give the impression of being deeply introspective or very excited by ideas or of attempting to stretch her intellectual wings . . . I don't mean to suggest shallowness or superficiality; on the contrary, Lisa is definitely a thoughtful person who understands herself and her world quite well. What I am hinting at is perhaps too easy acceptance of that world.

Ron is one of my favorites! He's extremely sensitive and thoughtful, also one of those most willing, most compelled to talk about very personal concerns. Calm and mature, he seems much older than many of his peers. I imagine that his friends turn to him for support. He must also provide important emotional support to his family. Consistently warm and friendly. Getting to know Ron has been one of the high points of this study!

Background Characteristics of Strivers

Gender. The intermediate position that Strivers occupy between Careerists and Intellectuals is exemplified by the gender composition of this group. While Careerists are mostly men and Intellectuals mostly women, the two sexes are present in equal proportions among Strivers. This orientation offers an option to both sexes who wish to avoid a narrower emphasis on intellectualism or careerism. Nonetheless, there is a difference between the two sexes as to which end of the educational spectrum they are drawn from. Men who become Strivers are more like Careerists with an additional element of intellectualism; women who become Strivers are more like Intellectuals with stronger career interests. Examples from interviewer reports:

What Rebecca wants from undergraduate education is a good background that will be rigorous, that will enable her to be admitted to a good law school, something she has wanted to do since her junior year in high school . . . She wants to learn to read, to write, to speak effectively: "If I do that, then I have fulfilled my objectives. I would like to learn to be constructively critical and to be logical and to balance those things out with some general knowledge of science and some appreciation of the arts."

Alex wants to pursue a degree in law or business after graduation. While he is keen on obtaining a good liberal education, he does not want to graduate without a marketable skill that will allow him to do something interesting and worthwhile, while at the same time earning enough money to do the kinds of things he wants to do . . . He is unhappy with some of his classes and feels uncertain about his major. Part of the problem is the conflict between his wish to obtain a broad liberal arts education while so many others are preparing to learn how to make even more money than their families already have.

Ethnicity. Ethnic minority students are especially likely to be Strivers. Some 35 percent of Black and Chicano students and 36 percent of Asian-American students are Strivers, compared to only 22 percent of Caucasians. Of course, as with all other categories, the majority of Strivers are white, but ethnic minorities are by far the most prominent among Strivers, comprising 27 percent of this group but only 11 percent of Intellectuals and 19 percent of Careerists and the Unconnected.

The relative paucity of minority students among Intellectuals and their overrepresentation among Strivers suggests that even for those minority students with a strong interest in liberal education, career concerns remain compelling. This is quite understandable given the less advantaged backgrounds of many of these students, and it is consistent with the greater push for upward social mobility shown by those in the lower socioeconomic groups.

Socioeconomic Status. Being a Striver is inversely related to socioeconomic standing. This is true for all students, not just ethnic minorities: Students from the top third of the SES ranking are especially unlikely to be Strivers (18 percent); students from the bottom third are most likely to be of this type (27 percent); while students from the middle third are in between (23 percent).

This finding is further corroborated by specific SES indicators. Fully one third of all students from the bottom third of the family income scale and 46 percent of students from families having less than $20,000 income are Strivers, compared to only 23 percent of the top third. Students identifying themselves as being of upper-middle- or upper-class status are much less likely to be Strivers than students who say they are of lower- or middle-class status (20 percent compared to 34 percent). That being a Striver is related to the drive for upward mobility is exemplified by the children of blue-collar workers; though we have information on only nine such students, six of them are Strivers.

The one exception to this pattern is that students from the highest professional levels and social backgrounds may also be Strivers. For instance, 39 percent of the children of physicians are Strivers, as are 29 percent of students from families in the top income bracket (over $100,000 a year), compared to 24 percent of all students. Also, 32 percent of students whose fathers have doctoral-level degrees are Strivers, compared to only 16 percent of those whose fathers have master's degrees (and 33 percent of those whose fathers have less than a college education). Thus, the Strivers are to some extent bimodal: Both students of relatively low socioeconomic background (including a high proportion of minorities) and students of very high status background are likely to be in this group.

Strivers from high socioeconomic backgrounds are exemplified by David, whose family had extensive financial interests in the entertainment industry. His travels, social contacts through his family, and elite prep school education imbued him with considerable sophistication. David enjoyed a similar advantage with respect to his career. He helped manage some of his father's global enterprises during the summer, often carrying a level of responsibility that many of his peers were unlikely ever to attain. Both David and his father were proud of his vocational drive and competence, which was so much in keeping with the family style. The purpose of striving in his case was not so much practical as it was symbolic.

The situation was very different for Billy. He came from a very small evangelical Christian college. His father worked fourteen hours a day in a print shop. Neither of his parents had been to college. Billy worked as a hasher and cooked his own meals part of the time to save money. Coming from an extremely sheltered background, he felt "socially inexperienced." Over the four years Billy's social horizons greatly expanded. He was very serious about getting a liberal education but he also wanted a profession that would secure his financial future. His "ultimate dream" was to get into a J.D.-M.B.A. program. Though he felt a bit self-conscious about wanting to make a lot of money, reading Ayn Rand helped him to come to terms with it.

Academic Background. Academic background is closely related to being a Striver but not in the way that might be expected. Given the huge level of ambition that characterizes Strivers, concomitantly high abilities would seem called for. This is not the case. It is students with relatively low verbal or mathematics SAT scores who are likely to be Strivers. About 30 percent of the lower-scoring students on each dimension (below 610 for verbal, below 600 for math scores) fall into this category, compared to only 20 percent of the high-score students. The overall effect is that students having below-median scores in *both* dimensions are more likely to be found among the Strivers than any other type. This finding indicates that the aspirations of Strivers are often not commensurate with their academic abilities.

Why is it that the students who have relatively weak academic backgrounds are precisely those who aspire to get the most on both counts—education and career? Why is it that students of the strongest academic backgrounds are not the ones most likely to be Strivers?

There is no easy answer to these questions. Some of the most able students, in fact, do become Strivers, making a spectacular success of this orientation to college (as exemplified by Pierre in profile 6.2). But they are few in number and it is not they who set the standard for this group as a whole. Some students with strong academic backgrounds may shun the Striver orientation because they see the danger of trying to accomplish too much and hence missing out on both educational depth and career prospects. Other highly competent students who could make a success of Striverhood do not have the diversity of interests that is the hallmark of students in this group, as exemplified by the following case:

The son of a retired Air Force master sergeant from the South, Rhett could have been a Careerist or an Intellectual with equal ease. He was ready to declare his major in biology in the fall quarter of his freshman year since he had intended to pursue such a major long before he arrived at Stanford. For the sake of protocol, however, he waited until the spring. He had done extensive study in biology in high school and *had worked as a technician in a neurophysiology lab. He obtained similar employment at Stanford as a lab technician and research assistant.*

By his junior year, Rhett thought of himself as a neurophysiologist and was as well integrated into the biology department as many graduate students. Alert and enterprising, he wrote to an incoming faculty member and arranged to work with him following his arrival at Stanford.

Rhett was also a singer and music was as important to him as biology. He sang in choirs and performed in four operas, four Gilbert and Sullivan operettas, two musical comedies, and one rock opera, with leading roles in eight of these. He also worked as technical director, master painter, makeup artist, and in other capacities. He planned to go on to a Ph.D. program hoping eventually to teach and do research in a major university and sing on the side.

The students who predominate among the Strivers strike us as being quite capable even though their academic backgrounds may be weaker. They are aware of their deficiencies and are highly motivated to correct them by taking advantage of every opportunity available to advance their education and career prospects. If they do not fully succeed, it is not for lack of trying.

As we saw with the Careerists and Intellectuals, the findings with respect to academic background are different for the two sexes. For men, the crucial factor related to being a Striver is a low *mathematics* SAT score, with men having high math scores more likely to be either Careerists or Unconnected; verbal scores make little difference. For women, the mathematics score, as such, is relatively unimportant; it is a low *verbal* score that is most strongly associated with being a Striver, particularly when it is coupled with a high mathematics score. Thus, almost half (47 percent) of women with low verbal and high math scores are Strivers, compared to only 16 percent of men with the same combination.

Sources of Influence on Strivers

Parents. We have seen that the Careerists are strongly influenced by their families, while Intellectuals are strongly influenced by the faculty. Strivers once again share an affinity with both groups by being receptive to influence emanating from both sources. Students whose academic and career decisions are strongly influenced by their families are almost as likely to be Strivers as Careerists (30 percent as against 34 percent), and only 19 percent of students expressing weak family influence are Strivers. Similarly, students who are strongly influenced by the faculty are more likely to be Strivers (29 percent), while only 23 percent of students showing weak faculty influence are in this group.

The interview reports indicate that the parents of Strivers reinforce both Careerist concerns and broader educational aims, as illustrated by these excerpts:

Out of his growing sense of engagement with college came his conviction that he wanted diversity, "the license to explore." He admitted that his mother's emphasis on the liberal arts was a strong influence.

He said his dad has always pressured him to figure out what he wanted to do: "He told me over spring break that if I don't get a job in my field this summer, it's probably not worth coming back for my senior year. It's been bothering me since he said it."

His many and varied interests seem patterned on his father, a translator for an oil company who "speaks fifteen languages and says he can play the piano with his toes. He was a priest and then a Methodist minister, did social work, ran a parochial school and then a Hebrew camp. . ."

Faculty. Overall, family influence has a larger impact on being a Striver than does faculty influence, but it is the combination of these two sources of influence that is most likely to produce a student of this type. As with the Intellectuals, greater Striver involvement with the faculty may be more effect than cause. The Strivers go to greater lengths to develop relationships with faculty members, thus giving the faculty the opportunity to influence them. This interpretation is supported by the related finding that Strivers indicate considerable influence of course work on their major and career decisions; students indicating that course work is a strong influence are very likely to be Strivers (32 percent, compared to 20 percent of students indicating weak course work influence).

The following excerpts from interview reports illustrate the generally close relationships Strivers have with members of the faculty and their regrets when such relationships are lacking:

In her freshman year Betsy took a philosophy class, where the subject and the professor "just opened me up . . . I'd never had such an experience." Since then, "I've been doing a lot more thinking about myself, my values, and my relationships with others."

"Every class I have taken here has been my best class." He went on to talk about his individual professors in rave terms: "The brilliance of that man is amazing . . . I know I'm getting the best . . . all superb in their own ways."

He said that he also has good contacts with the business school where he works for one of the retired professors: "He's kind of leading me by the hand."

Although he thinks he could do the long-range planning on his own, it would be nice to have a "guiding hand" who would at least be able to point out areas that he might have overlooked due to lack of experience.

Mark regrets that faculty do not provide much direction to students and is disappointed that no member of the faculty has taken a real interest in him. He appreciates the university's efforts to promote student-faculty contact but feels that such interactions can't be forced. Arm twisting won't work; what is necessary is sincere interest.

The faculty sponsor for the experimental course Fred put together is a professor from the business school, who has been exceptionally helpful to Fred: "He will do anything for you!" This has been Fred's most rewarding faculty relationship.

Other Influences. The impact of fellow students on the educational and career choices of Careerists and Intellectuals is quite small, but for Strivers a more significant effect is evident. Some 28 percent of students who are strongly influenced by their peers are Strivers, compared to only 19 percent of those who are weakly influenced. Our suspicion that student peers tend to reinforce both career and intellectual concerns is confirmed, particularly in light of the fact that the Unconnected say that peers have little effect on their decisions (Chapter Seven). The overall picture is one where these students are highly engaged in all aspects of their lives and are therefore likely to feel that many different sources of influence play a part in their decisions.

This picture is given added depth by the finding that the Strivers are especially likely to be strongly influenced by both their knowledge of the job market and their past work experience. They show as much influence of their knowledge of the job market as Careerists do and as much influence of work experience as do the Intellectuals. Once again, Strivers reveal a tendency to cover all the bases. They are concerned about high-status careers, so they pay attention to job market prospects. But since they are not willing to settle for careers that offer only external rewards, they also evaluate their career choices in light of what they have learned from jobs they have held, looking for an occupation that will offer intellectual satisfaction as well as material benefits. In general, then, the Strivers exhibit a high degree of susceptibility to influence whereby family, faculty, peers, work experience, and the job market are all important considerations to them in their choice of major and career.

Major and Career Choices of Strivers

With respect to major choice we find Strivers to be fairly evenly distributed across school divisions. They are somewhat more likely to major in engineering than other students (21 percent, compared to 16 percent of all students) and less likely to major in the humanities (12 percent, compared to 19 percent), but in other areas they are proportionately represented. In their major choices they resemble Careerists more than Intellectuals, but they are less extreme than the former: Fully 24 percent of the Careerists choose engineering and only 6 percent choose the humanities. Since there is no set way of combining an interest in liberal education with the concern for career success, Striver students follow many different pathways to that end.

Unlike other types, Strivers show few sex differences in choice of major. Similarly, in terms of changes in major choice between the freshman and senior years, Strivers follow the same pattern displayed by other students: There is a net loss of students majoring in the natural sciences and a net gain in the humanities.

The postbaccalaureate aspirations of Strivers are on the whole also quite typical: Forty-four percent plan to obtain doctoral-level degrees and 50 percent plan to obtain master's degrees. But there is an important sex difference here that shows the ambitions of women in this group to be considerably higher than those of men: Fifty-four percent of the women, but only 33 percent of the men, plan to pursue doctoral-level degrees. In fact, women Strivers far exceed women in the other groups in this regard while male Strivers fall below all other men. This is an intriguing and puzzling finding. While it makes sense that Striver women should have high aspirations, since the group is highly achievement oriented, why should the aspirations of the men be so low (fourteen percentage points below the figure for all men)? Let us look at patterns of career choice before attempting to answer this question.

As with choice of major, the career choices of Strivers are very similar to those of the entire sample. There are sharper differences, however, when Strivers are compared to Careerists, with whom they share a strong interest in careers. The contrast with the Careerists is particularly strong in medicine: Twenty-two percent of Careerists are planning to enter this profession, as compared to only 8 percent of Strivers. The Strivers are also much more open to careers in the nonstandard fields: Twenty-six percent of the Strivers plan careers in these occupations, compared to 8 percent of the Careerists. On the other hand, the career choices of Strivers are much more conventional than those of Intellectuals; half of the Intellectuals aim for nonstandard fields, and they are much less likely than Strivers to plan to enter law and engineering.

Are the career choices of Striver men and women equally diverse? Clearly not; women in this group make more diverse choices than men, and the nature of their choices explains the higher educational aspirations they exhibit. Nearly two thirds (63 percent) of the men choose either business or law, compared to 48 percent of the women. Furthermore, men are notably less likely than women to plan careers in medicine (4 percent of men, 12 percent of women), and women are generally better dispersed across the other categories. The very high proportion of men planning to enter business (42 percent) means that most of them will pursue master's-level degrees (mostly M.B.A.s), while the women are more likely to plan careers as physicians, professors, and researchers, all of which require doctoral-level degrees.

There is an interesting contrast here with the Intellectuals, with whom the Strivers share a high regard for liberal education. Intellectuals in general, and Intellectual women in particular, are likely to choose nonstandard fields, for many of which a doctoral-level degree is unnecessary. Striver women, however, are drawn largely to fields such as medicine that offer more certain material rewards and prestige and that require a doctoral-level degree. Thus the aspirations of Striver women for further education are considerably higher than those of Intellectual women, not because the Strivers value education more but because they choose careers that make doctoral-level education necessary.

The difference between Striver women and men is more straightforward. Men who combine career and educational concerns lean toward the more Careerist occupational choices. Women seem freer to pursue their intellectual interests and make career choices that entail intrinsic rewards more than external symbols of success. Thus Striver women make more varied career choices than their male counterparts and are more likely to choose nonstandard careers, even though compared to Intellectual women they behave more like men in their career decisions.

Strivers shift career direction between the freshman and senior years in a pattern largely typical of their classmates, with one exception. Like the Careerists, Strivers are especially unlikely to stay with a career choice in one of the nonstandard fields—only 46 percent stay with a nonstandard field, about the same proportion as the Careerists (43 percent) and well below the Intellectuals (73 percent) and Unconnected (60 percent). However, the Strivers are much more open than the Careerists to moving from standard to nonstandard fields; 21 percent of the Strivers who initially plan on a standard-field career end up in a nonstandard field, compared to only 3 percent of the Careerists.

Considering the frequency of change in career plans, Strivers are again very typical, averaging .8 changes per person. But some 59 percent of the Strivers never change their career plans at all, a figure higher than the mean for all students (51 percent) and far above that for the Unconnected (34 percent), who are least likely to stay with an initial career choice. This indicates that a small proportion of Strivers change their career plans relatively often.

Some Strivers show great entrepreneurial aptitude. For instance, Monty and a friend set up a small business selling sandwiches on campus. They were assisted in this venture by a professor from the business school, who proved to be most helpful. Monty learned a great deal through this practical experience. He then developed an undergraduate course dealing with small business management, which he offered the following fall as an Undergraduate Special. (Monty was admitted to four M.B.A. programs, accepted by one law school, and placed on waiting lists for two others.)

On the negative side, one of the characteristics of less successful Strivers is their vagueness as to their career goals compared to Careerists (and educational goals compared to Intellectuals). Thus, not only do they tend to overextend themselves—trying to accomplish too much, they accomplish too little—but this is further compounded by their lack of specificity as to what they want to accomplish, at least within the realm of possibility. For instance, Nora was in such a rush to graduate that she was taking a large number of courses but then failing some of them. Nor did the passage of time make things clearer ("the closer I got to graduation, the less I knew what I wanted to do").

Strivers bring to their career choices much of the same sense of exuberance that they manifest in other aspects of their lives, while displaying attitudes that are a mix of Careerist and Intellectual tendencies. The following excerpts from interviewers' reports are illustrative:

He highlighted this year by being selected from among thousands of people who auditioned to perform in Marriott's Broadway Musical Review. His dream is to work with an international touring company related to Disneyland Productions.

Although she isn't moving inexorably toward any concrete goal, she does seem to know the general lines she hopes to pursue. She's engaged to be married to a graduate student. They will be attending the same law school. After five years, she plans to take some time off to have two children, work part-time from her home, and "read everything in sight." She hopes that the law, its practice and study, will be a "binding force" in her marriage.

Catholicism has been a source of great comfort to him, because he feels confident that no matter what happens in the future, "I would be okay; I would be taken care of." This aspect of Anthony's life became progressively more dominant in his undergraduate years, eventuating in his decision to become a priest.

His honors thesis is on the application of marketing techniques to social causes such as the promotion of family planning through TV. He says, "I'd like to land a lucrative career by the time I am thirty."

He is thoughtful and concerned about the future, but he seems to have arrived at a way of being comfortable with the fact that his plans are largely unformed.

During his Washington internship, he went from intern to legislative assistant almost immediately because of his excellent communication and interpersonal skills. They would have been happy to lure him away from school for a permanent job . . . He lamented the fact that he didn't have more time for reflection. When talking about the possibility of his becoming an international diplomat, he noted that one of the sacrifices would be that of marriage. He could not see traveling around the world and asking his wife to give up her own career to travel with him.

A wide range of interests and involvement in numerous activities help determine career choices, as shown by statements from two Striver students:

"I am a shoo-in for business school. I have directed a play, I've done management work, and I have lots of extracurricular involvements plus some applicable experience in banks . . . my academic background would fit well too."

"In five years' time I could possibly be married. I'll definitely still be working. I'd die of boredom if I didn't."

The high degree of academic diversity and unusual combinations and shifts of majors and careers are characteristic features of Striverhood. Wayne explored a number of major and career prospects, finally graduating with a double major in political science and economics. He was initially interested in law but decided to go on to graduate school in sociology and become a professor. Gregory successfully finished an electrical engineering major and went on to a top flight law school. He comes from a family of lawyers and planned to become a patent lawyer, thus combining his technical background with his legal education. Cheryl was a varsity golfer who despite the enormous time demands of her sport obtained a solid liberal education and was admitted to law school. The story of Kevin is even more unusual:

Described by his interviewer as a "big grinning farm boy from Oregon," Kevin came to Stanford having done everything from manual labor to assembling a computer. His career options were farming, working for the Foreign Service, engineering, and veterinary medicine. At first he felt a bit out of place at Stanford but after a year in Vienna, Kevin returned speaking German, French, Russian, and Romanian. He had spent two quarters at the Stanford campus and one at the University of Vienna. He attended a concert "almost every night" and went to a dozen Viennese balls (his roommate came from a prominent family). He traveled through Poland, Hungary, and Yugoslavia.

During the summer of his junior year Kevin worked on an eastern Oregon desert construction site and lived in his own camper for the whole summer. He had no radio, telephone, or television so he read twenty-three books in several languages and the entire collected works of William Shakespeare. The interviewer called him "a perfect example of the early pioneer American—adventurous, ingenious and self-reliant."

Following graduation Kevin planned to work on his father's farm during the summer. In the fall he would go into a J.D.-M.B.A. program. Eventually he thought he would go into private business, perhaps managing his father's mechanical contracting company. In ten years he would have paid off all his debts and would be living in some semirural area with his family.

The interviewer called Kevin "the most impressive student I have interviewed. His academic and social growth have been exponential."

Pursuing a Liberal Education

Strivers share with Intellectuals a high regard for liberal learning. But their educational aspirations are tempered by a concomitantly active interest in careers. This diffusion of purpose results in Strivers being less certain of their educational aims and somewhat more superficial than Intellectuals. Where Careerists choose majors and courses for instrumental purposes and Intellectuals for interest, Strivers try to extract double duty of them. This usually entails some dilution of focus.

Strivers may lose out to Careerists in vocational emphasis and to Intellectuals on educational goals, but they manage to get a broader exposure than both. They neither shun the humanities as the Careerists do nor avoid the sciences as the Intellectuals do. The penalty they pay for breadth is a relative lack of coherence in their education. The following interview report excerpts typify their attitudes:

His classes have covered "a broad spectrum." On the other hand, he doesn't want to come out of Stanford being unable to "do something."

"I never really made use of my advisers, and my program has been incoherent, especially in my major. It would have helped me if things had been more structured. I wanted to get something out of classes that would do something for me personally."

His program has been aimless so far (sophomore year). He came to college for a broad general education and still wants to learn a lot about a lot of things and therefore finds it hard to choose a major. He is extremely frustrated by this whole process of narrowing down his interests.

With respect to her educational gains, she had "hoped for more . . . not sure what, just more."

Some Strivers are nonetheless very close to Intellectuals in their perspective on liberal education. They complain about some of their peers having the attitude that one does not "talk about

academic matters out of class." One ascribed the vocational
orientations of other students to excessive job concerns ("they feed
on each other's fears").

Like Intellectuals, Strivers also care about the quality of their
courses. Rita derided a survey course in literature that lacked
content ("you know it's Wednesday, so it must be Robert
Browning"). In contrast, she was enthusiastic about another survey
course about which she said, "That also is a survey course but there
is a text, there are contextual materials, there are primary works to
read, and it's taught in a purposeful way." The following quotes
from interviewers' reports provide further examples of the more
serious Strivers' perspective on liberal education.

*"Before I came to Stanford," she said, "I thought academics were
mathematics and science. But anthropology and philosophy have
broadened my outlook. I look at society differently now."*

*A lot of her classes are taken for interest. Fascinated with discussing
ideologies, philosophies, and personal values.*

*His academic plan is to experience as much as possible in a broad
range of fields. He can't think of anything more exciting than studying
Shakespeare while in England.*

*He spoke over and over again of his exhilaration at being in
college. He has discovered a new freedom that allows him to think about
things that he was never able even to question before. "I am learning
how to think for myself."*

Overseas Study. Despite the contributions to liberal learning
offered by overseas study, only one third of the Strivers avail
themselves of this opportunity, which is far below the figure for
Intellectuals (55 percent). In fact, the Strivers are less likely to go
overseas than all other types except the Unconnected. This is one
more instance where Strivers fail to have it both ways. With so many
irons in the fire something has to give, and overseas study is one of
the casualties.

Those Strivers who do go overseas appear to make good use of it, as exemplified by Kevin's Vienna experience discussed earlier. A number of others would readily agree with Jeanne for whom "the high point of the year was Florence." And at least some of those who do not go regret it: "I am sure I would have gotten a lot out of going overseas. It would have done me a lot of good."

Stopping Out. Strivers are also unlikely to stop out. Only 17 percent stay away from school for one or more quarters, less than half the proportion of Intellectuals who elect this option. The reasons for this are probably similar to the reasons more Strivers do not go overseas—they have too much going on right where they are.

On the other hand, we might have expected Strivers to stop out not only for stocktaking but also to relieve economic pressures by working for part of a year, given that many of them come from families of relatively low income. This does not seem to be the case, perhaps because many of them are eager to finish college and go to work or pursue other career goals.

Social Life and Extracurricular Activities

One might expect Strivers to be socially very active for several reasons: Their general enthusiasm for all facets of college life would lead them to become involved in a wide range of activities; their concern for intellectual issues would motivate them to be socially and politically engaged; and their desire to build impressive records would cause them to seek resume-enhancing activities. These expectations are only partially fulfilled.

The Involvement Index shows Strivers to be no more active than students in general and somewhat less active than Intellectuals. In particular, in such areas as the arts, organized campus activities, and off-campus involvement, the activity level of Strivers is very close to the mean for all students. Yet, these general indexes mask some highly active Strivers. For instance, one interviewer wrote: "Tom spent more than forty hours a week in a student theatrical production. He directed the show, wrote and orchestrated the music, conducted the orchestra and was very involved in all other aspects of it. For all intents and purposes, he *was* the show."

The energy level of some of these Strivers is astounding, as shown in these reports by interviewers:

Brenda can move with ease from a vigorous tennis match at 4:00 P.M., to formal dinner at 5:30 P.M., and a pretest chemistry study section at 7:00 P.M. She runs two miles each day, she swims on warm days, hardly ever misses the flicks, goes to lots of speeches to hear "great people that you would otherwise only read about," plays tennis, practices the piano, plays the flute in her dorm musical production, yet she still worries a bit that she may be missing some opportunities here. She doesn't mind the whirlwind pace—life would otherwise be quite dull.

Saturday morning Joel attended a fraternity party, then he went to a semiformal event that began at 5:00 P.M. and ended at 3:30 A.M. He came back to the fraternity to have breakfast and left shortly thereafter for a rock concert (a rush event sponsored by the fraternity) that lasted all day Sunday. When Joel got back to the fraternity in the evening, he spent a couple of hours studying and then spent from 9:00 P.M. to 2:30 A.M. cleaning the kitchen, which was part of the responsibilities he has as a hasher. Because this is the last week of rush, he has the rest of the week booked up with parties as well. Despite this hectic pace, Joel has done quite well this winter quarter, garnering a 3.9 GPA. He says, "I realize that I shouldn't be wasting time."

Strivers are noted for their involvement in academic work beyond the classroom (such as taking accredited internships) and participation in athletics. In these two areas they are the most active students. They thus attain more closely than others the classical ideal of "a sound mind in a sound body."

Strivers are also very likely to be involved in volunteer public service; 62 percent of those students indicate serious engagement in such activity, making them second only to Intellectuals (72 percent) and far ahead of Careerists (45 percent).

At the more personal level, the Strivers have a rich network of friends and social relationships ("I have *very, very* close friends"). The Strivers are the most certain of having intimate ties in the future: Only 2 percent say they do not think they will be married or in a committed relationship in ten years, comparable figures being 4 percent for Intellectuals and 6 percent for Careerists. These differences are, however, wholly generated by males—4 percent of

Strivers, 10 percent of Careerists, and 15 percent of Intellectual men, but none of the women in these groups, see themselves as unattached in a decade. With respect to having children, Strivers again emerge as the most positive: Ninety-eight percent say they plan to have children sometime. The corresponding percentage for Careerists is only 83 percent.

Academic Success and Satisfaction

A key answer to the question of whether Strivers can "have it all" is to be found in how well they do in their course work and how satisfied they are with their overall educational experience.

Academic Performance. Strivers are not as academically successful as students in the other groups. Only 3 percent (two of sixty individuals) earned the Phi Beta Kappa award, compared to 14 percent of Intellectuals, the highest group, and 8 percent of all students. Seven percent complete departmental honor's programs, which is very close to the mean, but they have the lowest rate of graduating with distinction (12 percent, compared to 20 percent of all students). Their overall grade point average is the lowest of the four groups (3.28), although this figure is only slightly below the figure for the Careerists and the Uncommitted (3.34). However, they get lower grades not just in general but in virtually all academic areas from the humanities to engineering.

Self-Assessments of Knowledge and Abilities. As might be anticipated from the fact that Strivers choose diverse majors, their self-assessments are just about average for most of the ability areas. Strivers give notably high self-assessments in only two areas of the Senior Survey: understanding non-Western cultures and understanding human development. The reason for the latter can be traced to the fact that a high proportion of Strivers major in biology, human biology, and psychology (35 percent of Strivers, but only 25 percent of all students), fields where such understanding is fostered.

The high rating for understanding non-Western cultures derives from two factors. First, Strivers contain a higher proportion of minority students who have their ethnic roots in non-Western cultures; this is particularly true for Blacks and Asian Americans.

Second, the commitment of Strivers to a liberal education leads them to learn about other cultures, irrespective of their ethnic background. For the same reason Intellectuals are also high on this dimension, even though ethnic minorities are underrepresented among them.

One further finding about Striver self-assessments is worthy of note: These students give the highest overall ratings for the *importance* of the various ability areas. Hence, they seem to be more engaged and care more than other students about what they learn even if they do not perform as well in the classroom.

Satisfaction with the Undergraduate Experience. In their questionnaire evaluations of the senior year, Striver assessments are quite high. They give the highest overall responses on four out of nine items, including the development of career plans, sense of belonging, and overall level of contentment, where they have a mean of 4.2 compared to 4.0 for the Intellectuals, the next highest group, and 3.8 for the Careerists. The only area where they express less-than-average satisfaction is getting the desired grades.

The Senior Survey shows much the same pattern of responses. The Strivers give higher-than-average evaluations on many items, and none of their evaluations are significantly below average. They are particularly satisfied with their training for graduate or professional school (higher even than the Careerists), the contribution of their living situations to their intellectual life, and the faculty as researchers. They give slightly above-average responses concerning the overall quality of the education they have received, and their satisfaction with their liberal education is just about average but well below the rating given by the Intellectuals (4.2 for the latter, 3.8 for the Strivers).

These measures of success and satisfaction, no matter how objectively valid, fail to do full justice to the undergraduate experience of Strivers. We noted earlier the positive impression that Strivers made on their interviewers. But there is more to Strivers than likability. These students are described over and over again as healthy and mature individuals. Even though there is at times a tinge of "pollyannaish" exuberance to their overly positive views of the world, more often their contentment is the result of a balanced, positive view of life, as shown in these comments by interviewers:

She strikes me as an extraordinarily well-adjusted, healthy, and well-balanced person. She's bright but does not come across as a heavy intellectual; she has distinct professional ambitions, but she is not out to conquer the world; she knows what she wants in a career yet simultaneously has definite aspirations for her personal life. In short, what is impressive about her is not one or another isolated characteristic but the overall balance and harmony that she conveys.

There is an energy level here that makes itself felt in the dorm and among friends, without Joshua's being an organization man or a leader. He floats freely through various social strata and contributes his talents in a number of ways while appearing to think seriously about his own needs and actions. He seems mature and thoughtful, at least about his personal life if not about his academic involvements.

A gregarious and ebullient person, Donald looks healthy, happy, and robust. He seems always to make the best of any situation and I can't imagine his ever whining or complaining. Seems exceptionally mature without being overly sophisticated. He exudes a sense of confidence with no trace of snobbishness or overbearing personality. "I never felt overwhelmed—only momentarily upset. I know I can do things. Even though my future feels nebulous, I feel confident about it."

Dawn strikes me as a very mature, levelheaded individual. She is vivacious and has a warmth about her that one instantly finds appealing. She enjoys her classes, yet her friends and family are very important to her. She has demonstrated a very positive outlook over the years and has a great sense of humor. It is apparent from talking with her that she is an individual who understands how to succeed.

"The epitome of the well-adjusted, well-rounded Stanfordite."

The Balance Sheet

The Strivers are the least complicated of the students we have discussed so far. Their educational aims are clear and broad. They defy the cleavage between career preparation and liberal learning. They combine the life of the mind with the cultivation of the body and social involvement. If a balanced approach to all that college has to offer is the objective of higher learning, the Strivers are the model students.

Strivers contribute more than most to making college an exciting and lively environment. Their enthusiasm is infectious, their loyalty unwavering. Had we included a more systematic examination of personality factors in our study, the Strivers would probably emerge as the best-adjusted group. They are certainly the most contented. One can hardly quibble with an interviewer's statement like the one that follows in determining whether an undergraduate experience has been successful.

Mark's response to the question "What are you taking with you?" was, "Everything." He sees his years at Stanford as being the most important ones of his life and feels very fortunate to have had such "fantastic experiences." He talked about intellectual growth and was glad that he "chose to question and to be involved. I could have been sterile socially but I wasn't." Stanford has made a difference in that he has grown socially and emotionally as well as intellectually.

The debit side of the Striver orientation, like that of Intellectualism, lies not in its conception but in its execution. This is a hard road to travel very successfully. It is made more difficult when the educationally less well prepared set out to be academically and vocationally more ambitious. Their level of satisfaction with their undergraduate education exceeds that of others even though their academic performance does not. Strivers may be the salt of the earth but they are unlikely to emerge as the seminal thinkers of their generation.

It is possible to fault Strivers for being uncritical judges of themselves and their accomplishments, but one must also admire their efforts to transcend both the artificial splits of academic life and their relative weaknesses. They embrace enthusiastically the prospects of learning and earning, work and play, the intellectual and the social. They would be shining models of a successful college education if they could integrate better the various facets of their lives and accomplish as much in depth as they do in breadth.

7

Unconnected Students:
Failing to Engage
in College

In the introduction to *The Uncommitted*, Keniston (1960) says, "This is a study of the roots of alienation in a group of Americans who have no obvious reason to be alienated." We could likewise say that the Unconnected are students who fail to engage fully in their college education for no obvious reasons.

We had more difficulty understanding this group than any of the others. If Strivers are the most straightforward in their academic orientation, the Unconnected are the most convoluted. The two groups can be thought of as polar opposites. The Unconnected students appear to be relatively indifferent to both career preparation and liberal education, while the Strivers are highly concerned about both. Strivers show the most enthusiasm for the educational enterprise and are the most highly satisfied with it, while the Unconnected show the least enthusiasm and are much more critical of it. But just as the Strivers do not represent a simple summation of the high careerism of Careerists and the high intellectualism of Intellectuals, the Unconnected are not just a negation of both. They rate low on intellectualism, like Careerists, but not because liberal learning is being sacrificed on the altar of careerism; they rate low on careerism, like Intellectuals, but not because of their devotion to institutionally endorsed intellectual aims.

Trying to define a group in negative terms is not easy. No wonder that we often felt as if we were sailing through a fog bank when dealing with the Unconnected. Time and again, when we thought we had found our bearings, we would get stranded. Assuming that in every race there must be a loser, we initially cast the Unconnected in that role, but then had to face the fact that these students get at least as good grades as the other types—and grades are a measure of success that is hard to disregard. We called them "uncommitted" for a time, only to realize that the group included some of the most committed individuals we were likely to encounter—they were merely not committed to the same goals as other students. Nor were most of these students uncommitted in the sense used by Keniston to refer to alienation from, or the rejection of, the dominant values, roles, and institutions of their society. We thought they were academic drifters but found that, their attitudes aside, their academic careers were, in fact, no more purposeless than those of quite a few others.

We finally saw the light in the realization that being Unconnected is not an academic orientation in the same sense that being a Careerist, Intellectual, or Striver is. There is merit in each of the just mentioned characterizations of the Unconnected, but no one of them adequately describes the group. What we have is a composite picture with a common theme but distinctive and often unrelated variants—there are many ways and many reasons for being Unconnected.

An easy way out in dealing with this group would be to consider them unclassifiable. After all, few typologies are perfectly exhaustive, and the recognition that some subjects do not fit would impart more credibility to our typology. But we have chosen instead to consider the academic orientation of these students as being insufficiently differentiated. Many of these students have a discernible bent toward careerism or intellectualism, but for some reason or another have not "connected" (a term borrowed from E. M. Forster) with these orientations—hence the "Unconnected."

The failure to connect may be due to active rejection or passive default. These students vary in the extent to which they are Unconnected, just as others vary in the intensity with which they are Careerists, Intellectuals, or Strivers. Students at the low ends of the other three categories are virtually indistinguishable from those who are least Unconnected. In many of these cases, additional information or a different reading of the interview reports could easily lead to a different classification of the student. But as with the other categories, we will not dwell on the attenuated forms but focus on those students who are more markedly unconnected to the institutional channels that lead to career paths and liberal learning. However, even when dealing with the purer types in the core group of the Unconnected, we must bear in mind that what sets them apart in our typology are their academic attitudes. Whether their behavior is equally distinctive is an issue we explore in the following section.

Before we delve into descriptions of the Unconnected as a group, it may be useful to present biographical profiles 7.1 through 7.4 of some individual students in this category and follow those with descriptions of the subtypes under this heading. We shall then explore briefly why these students as a whole do not become "ignited" to manifest the particular academic orientation toward which they incline.

Profile 7.1: Fred—Beating the System

Fred hates school and has done so ever since he "last learned anything meaningful" back in the sixth grade. Since then, he has looked upon education as the "game" it really is. Despite claims about the value of learning, the only thing people really want to get out of schooling is a "ticket" to future success. The "bottom line" to success (something he wants as much as the next man) is a set of high grades that convince those in the hiring or admitting system to promote you to the next step. Fred got straight A's in high school on the strength of his intuition and by figuring out what the teachers wanted to hear. He wanted to replicate the same success in college. Put simply, Fred would be happiest if he could get A's without going to classes at all. "I concentrate solely on getting by. Others concentrate on 'learning' and 'the educational experience,' but that's bullshit. It's okay if you believe in it, but I don't."

Fred implemented this strategy in his freshman year by choosing courses that would offer him the most units for the least amount of work. He took a fair mix of classes, concentrating on economics because of his *interest in business. But even then his choices were strictly utilitarian in nature. For example, he took an economics course that was quite similar to another he had already taken because of its "nice, high-sounding number." As for the education he was missing in the process, Fred's view was, "I am paying for the grades, not the classes."*

Fred's social interactions followed the same format. In high school he had been elected to positions of leadership in student government by telling "those voting what they wanted to hear." At Stanford Fred persisted with the same strategy and felt himself quite at home because he perceived Stanford's educational philosophy to be deep down as materialistic and self-serving as his own.

In his sophomore year Fred experienced a marked change in his orientation. This was partly due to his exposure to Taoism but also because of his active engagement with two professors in the humanities. This shift in consciousness resulted in his taking courses in subjects that he was interested in, irrespective of their practical implications for helping him make money in the future. He now began to let his life flow naturally, free from premeditation or planning. His ideology shifted from the hard-nosed, get-ahead approach to one of almost total aimlessness. When asked what his purpose was in pursuing a Stanford education, he responded, "There isn't one. I have no idea why I am here. I am just here because I am here."

As a reflection of his changed perspective, Fred declared a major in linguistics even though it struck him as the worst possible choice for purposes of professional security. But he was interested in the subject and did well in it. Yet, Fred's former self continued to intrude in his reformed life. He pointed out, for instance, that though linguistics sounded impressive as a major, it really was an "easy subject" with its basic concepts "self-evident" and the content of many courses overlapping. Furthermore, as one of the few students majoring in the department, he felt well attended to because "I am one eighth of their budget."

In time Fred became a calmer, more thoughtful, and gracious version of his former self. Yet he very much remained his own man. He did not attend many classes but only took the exams and did reasonably well. He spent most of his time reading (including textbooks for courses he was not taking), talking to friends, listening to music, and meditating.

Toward the end of his junior year Fred redirected his interest to more worldly career prospects. He now wanted to work in investments, and his ambition was to build up enough capital so he could retire at age twenty-five. Yet he knew he could not do this, nor was he interested in going to business school, since students "actually have to study there." So he took a year off and worked as a bellman in a motel managed by his father. On returning to school he faced the formidable load still required for graduation but by single-minded application to this task he accomplished it successfully.

To the very end, Fred maintained his cynical facade. He claimed to be satisfied with his Stanford education because employers would be impressed by his degree and because it had taught him how to behave at cocktail parties. Fred's interviewer, however, was not entirely taken in by the image he presented and wondered about the "more serious aspects of this apparently unabashed joyrider." Despite the seeming lack of clear educational or vocational purpose, one could not help but feel that Fred would be quite successful at whatever he chose to undertake.

Profile 7.2: Martha—Staying at Arm's Length

Martha's choice of Stanford was an act of defiance against her "ultraconservative and restrictive" mother, who was worried about "all the radicals." It was also an attempt to get away from the East Coast where the family lives ("you can only prevent a person from doing what she wants for so long"). In high school she was hardly challenged academically nor did she particularly enjoy her social life, describing herself as self-centered, withdrawn, shy, and an "outie."

Martha started her freshman year without clear academic or career goals. She was primarily interested in "doing things for the experience." Her plans had to be defined with respect to "an appropriate life-style." Courses were "taken at random," because "I was kind of tired of basic courses in high school." She was hardly challenged by the courses she took, but that did not bother her because "who needs rigor for rigor's sake?"

Not only did Martha keep her family at arm's length, she hardly had any contact with her academic adviser or other members of the faculty. In her sophomore year she declared psychology as her major even though she was neither taking any courses in it nor did she have a clear idea of why she made that choice. She gave even less thought or concern to career prospects.

Martha stopped out for part of her sophomore year. The decision was "very spontaneous." During a weekend of horseback riding with a friend she decided that she was going to "learn on her own" since she was "tired of being spoon-fed and wanted to be challenged." When asked if she had accomplished that aim in her quarter out, she admitted that she hadn't and said: "I will but not now." She considered transferring to a small liberal arts college because "it has a more intellectual atmosphere, and I belong on a small campus." She was accepted, yet decided to stay at Stanford because it is a "more worldly place."

By the end of her junior year Martha settled on an English major since it provided "more leeway for creativity" and because she enjoyed writing. Nonetheless, she remained uncertain ("I'm not sure what I want"). She was far from integrated in the department, had very little faculty or student interaction, and hardly any dealings with her departmental adviser. Her living arrangements were equally fluid ("she seems to move every quarter").

Although Martha was, in principle, interested in social and political issues, she never managed to get fully engaged: "I must mature socially and emotionally before committing myself to any activity." When she did get involved, she either alienated others in the group or stayed on its periphery. For example, she and her boyfriend joined a vegetarian living group, then upset everyone by cooking meat in the dormitory.

The senior year found Martha mellow and contrite. She admitted to having wasted a good deal of time and was quite disappointed with her undergraduate experience (the interviewer called it "great expectations unfulfilled"). Yet she had no interest in graduate school ("it is not necessary for my purposes"). Her immediate future was tied to her boyfriend's plans (he was graduating in a highly sought-after field). She was considering work in some administrative capacity, either within community services or in business. These uncertainties notwithstanding, Martha impressed the interviewer to the very end as being "quite comfortable with herself."

Profile 7.3: Patricia—Fighting the System

"Patricia came closer to looking like a Bohemian than anyone else I've ever met," wrote the interviewer in the freshman year. She was wearing "a pink-and-black spotted bandana pulled awkwardly around her head, a black vest over a multicolored T-shirt, another bandana for a belt, and a good old-fashioned pair of work boots hidden under her rather baggy pair of blue jeans." Given her attire and hard, staccato speech laced with earthy vernaculars, "this conversation would have seemed better set in the coffeehouse," noted her interviewer.

From an affluent suburb of an Eastern city, Patricia was admitted to half a dozen select colleges and universities to which she had applied from an equally select prep school. She narrowed the choice down to Yale and Stanford and opted for the "laid-back mentality" of the latter as against the "intense ratrace" of the former (much to the dismay of her family, which has old ties to Yale).

Patricia was bitterly disappointed in Stanford. For two years she complained about everything. She could "not figure out why I'm getting less out of college than boarding school." Her classes became flat, dull, and boring by the fourth week, and left her wondering how the

professors managed to kill the initial excitement. They had a "terribly
narrow-minded approach" in their thinking. Advising was "completely
awful." Residential education espoused "mush-minded" standards and
promoted "mush-minded housing." She had "expected people to be
shallow" but not to the extent she found them to be. Stanford students
were neither "academically active" nor "intellectually stimulating," but
"too Californian" and "too much alike." Only a small group of students
and a few faculty shared her "leftist" perspective to think progressively,
to question the status quo, and to transcend the classroom in order to
address the problems of the world.

Patricia stopped out for a quarter in her sophomore year,
considered transferring to Yale, then decided to take off a full year. She
worked in boat yards and on boats in the Caribbean, was a waitress for
a while, got her coast guard license, then attended an art school in the
south of France. When contacted by the Cohort Study staff, she wrote a
gracious letter explaining why she was away and her eagerness to stay
with the study ("because studies like this are of great importance"). She
said the year off had been "fantastic." She looked "forward to coming
back to Stanford and to working really hard—which I am now ready to
do." She had concluded that "the problem lies more within myself than
with the university."

She did come back and apply herself wholeheartedly to her
education, but the problems were still there. She found her courses to
be poorly taught, and there was no "real" adviser to help her find
academic direction. But this time Patricia stuck with it and things began
to fall into place. Though she still did not feel committed enough to any
particular direction, she could now entertain concrete career possibilities
like journalism or law. She became very active in the arms control
program and though discouraged by how intractable the problems of the
world appeared to be, she was willing to persevere in addressing them.
She got involved in student government and was elected to the senate.

In her senior year, everything came together for Patricia. She had
no trouble taking the right courses and finding the right professors. She
was happy being at Stanford. Life was now interesting, not a drag. She
completed her major requirements in political science and wrote an
honor's thesis on the political ideology of punk rock. She found a mentor
in her thesis adviser who helped her explore the roots of alienation in
society and in her own life.

Patricia was not "tamed" by any means. She remained quite
conscious of the deficiencies of Stanford and the world outside it. She
was especially sensitive to the problem of women finding meaningful
career direction, getting established, and learning to function
independently of men. But in facing these tasks she now could count on
the help of her parents, teachers, and friends. So she gave herself two

more years following graduation to figure out whether to go on to graduate school in political science or attend law school.

Profile 7.4: David—Waiting to Be Free

David had been a freshman for but a short time when he began to make plans to transfer to another institution. The reasons for his disaffection were not easy to determine. On the one hand, he claimed to be thoroughly disenchanted with what he called the "liberal education bias" permeating Stanford while he was simultaneously denouncing the high achievement and competitive orientation of Stanford undergraduates ("disgusting"). David claimed an interest in accounting as a career and very much wanted an undergraduate degree in business (which he knew Stanford does not offer). He also had a vague interest in medicine with the aim of becoming an ophthalmologist. Yet at the same time he felt drawn to English as a major. In the context of such uncertainty, David mainly took courses in an attempt to be introduced to various fields. He then stopped out for part of his sophomore year to attend his home-state university. The experience prompted him to head back to Stanford, where he declared English as his major but remained vague with respect to longer-range plans and career aspirations.

The high point for David was the time he spent at the overseas campus in England. He was glad to be out of the country, living in Europe, and seeing that the United States is not the only viable society, let alone "the center of the world." The courses he took there were excellent and closely tied to his major. Yet even with respect to this successful experience David showed relatively little enthusiasm. He expressed no interest in further travel for its own sake, no burning desire to see the rest of the world, nor did he manifest the nostalgic reactions of students when they get back from their first trip abroad. Another positive experience for David was living in a cooperative residence. He liked the people there, the autonomy they enjoyed, and the collaborative decisions they made.

David reached his senior year without much enthusiasm over either his educational experiences or his career prospects. Though he remained fairly satisfied with his major, he had never gotten involved with the department to any great degree and had little to do with his adviser. His career prospects were even more vague. He thought of teaching English in the Peace Corps, a prospect that did not please his career-oriented parents. As an alternative he thought of spending some time on a kibbutz. While thinking over these choices, he hoped to find "some way of supporting myself that I can stand." The next few years would thus be spent as a transitional period, during which time he hoped to become independent of his parents. Graduate school remained a long-

range possibility but he thought he would never do it unless he had some specific purpose in mind. Though he's a fairly accomplished musician (guitar and piano), he could not really see himself seeking a musical career.

Reflecting on his undergraduate years, David wished that he had not come to college immediately after high school or that he had stopped out for a longer period until he found "what the point of it is." Although David was quite uncommunicative about his more intimate relationships with his parents, the interviewer got the distinct impression that David had considerable conflict with them over his inability to settle on a career. He is the third son in a career-oriented family where his two older brothers are also not pursuing careers rigorously, so the family is running out of sons to fulfill their ambitions.

David seemed like the type of student who would have passionate political involvements, yet when questioned about activities in this regard, he could only respond that he was "not very active but very aware." His very long hair, worn-out clothes, and general style of relating made him look like a throwback to the late sixties. His interviewer thought David would have been a "first-rate hippie" were he living in the 1960s. Now that there isn't the social support for that "searching life style," he needed to do it more on his own.

David remained something of an enigma to the very last. As the interviewer concluded, "It's hard to get a sense of how bright or talented he may be, because he is extremely low-key, nonassertive, and not at all lively. I also thought that he's fairly thoughtful and concerned about leading a life that he can feel both contributes to the greater good and is intrinsically satisfying, and until he feels certain that he has found a career line to pursue that is his own choice, he won't begin to pursue it. My reading of him is that establishing independence from his parents is a rather important need at this point and that pressure on him to get into a standard success-oriented career has led him both not to do so and to feel stymied as to what he really wants to accomplish."

Component Subtypes of the Unconnected

Potential Careerists. The potential Careerists include some students whose career interests are quite vague but who manage to get on to a vocational path sooner or later. Others show distinct career aptitudes while manifesting or feigning disinterest (providing good examples of "how to succeed in business without really trying"). In the following descriptions Pamela illustrates the former case, Timothy the latter:

In the freshman year, the interviewer thought Pamela was "a rather lonely and insecure young woman who, for whatever reasons, has not yet been able to get a fix on what she wants from herself and thus from college either." In her junior year she was still seen as "an attractive and pleasant person, who appears to lack involvement in or genuine commitment to any of her activities. Her major objective seems to be to have a good time." Nonetheless, Pamela managed to get a job following graduation and was thinking of applying to business school.

Timothy was described as a bright freshman with a strong academic background who nonetheless showed little active interest in academics, which he characterized as a "give-and-take affair—Stanford gives and I take." He majored in economics but had yet to meet his adviser by the junior year. He claimed to spend much of his time being "hedonistic and decadent." His senior year was mainly "read, run, swim, and sun." However, beneath his "hail-fellow-well-met" image, Tim had a strong Careerist bent. He acted as a consultant to a local business, was a partner in a venture started by his father, befriended several business school professors, and was admitted to one of the top business schools in the country. He planned to eventually set up his own business in Australia because "you can win more games in the minors than in the major leagues."

These students may strike interviewers as being at sea when they are actually pursuing their own private interests. For instance, Boris was described by his interviewer as follows: "This guy is here physically but not engaged in any way with the purposes of the university. Bright and glib. At least *he* knows he is not getting much out of this place even if our faculty doesn't. He makes no demands on us; nor, apparently, do we make any on him. What a shame." Yet Boris was fanatically dedicated to filmmaking. He did not think of it in Careerist terms but in fact it was the career he intended to pursue. The same was true for Rodney and music; he had his own band and was planning to be a professional musician. His interviewer thought him "glib and smart; vague about future career."

The unconnectedness of some potential Careerists is based on a rejection of the central values of that orientation. For instance, Gary was undecided between chemical engineering and law. In either case he wanted to make money but with qualifications:

"Money is important, but I have to live with myself." This attitude is not distinctive for the Unconnected; many Intellectuals and Strivers also feel this way, so it does not explain unconnectedness in and of itself.

Potential Intellectuals. These students give low responses on the questionnaire items concerning intellectualism because their values and commitments do not mesh with the framework of the questionnaire, which reflects the institutional perspective. They may be highly committed to intellectual values as they define them, but their definition does not square with that underlying the questionnaire items used to measure their intellectualism. To the extent that they deviate from the mainline institutional norms, these students could be thought of as academic dissenters. For some, but not all, this is part of a larger pattern of social alienation. Patricia (Profile 7.3) and Alan, described as follows, illustrate these patterns.

Alan showed a chronic and deep-seated negativism with respect to most everything he encountered in college. He did not get along with his roommate and felt ostracized in his freshman dorm because he could not stand the noise, and so he stayed away much of the time. He chose industrial engineering as his major without being particularly interested in it; he knew he could get a good liberal education but claimed he did not want to. He had "reservations about corporate America" with regard to issues like environmental pollution, the treatment of minorities, and holding the profit motive above all else. While this is the world he knew he would have to live in, he hoped to avoid contributing to its problems. He fantasized about a "creative vocation" that would include writing fiction of the Kurt Vonnegut–type and composing music. Yet he knew that both of these pursuits were out of his reach. So he planned to travel and work for a while after graduation as he sorted out his future plans. The senior year interview report concludes as follows: "His left-wing and progressive outlook on American society set him apart from most other students. I think that he feels pretty alienated from society and has a hard time seeing how he can ever find a place that will allow him both to have financial security and to do something that he considers worthwhile."

Truly Unconnected. These students "cruise about" through courses and majors with little discernible rhyme or reason; they float over their career prospects without really dipping in. Some of these students are charming, intelligent, and full of life; others are bland, nondescript, "laid back." After four yearly attempts of trying to draw out one of these students, her interviewer said in exasperation, "She must be enthusiastic about *something!*"

Others are in college for primarily social reasons. They want to have a good time, make friends, maybe even find a spouse. They are unwilling to put in the time and energy necessary for serious academic commitment; they do not want to let education or careers interfere with their lives ("I am too busy to worry about a job"). Bright and able, these students do not come across as goof-offs because they do well in their courses without being fully engaged in them. Examples:

A hard fellow to get a handle on. He is a go-with-the-flow type who defies the frat-rat image and certainly is not a scholar. Majored in history but without much evidence of intellectual involvement in either the subject or a broader liberal education. Yet coming well prepared from a select private school, he did fairly well nonetheless. He was interested in business and law but decided to take a couple of years off before making up his mind. At the time of graduation his primary concern was to be as independent as possible.

Bright and gifted young woman who came to Stanford without any particular aim or purpose. Much of the freshman year was spent in trying to find her place and define her goals (while she made adequate academic progress). A certain fluidity and vacillation continued to mark her sophomore year when she was neither happy nor unhappy, neither satisfied nor dissatisfied. A year off that she spent working and traveling in Europe was remarkably maturing for her. It put more meaning into her academic orientation and clarified her career goals, which finally led to law school.

One must be careful when dealing with these Unconnected students not to confuse style with substance. George looked as distracted as they come. He was from a small farming community ("a sleepy town"), was notably uncommunicative, and was a hopeless procrastinator; at the end of his junior year he had yet to declare a major and get an adviser. He bored the interviewer to tears: "Last year I made the comment that interviewing George was about as exciting as watching paint dry. I would alter that statement this

year and say that watching paint dry is definitely *more* exciting."
Nonetheless, George was not only admitted to five law schools but
also managed to get a very good liberal education. We would have
to call him a Striver if the proof of the pudding is in the outcome.

We have not made a formal division of the Unconnected into
these subtypes in our data analysis, for two reasons: The criteria for
separating the three groups are hard to define precisely, and a
further division of the types reduces the number of cases so much
as to make meaningful comparisons impossible. But we shall meet
these subtypes again at various points in the discussion that follows.

Interviewer Impressions of the Unconnected

The contrast between the Unconnected and Strivers is quite
striking in the impressions they made on interviewers. Where the
Strivers charmed them, the Unconnected more often evoked
perplexity, boredom, concern, and irritation. These students are
generally more difficult to interview; they are not as articulate,
spontaneous, or candid as the others. They come across as shallow,
aimless, and lacking in enthusiasm. "Not much here, folks," said
one interviewer. Immaturity is another theme that crops up in the
interview reports: "A woman/child"; "I thought I was talking to a
thirteen-year-old." Though interviewers were not expected to make
psychological assessments, several students seemed disturbed
enough to elicit almost alarming comments: "She seemed rather
depressed—didn't show much life, spoke very softly and slowly";
"He had a crazed expression in his eyes and looked a wreck . . . I
was so frightened that I was afraid to shut my door."

Some students disconcerted interviewers by their unconven-
tional behavior: "She started out sitting on a chair and then moved
to sitting on the floor because she said that the chair was sticky, and
then finished up lying flat on the floor." Others provoked them by
their strongly opinionated views and abrasive behavior. One
interviewer (the kindest of men) was driven to say, "I would like to
go on record as having had the urge to throttle Linda at various
times in our conversation . . . flip, smug, unkempt, uncooperative,
unpleasant, haughty, egotistical, curt—a real sweetheart."

Despite all, the interviewers were by no means entirely negative in their perceptions of the Unconnected (just as they were not unreservedly positive about the Strivers). A common remark is that there is probably more to these students than meets the eye. They are not lacking in intelligence ("very intelligent, if not intellectual"). Beneath the confusion, there is, at least for some, a sense of knowing where they are going, however unorthodox their direction ("Peter's road is not exactly a well-traveled one"). These special qualities moved one interviewer to conclude, "Murray is just the kind of student Stanford should be proud of." Additional interviewer comments:

He needed some prodding . . . there were more silences between questions than with most students I have seen. Neither quick to smile nor eager to open up, he struck me as someone who likes to fly pretty much by the seat of his pants. He takes things as they come; and so far, they've come pretty easily for him. He probably will do just fine in life—and without picking up any ulcers along the way.

(Freshman year) she said she was lost. Her high school was so small and Stanford seemed so big . . . she was really scared here . . . doesn't know what she wants to do. I don't get the impression that she works very hard. Her energy level seems low even to the point of her being almost totally unconcerned about the future.

She's probably got just enough smarts to go through okay, but I think her social life is the big thing to her. If ever there was one with room to grow, Laura is the one. She likes to give off airs of "being above it all," but if you talk with her a while, it's clear she isn't as mature as she pretends (or would like) to be. I didn't sense that anything excited her intellectually or even academically, but I could be mistaken.

An unusually relaxed individual, one who seems to "have his head together" . . . calm, patient, trusting, straightforward, and self-aware. There's no way to explain why some people's indecisiveness seems dangerously linked to confusion. It's even harder to convey what it is about a person like him that makes that same indecisiveness seem so mature, healthy, and well considered. I'd say he struck a peaceful bargain among life's many commitments at an unusually early age.

It takes him a long time to get a complete thought out since his sentences and paragraphs are full of hesitations . . . academic purpose is serious but not yet clear. I doubt that he'll be very clear about that for a while yet. He seems immature, impressionable, and a bit adrift. His descriptions of life at Stanford convey a scatteredness, a playing at growing up more than doing it . . . Yet he is also undeniably clever, able, and intelligent.

He has learned to think independently . . . cares about his formal education as well as his personal relationships . . . a warm, friendly, bright young man . . . an outstanding individual—one of the very best, most interesting, and most delightful of my group! A pleasure to talk to!

Background Characteristics of the Unconnected

Gender. Men are somewhat more likely to be Unconnected than women; 31 percent of men and 24 percent of women are of this type. This finding allows us to infer that it is the factor of intellectualism and not careerism that is central to the sex differences in the typology: The groups where men are overrepresented (Careerists over the Unconnected) are both low in intellectualism; the groups where women are overrepresented (Intellectuals over Strivers) are high in intellectualism but not necessarily low in careerism. Therefore, the more influential factor would appear to be the greater commitment of women to intellectualism, rather than their lesser commitment to careers. This inference is confirmed by the scores on the careerism and intellectualism scales, which show very little difference in the career dimension between men and women but significantly higher mean scores on intellectualism for women.

Ethnicity. There is virtually no relationship between ethnicity and being Unconnected; close to 28 percent of each ethnic group are of this type. There may be ample cause for ethnic minorities to feel alienated but they do not commonly express it by becoming Unconnected.

Socioeconomic Status. The SES Index shows only a modest relationship. Students from the bottom third of the ranking are most likely to be Unconnected (30 percent); students from the middle third are least likely (22 percent), and the top third is in between (26 percent). This finding is repeated for family income, where the lowest third of the income ranking is overrepresented among the Unconnected (32 percent), the middle third is underrepresented (20 percent), and the top third is in between (26 percent).

Looking at specific occupations, we find that the children of engineers are most likely (46 percent) and the children of physicians are least likely (18 percent) to be Unconnected. No other specific occupations stand out in a similar manner. The socioeconomic background that is most likely to produce an Unconnected student, then, is one where the father is in a purely technical field or one of a relatively low status. These paternal occupations rank low in the organizational hierarchy and generate relatively low income.

Paradoxically, these characteristics are very similar to the parental conditions that also produce a high proportion of Strivers, the very antithesis of the Unconnected. There are thus two highly disparate paths traversed by students coming from such families. One involves a reaction to modest social circumstances in the form of a push for upward mobility and enthusiasm for all that college has to offer. The other seems to be a resignation to that background, reflected in negative attitudes toward both career and intellectual achievements.

Academic Background. There is a very strong effect of verbal SAT scores: Thirty-seven percent of students having high verbal scores are Unconnected, compared to only 18 percent of students having low verbal scores. This is the strongest SAT correlation we have in all of our comparisons. The mathematics SAT score has no bearing on this group as a whole: Students of strong verbal ability are more likely to be Unconnected regardless of their mathematics ability. There is, however, an important sex difference. For women, high verbal ability combined with *low* mathematics ability is more likely to result in an Unconnected student; 46 percent of such women are of this type. Their male counterparts are most often Strivers. For men, high verbal ability combined with *high* mathematics ability often yields an Unconnected student (39 percent of such men). Their female counterparts are most often Intellectuals.

As we shall see, the Unconnected generally do quite well in their course work, as one would expect from their strong SAT scores. Their competence in both the verbal and quantitative dimensions allows them to coast along without the need to make strong commitments to either career or intellectualism. But that does not explain why they shun such commitment. Is it because the institution fails to challenge them? Are the choices made available to them such that some of the students with the greatest potential are least able to realize that potential?

Sources of Influence on the Unconnected

We found Intellectuals to be strongly influenced by the faculty but not their parents, Careerists to be influenced by their parents but not the faculty, and the Strivers to be influenced strongly by both faculty and parents. By contrast, the Unconnected are largely insulated from both sources of influence.

Parents. Some 37 percent of students who indicate weak family influence are Unconnected, as against 21 percent of those who indicate strong family influence. The interview reports provide many examples of the greater independence and distance the Unconnected have from their families. On the other hand, there are numerous cases that reflect closer relationships with parents, both happy and unhappy. Here are comments from interviewers' reports on parental relationships of Unconnected students:

His folks have always encouraged him to be independent. "I choose the courses I want to take and write home after the quarter to tell my parents what I took and how I did."

"My father doesn't push me. He is glad I'm in college. We argue, trade books, and exchange ideas."

Commenting on the flight to Stanford that Alma took with her parents, she said, "What a bore. Everybody around me was having fun and I had to sit there with my parents."

The father had pushed his kids fairly hard: An older brother is a professor, another is in medical school. Her reaction is neither to fall in line and do what is expected of her nor break away and do the "wrong thing" since she does not have a clue as to what she really would like to do.

He keeps his parents mostly in the dark about his shifting values because "nothing would be served by shaking them up and upsetting their relationship needlessly."

He came to Stanford to please his family.

He is unabashedly close to his family. "I have been blessed with wonderful parents and I love them deeply."

Her family is very supportive; she spends at least an hour a week on the phone with them.

Faculty. Thirty-seven percent of students who experience weak faculty influence are Unconnected, compared to 19 percent of those indicating strong influence. The absence of interaction with faculty is reflected in the interview reports. Although the Unconnected are not the only ones lacking in such interaction, they are less likely than other students to complain about it. Even when there has been interaction, it often appears that some obstacle has had to be overcome to achieve it: "Good professors put up with me until I got my head together." Or the relationship is redefined: "He has never used his adviser as an adviser but just as another good friend whose opinions he weighs against those of others." All too often the experience is unsatisfactory, as shown in the following examples from interviewers' reports:

Carol asserted that all of her difficulties or bad academic experiences were due to bad advice she received.

He says "there's no reason to talk to an adviser."

He did not have an adviser and didn't care about having one. He thinks asking questions of faculty is a little like "cheating"—it's up to him to learn what he wants and to find the answers.

"I've had a lot of good luck in courses," he said, and added that it really has been luck because he's gotten no advice about course selection.

He took a political science course that was the highlight of the term for him. He didn't remember the professor's name but did light up just reflecting back on the course.

Alex hasn't gotten to know any faculty members at all . . . So far this doesn't bother him.

She has had virtually no interaction with other students or faculty members in her department. "I am very individualistic so there hasn't been much interchange with others." She rarely sees her adviser and, in fact, has forgotten her name.

She says of her adviser: "I never see him. I used to like him, now it's almost a bother to go and see him."

He may actually graduate without ever having met with an adviser in his major department.

Other Influences. The Unconnected are also less influenced by their peers and more impersonal factors such as knowledge of the job market. A third of those who say their decisions are only weakly influenced by peers are Unconnected, compared to 24 percent of those saying fellow students strongly affect them. Likewise, 37 percent of the students in this group indicate weak influence of the job market on their decisions, and only 17 percent say this factor strongly influences them. The same pattern holds for the influence of course work. Thus, students who say that parents, faculty, the job market, course work, and fellow students are all relatively unimportant in their academic and career decision making are almost certain to be Unconnected. Why do these students surround themselves with curtains of impermeability and avoid being influenced by anyone or any agency with which they have regular contact?

Two different interpretations of this finding are possible. The more positive view is to see these students as self-directed, with a strong sense of individuality motivating them to find their own paths. They know their own minds and they do not want their decisions to be unduly influenced by the opinions and urgings of family, friends, faculty, and advisers. They want to carry out their own, not someone else's, concept of what they should do with their lives. This view would best characterize the academic dissenters found among the Unconnected Intellectuals. The more negative view (which best fits the truly Unconnected) is that they are uninspired, disengaged, and withdrawn, and hence have distant relationships with their parents, faculty, and fellow students.

Major and Career Choices of the Unconnected

About one out of four (27 percent) of the Unconnected major in the humanities. This proportion is second only to the Intellectuals and far above the other two groups. However, they are no less likely than others to major in the natural sciences and engineering and are far more likely to do so than Intellectuals (31 percent of the Unconnected but only 16 percent of the Intellectuals are in these two areas).

The choices within the humanities made by the core Unconnected include the more common major selections like history and English. But there is often a sense that these are choices of convenience that are not motivated by any particular affinity to the subject. These students are also attracted to "flexible" programs because, as one of them put it, "It's a major you can decide on without really deciding." In other cases their choice of major seems highly unusual, if not positively incongruous, as illustrated by Fred (Profile 7.1).

There is a similar pattern in the choice of careers. The Unconnected are second only to Intellectuals in their avoidance of standard career paths. Only 58 percent choose them, compared to 50 percent of Intellectuals and 68 percent for all students. They are the least likely to choose business (20 percent, versus 31 percent of all students) but almost as likely as others to enter medicine and engineering. Their choices of nonstandard professions include communication, writing, and the arts (16 percent of Unconnected students, only 12 percent of all students); teaching (14 percent versus 9 percent); public administration and the social sciences (10 percent versus 7 percent). As with their choice of major, the specific career choices are often unusual and sometimes fanciful: "My secret dream is to be a cocktail pianist on a cruise ship to Tahiti!" In short, their career choices are often highly varied and interesting, hardly what one expects from students who supposedly care little about education or careers.

But this is only part of the story. The students we have described so far are those who have made a career commitment. For a substantial proportion of the Unconnected there is no such commitment. This is most strikingly illustrated by the interview reports of the core Unconnected. Of the twenty-seven Unconnected students in this subgroup, only one third had reasonably certain career plans by the spring of their senior year. By contrast, two thirds of Intellectuals and virtually all of the Careerists and Strivers had definite vocational expectations. There is an important sex difference here in that Unconnected men have more definite career choices than women (and their choices are spread over a wider spectrum of occupations). The Unconnected men were much less uncertain than the women as to what they would be doing after graduation, although the proportion of such men was still high compared to the other types. However, as the following excerpts from interviewers' reports on their career attitudes illustrate, the Unconnected are typically postponing career decisions, not neglecting them outright:

He is vague about his future career and not a bit worried about being vague.

Rather noncommittally anticipates something developing in either law or business although the business world seems a bit "sleazier" than he would prefer and likely to demand too many moral compromises.

Linda isn't sure she wants a career, and if she is to have one, she wants many careers—she can't see doing something "forever." She has faith that something will come along that interests her . . . she doesn't want to plan too much in her life . . . looks ahead only six months at a time. "I'm going to live a long life and there's no reason to press it right now." Planning too much wrecks all the surprises and runs the risk of disappointments if plans do not work out.

He does not want to be tied down to one thing . . . After the investment of time, money, and hard work required for a career like medicine, it would be difficult to "walk away from it."

Her friends want financial security and are drifting toward business. She is "not afraid of being poor" and doesn't see it as connected to happiness or self-fulfillment. Nonetheless, she has a "terrible fear of ending up as a secretary or bank teller."

He has shed the so-called success compulsiveness and is able to live life as it is and as it comes. He feels mildly uncomfortable at times because he does not have specific vocational goals, but that appears not to stop him from savoring every book he reads, every hour he spends playing his instrument, and every friend he has made.

He is something of a true romantic and enjoys things for their intrinsic value and seems not to get uptight about the future, about his career, about making every minute count in some practical way.

Arthur has no concrete plans beyond the next year. He and his parents feel comfortable with his taking two years for manual labor–type experiences. After that, he feels that he will surely have to settle down, get a job, perhaps go to law school, or perhaps find some other area for further study. All of this sounds very loose and self-serving, but in fact there is a very honest quality about his plans.

He's not really interested in getting a high-paying job right now. "I want to spend one to two years deciding whether to go into law or business school . . . I have a general plan, but I think it's bad to try and plan everything . . . It's important to me to find what I enjoy."

Fewer of the Unconnected students stay with their original major choice than any other type (57 percent, versus a mean of 67 percent). Their pattern of major changes is distinctive in that far more of them move into the humanities than is the case for other types. For all students, there is a shift from 16 percent in the humanities the freshman year to 19 percent the senior year, but the figure for the Unconnected increases from 17 percent to 27 percent. They are also more likely than other students to leave engineering and earth science majors.

The Unconnected are much less likely to stay with their original career choice. Only 34 percent graduate with the same choice they had during the freshman year, compared to 51 percent of all students. Further, they are less certain of their career choice than any other type; on a scale ranging from one to five ("not at all certain" to "very certain") they give a mean response in the senior year of 3.7, while the most certain group, the Strivers, have a mean of 4.1.

The pattern of changes in career choice is unusual for the Unconnected in that they are drawn to law and humanities-oriented careers in far greater proportions than other students; their representation increases in these two areas while for all other students there is either a decrease (in the case of law) or no change (in the case of the humanities.) Unconnected students are also less likely than other types to stay within the four standard fields (67 percent, versus 82 percent of all students) and relatively unlikely to leave a nonstandard field for a standard one.

A surprising finding is that the Unconnected are *not* overrepresented among those who are undecided about their career choice in the freshman year. The basic difference between the Unconnected and the other groups is therefore not that the Unconnected are less likely to have vocational plans when they begin college—their level of uncertainty at the entry point is comparable to that of other students. But whereas the others progressively become more certain of their career choices as they move along, the Unconnected lag behind in this respect. This may mean that the propensity to be Unconnected is a reaction to the institutional milieu rather than a tendency that students bring to college. This is an issue we shall return to at the end of the chapter.

The seemingly greater difficulty that the Unconnected have in making definite career choices does not affect their postbaccalaureate educational aspirations. These are very close to average, with some 39 percent planning on obtaining doctoral-level degrees, compared with 42 percent of all students. In the face of so much apparent uncertainty, how is it that the Unconnected plan on continuing their formal education just as other students do? The answer seems to be that the similarities between the Unconnected and the other groups are more fundamental than the differences. The Unconnected are ensconced in the same academic environment as other students and are bound to very similar long-term goals. Nine out of ten of the students in our sample plan on eventually obtaining some advanced degree; they mainly differ on when they will pursue it and whether that degree will be at the doctoral level or not. In trying to highlight the basic similarity of this group to the rest of the Stanford student body, we are reminded of the parallel situation with respect to Keniston's Uncommitted students: "Their admission to Harvard College alone attests high achievement in high school, innate talent and the fact that their parents could provide the cultural advantages indirectly helpful for admission to college and the financial support necessary to stay there for four years" (Keniston, 1960, p. 18).

Pursuing a Liberal Education

Given the varied characteristics of the Unconnected, their educational aims and attitudes are even more difficult to pin down than their career choices. We already know that the Unconnected have certain affinities to the Intellectuals in that humanities majors are overrepresented among both. This affinity carries over into areas like literature and music: "He dearly loves to read and to write"; "Music continues to be the center of his life." There is a common yearning for educational breadth, which is not always satisfied: "John loves art, travel, studying, and the other pursuits that make him a Renaissance man, yet sees no way of integrating these into his work in any meaningful way"; "Mark is something of a closet intellectual."

A few of the Unconnected are disdainful of the humanities and of anything remotely suggestive of liberal education. One student, though quite bright and gifted, went to considerable lengths to avoid "intellectualism." Hank claimed that nothing he learned in college had any applicability: "Oh sure, classes might teach you to think a little better but you don't need to come to Stanford to do that." His first priority was "fun" and what kept him in college for three years was his fraternity. Whatever he learned was through the "academic environment" outside the class, which "kind of rubbed off on me." There are some among the Unconnected who sound like Strivers about their classes yet somehow their enthusiasm sounds hollow: "I chose my classes for fun. I just go for fun!"

The Unconnected are more likely than Intellectuals to be exposed to the natural sciences and technology. This is sometimes due to conscious choice, sometimes the result of their meandering through a broader range of fields. The following comments from interviewers illustrate some of the more general attitudes of Unconnected students to liberal education:

> He never plans more than a quarter at a time . . . doesn't want to take any classes before 10:00 A.M. . . . and in the spring he wishes to have as few classes as possible in the afternoon. He began the quarter by attending a third of the lectures, taking few notes, and finding the classes boring because the material was presented either in too abstract a way or as if it was being read directly out of a book. In one course he did none of the readings, took maybe one page of notes all quarter, slept through the lectures, and still got an A. Not only could he not tell me the rationale behind other courses he took this year, he literally could remember only one other class he had taken.
>
> He feels that his aim should be to get as extensive an exposure as possible during these four very short years. He chose his major simply because it was the only department in which there were enough interesting courses to complete requirements.
>
> He doesn't worry much about the vocational or the practical aspects of English. He majors in it because he likes it.

These attitudes are further supported by comments from Unconnected students.

"I don't love school, as I know many people here do."

Alison, a varsity athlete, says, *"My grades have been terrible . . . my study habits are terrible. I practice three hours a day and I keep on saying I'm going to do better next quarter, but I do too many other things. I don't see the usefulness in studying. I think I can do anything if I apply myself, but it gets me down when I do poorly in my classes. I don't want to face the next year. I don't feel I want to be here. I'm just sick of it. But I'll probably come back because of the team."*

"Grades are not important . . . because of my priorities, I'm not able to spend a lot of time on studying."

"I resented the fact that I had to study that much to do well in it. Stanford hasn't really given me any kind of direction. I don't know where I'm headed."

"Education should be a part of a way of life rather than something you do for the exam . . . A lot of people put off until after college decisions about what sort of a person they want to be and what sort of life they want to lead."

The potential Intellectuals among the Unconnected voice some of the most astute objections about the ethos of college education. One student in an engineering course was dismayed at the mechanical way in which their knowledge was being evaluated: "The students with the better calculators got the better grades." So, in one exam, he answered each of the technical questions by writing a small short story. He said he had immense fun doing this and the professor enjoyed reading his examination very much. But in the end he received no credit in the course because he had not demonstrated that he knew anything about small-scale energy systems.

The dissenters among these students are often hard to distinguish from the true Intellectuals. They can be equally passionate about intellectual issues, yet there is a certain iconoclastic and angry quality to their world view. That in itself would by no means disqualify them as Intellectuals in the strict sense of the term, but it does so here because our typology is based on the attitudes these students exhibit in their questionnaire responses. The interviewers are also less sure of the depth and authenticity of the intellectualism of these students as compared to those of the Intellectuals; that, however, may be but another manifestation of the institutional bias these individuals share.

Patricia (Profile 7.3) is a good example of the dissenter whose disaffection is framed in political terms. In the case of Joshua the same basic posture is expressed in somewhat different terms.

Joshua is a New Yorker. In their first encounter, the interviewer noted his "long hair and couple of days growth of beard." He seemed "to combine a degree of physical awkwardness with a more than compensating intellectual and psychological assuredness." Joshua signed up for the Structured Liberal Education program—one of the more intensive freshman intellectual experiences available. He gave it some grudging praise ("it forces you to get some background") but then condemned it as "elitist." His course in philosophy was "less than inspiring." He was disillusioned with the outlook of political activists on campus because "they are very sanctimonious and very impractical . . . They seem to be using the problems of the people in South Africa so they can feel good about themselves." His broader outlook on life as a freshman: "I've seen too many bad things to think the world is peaches and cream."

In and out of the classroom, Joshua was immersed in the life of the intellect. He went to concerts and lectures but his main source of stimulation was reading. He subscribed to the New York Times and the New York Review of Books. He read Husserl as part of a "reawakening of my interest in phenomenology." He also told the interviewer, "I am relearning to hate Tolstoi." When asked, "Why then keep reading it?" he answered, "It's like playing with a scab," and went on to elaborate on Tolstoi's motivation.

Joshua had trouble deciding on his major; human biology, philosophy, anthropology were considered but not settled on. "Graduate school would be difficult for me because I don't like school, never have." VISTA or the Peace Corps would provide the opportunity "to transcend my assumptions."

The sophomore interview sums up Joshua as follows: "It's hard to tell whether Joshua is a very smart fellow, a dilettante, both, or only a moderately bright dilettante. It does seem, to hear him talk, a minor miracle that he found his way to college. He seems put off by most of what he sees around him (I think he relishes his 'outsider' act), pursuing instead whatever takes his fancy but leaving as anyone's guess whether the pursuit is to discover a new law of human nature or to dazzle those who come within earshot at cocktail parties."

Joshua left Stanford in the fall quarter of his junior year. His interest in continental philosophies was not well served by the philosophy department and the "unreality" of Stanford got increasingly hard to take. As we quoted him earlier, it was "not a healthy place for a roadside weed like myself to grow up." He "knocked around" New York for a while, then enrolled part-time at Columbia, and got a job teaching remedial subjects to disadvantaged kids in a housing project. In the long run, he would like to write fiction but did not have a clear sense of how his future would shape up and was not troubled by the uncertainty.

Overseas Study. On some fronts the Unconnected differ sharply from Intellectuals. Overseas study is a case in point. Intellectuals are the most avid participants in the overseas study programs, with fully 55 percent of them attending an overseas campus. In contrast, only 28 percent of the Unconnected avail themselves of the opportunity, the lowest percentage among all four types. One likely, if not full, explanation for this has to do with the logistics of going overseas. It takes forethought and planning, which is not the strong suit of Unconnected students.

Since the Unconnected are not prevented from going overseas because of curricular constraints (as is the case for engineers) and self-imposed obstacles (such as with Careerists), they do not tend to complain about their missing out on the experience. Those of the Unconnected who do go overseas seem to make good use of it.

Stopping Out. The Unconnected are above average in their propensity to stop out for one or more quarters (31 percent, compared to 24 percent for all students). However, they are not as likely to stop out as the Intellectuals (36 percent), and their reasons for doing so appear to be different. The Unconnected are more apt to say that they are dissatisfied with their courses, need to work on personal problems, and are uncertain about their purpose or direction in college. The Intellectuals are likely to stop out for more positive reasons: to reflect further on their life purposes, to see the world, and to find out what can be learned on an experiential basis.

It is also revealing that the Unconnected stop out for longer periods of time than the Intellectuals: Some 42 percent of them stop out for more than one quarter, compared to only 14 percent of the Intellectuals. The Intellectuals almost always take off just one term, as a limited and planned break that is integrated into their overall

program of study. The Unconnected more typically take two
quarters or even a full year before they face the university challenge
again. Their staying away would seem to be more of an interruption
of their academic career both in terms of length of time as well as
what is accomplished through it.

Social Life and Extracurricular Activities

The Unconnected students participate in extracurricular
activities to a lesser degree than any other type. They average only
3.4 activities on the Involvement Index, below the general mean of
4.0 and far below the mean for Intellectuals of 4.6. Only 40 percent
of the Unconnected engage in academic work outside the classroom,
compared to 74 percent of Strivers; 48 percent get involved in public
service activities, compared to 72 percent of Intellectuals.

Why this relative lack of engagement in college life? The
Unconnected are not pressed for time any more than others, and
they are less driven by educational and career goals than most. So
where do they spend their time? The following interview excerpts
suggest that much of the social life of the Unconnected is carried
out in private and informal ways and does not show up as an
"activity" on our scales.

*She likes sports and spends a lot of time on the beach. "I like to
have a good time," she said, and combed her long blonde hair with her
fingers.*

He has some intense love affair at least once or twice each year.

"People make the experience."

She likes "lazying around."

*He spent many hours a week working with handicapped kids and
put in a great deal of time for his church when he became an ordained
minister. His pastoral work involved preaching, counseling, visiting
parishioners, and door-to-door evangelism.*

When asked how he spent his time, he said, "Last year I'd get high every afternoon on good grass, then play Frisbee or otherwise waste time."

He began to savor new and different life styles, and academics became quite secondary to his campus life this year.

Interested in "anything weird."

Though the Unconnected, as a group, are less likely than others to get involved in political and social issues, the more intellectually oriented among them pursue such aims and are critical of the lack of involvement and concern on the part of others, as shown in these excerpts from interviews:

Pierre is struck at how little social consciousness there is here and how unaware many students are of the differences between them and the people who provide them services on campus. According to him, the prevailing attitude of other students toward life is materialistic ("the work-study-get-rich ethic" is indicative of the "late 70s new conservatism"). As he sees it, there are no intellectual concerns at Stanford University, no interest in abstract ideas—"nothing!"

He is involved in an "ongoing search for meaning, for what my relationship to God should be."

"Selfish is a pejorative term, and I don't want to put people down, but the values I see reinforced here are for people to act primarily for themselves. The major and unquestioned assumption is 'Pursue what you want without concern for others.' Future jobs, future money, future inclusion in the American way of life. These are the values into which students get assimilated." In the summer, Joshua does manual labor. "It's a good place to work off a hangover. And it gives me a feel for Marx. When he talks about labor, I can react intuitively."

Despite their relative lack of social engagement, the Unconnected are by no means social recluses. They invest a great deal of time and energy in personal associations and ventures. Becky, for instance, who grew up on a farm in Kansas, spent an entire year in Brazil on her own, with very little assistance and guidance from the university, and had a great time. When Becky was leaving Brazil for the United States, she was befriended at the airport by a transvestite who loved trying her dresses on. But then when she was away briefly, he fled with all her belongings. This is the third time she was robbed, yet she told the story with such flair that the interviewer was in stitches. His conclusion: "I find Becky to be one of the most interesting and unusual persons among my cohorts. She really is different from most of our students and oddly combines solid roots with a willingness to experience—not adopt— almost anything. She's obviously not fragile, nor is she by any stretch of the imagination cocky. Those who had the chance and did not get to know her here wasted their time."

The Unconnected do not suffer from lack of personal commitment and they do not expect to in the future. Only 4 percent of them envisage being unattached in ten years (same percentage as for all students), although the only women who do not expect to be married or in a committed relationship in ten years are found in this group. The percentage of Unconnected expecting to have children (94 percent) is similar to that of Intellectuals and intermediate between the figures for Strivers and Careerists; for this variable the Unconnected women are not different from other women.

Academic Success and Satisfaction

On the basis of what has been said so far, one may suspect the Unconnected to be neither very successful nor very satisfied. Such expectations turn out to be only partly true.

Academic Performance. The Unconnected students are just about average in their grades and academic performance. They are as likely as other students to earn election to Phi Beta Kappa (9 percent), about average in earning distinction at graduation (18 percent), and only slightly below average in participating in departmental honors programs (6 percent).

While it is certainly not the case that the Unconnected do worse than other students in these dimensions, their classroom performance is definitely not as good as many others. They have lower grade point averages (3.28) than all other types but the

Strivers, and in most separate academic areas their grades are lower than those of the three other types, engineering courses being the only exception. Thus, although some of the Unconnected do very well and earn academic honors at graduation, on the whole they are not superior students.

Self-Assessments of Knowledge and Abilities. Since their major choices are quite varied, the Unconnected would be expected to have average assessments in most areas. But they do not. They give the lowest self-assessments in nine of the fourteen substantive areas: writing English; understanding Western culture, non-Western culture, literature and the fine arts, philosophical and religious thought, social processes, government, and international problems; and using computers. They also give the lowest self-assessments for the two more general items: using their creative faculties and absorbing and analyzing information. For four of the five remaining areas, most of which are technical in nature, they give the second-lowest responses. These negative tendencies are reinforced by the low ratings of the importance of the ability items given by the Unconnected. They give the lowest importance ratings on eleven of the substantive areas as well as the two more general areas, and they are below average on two of the remaining three areas.

Satisfaction with the Undergraduate Experience. The Unconnected are less satisfied with their undergraduate education across a host of dimensions. In the Cohort questionnaire evaluations of the senior year, they are less satisfied than any other type on six of the nine items: interaction with instructors, intellectual discussion, social interaction, interest in courses, career plans, and sense of belonging. They are less satisfied than all but one type (the Careerists) in two dimensions, overall contentment and time management. They are more satisfied than any other type in only the one remaining dimension, getting the desired grades (which may reflect lower aspirations on their part).

On the Senior Survey their responses follow much the same pattern, though they are slightly less negative. They are the most dissatisfied type in five of the twelve dimensions: liberal education, contribution of their living situation to intellectual life, faculty teaching, individual access to the faculty, and teaching assistants.

They are less satisfied than all but one type in four of the remaining dimensions, including the overall quality of undergraduate education, and they are at or near the mean for only three items: the quality of the faculty as researchers, the opportunities for individual work with faculty, and their major advisers.

A similar picture prevails with respect to the importance the Unconnected students assign to these items. They give the lowest importance ratings for ten of the twelve items concerning undergraduate education. For only the overall quality of undergraduate education do they express as much concern as students on the whole, but for such items as the faculty as researchers, individual work with faculty, their initial advisers, and quality of courses in the major, they are far below the mean.

Roots of Unconnectedness

The behavior of the Unconnected is more puzzling than that of students in the other groups. We will therefore make an attempt to point out some of the more salient conditions that appear to lie at the root of this orientation.

The unwillingness or inability of these students to settle on academic choices and pursue concrete career aims results from a variety of factors. Some of these students fail to connect because of uncertainties over their choices; being unable to decide what they want to do, they cannot get very enthusiastic about anything. Jackie was interested in subjects like sociology and anthropology but felt that these fields did not embody "the best of the university," since they are so easily popularized. On the other hand, subjects that appeared more substantive to her, like economics and statistics, did not interest her.

The seeds of Unconnectedness are sown when students come to college under parental pressure or for lack of something better to do. There are also those who are so burdened with psychological conflicts that they cannot become engaged in their undergraduate education. Such conflicts typically revolve around emancipation from parents, problems of identity, and a search for meaning. Not knowing who they are, they have trouble deciding what to do (which in turn complicates the task of defining themselves.)

In some of these cases, it is quite clear that the unconnectedness is due to a developmental lag. These students do not connect because they are not ready to; and unlike their counterparts in the other groups, they refuse to do so prematurely. Murray admitted in his senior year, "I wish I could start school again and put academics first." But given all the catching up he needed to do socially and emotionally when he came to college, he simply could not concentrate on his studies until late in his undergraduate career. The following comments from a senior interview report further illustrate these points.

Michael's career as a Stanford student has been to be in Stanford but not of Stanford. He's been a sort of academic drifter always out of the mainstream swirling in his own currents, touched from time to time by the momentum of the curriculum and spun into an eddy before drifting back into his own personal flow.

Michael is not someone who felt himself a part of undergraduate life at Stanford. He had, in my judgment, a lot of finding of himself to do and he has matured a good bit. He has always impressed me as introspective, but the quality of his explanations has grown in insight and apparent validity. He seems still to be existentially afloat (I was going to say "at sea" but that would overstate the case) . . . nevertheless he seems to have a good deal of unfinished business about who he is and where his motivations come from . . . My guess is that his education and the way he pursued it was a way for him to sow many seeds in the soil of his life without having to confront any fundamental facts about his motivational goals. This may have been astute, a way of giving himself more time to grow up, to let nature, in a way, take its course according to which of the seeds prospered and what sort of a garden grew. At any rate, I think Michael's experience at Stanford was a highly personal one. There was no enculturation into any mainstream, intellectual, social, or otherwise. For him, it will be more interesting to speculate about the influence of his Stanford experience five, ten, or forty years hence than now. Instead of being a major and immediate force in his life, I think what has happened in Stanford's classrooms and dorms will be like a time-release capsule. We'll have to wait and see.

A lack of challenge causes trouble for other students in this group. Robert came from Andover, where he had done very well. Having already been away from home and in a demanding academic setting during prep school, college was not a particularly novel experience for him. In his freshman year he said, "It isn't right if someone can goof around like I have, cram just before final exams, and pass." Yet that is what he did. In his junior year he continued to be plagued by lack of motivation. He declared a major in English but had to do relatively little work. Writing came very easily for him; he could go through the entire reading list for a quarter during the last week before exams and come out with a very respectable grade.

Ronald was brilliant. He came to Stanford with forty units of advanced placement credits, a math SAT score of 800 and a verbal score of 720. He had an intensely intellectual orientation to life and only the vaguest of career interests—the perfect combination for Intellectualism. Yet Ronald did not connect to the institution's intellectual lifelines. He majored in physics (earning all A's) but was disinterested in the subject; he took a set of demanding courses in the humanities but expressed little enthusiasm for them. Withdrawn and inarticulate in the interview situation, he appeared to be socially undeveloped and lonely.

In principle, the mere fact that Robert and Ronald were very intelligent cannot account for their being Unconnected. Surely, there is no lack of expertise among the faculty to challenge and occupy such students. But that would have called for someone taking a special interest in these students or their taking the initiative to put together a more personalized education suitable to their special talents. But even then, matters do not always work out and there is often more to the lack-of-challenge issue than meets the eye. The following case is illustrative.

Christopher is an unusually gifted student from a socially privileged background. By all indications he should have fitted naturally into Stanford academically and socially, but he did not do so until his senior year. The fact that he could have so easily melded in earlier robbed him of any sense of accomplishment when he finally did start to make sense out of things.

Initially, Christopher's problems were presented in the context of the difficulties he was having in gaining approval for his special program of study. But then his own self-doubts were let loose in a torrent. Underneath the decisive facade he presented, there was a fuzzy sense of who he was and what he wanted to do. Frequent references to his "personal helplessness" revealed a state of decisional paralysis and a desperate need to reach out: *"I want to feel attached; I need to feel attached. I need to get outside myself."* [The interviewer had no way of knowing this at the time, but this is one of the most compelling statements of unconnectedness we encountered in the interview reports.] He took some comfort in the realization that *"I am not alone in feeling adrift."*

Since Chris had come with hefty advanced placement credits, he could have graduated, if he so chose, in three years. But once again what should have been an advantage only complicated his life. The accelerated pace, when combined with his unorthodox and demanding curricular choices, wreaked havoc with his undergraduate program.

It all finally came together for Christopher in his senior year. He completed his program. He scored 800 on the LSAT. He fell in love, and he was happy: *"Everything is just fine."* Yet, although planning to go to law school, he still felt that his future was unclear and full of conflict. He did not want to work for a firm to make *"big bucks,"* yet he did have ambitions to *"make a difference, become famous, have people know me and remember me."* Not yet able to resolve these conflicts, he hoped to work for the National Park Service for a while to find his bearings.

Some students fail to connect because they seemingly are so highly sure of themselves and secure about the future. Arlene came from a wealthy background and an excellent private high school. She kept up with her studies but without serious commitment to academic or career goals. She was critical of her highly achievement-oriented peers: "We should be able to convince students that there is more to life. It would make Stanford less of a sterile environment. There is very little romanticism here." She had no anxieties about her future. Looking ten years ahead, she said, "I hope to be married . . . will have a golden retriever . . . and I will have a secure position in marketing or public relations."

While it helps to be well-off, and there is an element of the ennui of the "idle rich" among students of this orientation, others from modest backgrounds have more personal grounds for self-confidence. Pauleen, whom we quoted earlier as being too busy to worry about a job, is the daughter of a gardener. She had fended for herself from an early age so the world of work held little fear or fascination for her. Her immediate goals were therefore to travel and enjoy life while she was "young and independent."

Women students face special challenges because of changing gender roles. Although there are women in all four categories who are concerned about reconciling the prospects of careers with those of marriage and family, the Unconnected are more likely to see this as a source of potential conflict: "I can't see being a housewife and yet it's important to do it right for children if you have them." Compare this with the more decisive stance taken by a Striver: "I'd like to have kids, but I don't want to be in a wheelchair when my kids are in elementary school. If I can't solve the problem of how to be a doctor and a mother at the same time, I'll build a nursery in the back of my office." This dilemma leads to unconnectedness for some women, as shown in the following excerpts from interview reports:

Molly had fulfilled her premedical requirements but hesitated to apply to medical schools. She has had a very difficult time reconciling her academic goals, her personal goals, and her career goals. Although she can perhaps express that confusion more clearly now, I don't believe that she has come any closer to resolving it. She hopes to enter a medical speciality where it is possible for her to be married, I presume, and to have a family. Yet, I am not sure she is the kind of woman who has the maturity to handle both of those responsibilities confidently and successfully.

Carmen came to college with very unformed ideas about education and only somewhat clearer expectations of learning some marketable skills to get a job. As she meandered through her undergraduate career and struggled to sort out her priorities, she met a man and got married in her senior year, which seemingly solved her problems.

Her vocational interests are compromised by her concern that a serious career commitment on the part of a woman is not consistent with being happily married and having a family. So her notion is that one ought to plan for doing some interesting work for pay for the first few years of marriage, then work at home with children and in the community. Career skills are important primarily as a good fallback in case of tragedy or failure of the marriage. With this frame of mind, she's clearly not terribly enthusiastic about either the educational or vocational side of her undergraduate career.

The Balance Sheet

Given the more negative tone of the Unconnected orientation, it makes good sense to begin with the debit side of the balance sheet. The Unconnected are clearly the least contented with the undergraduate experience. But before we try to explain why this is the case, their disaffections must be placed in perspective. Let us remember that despite all their complaints, the vast majority of these students rate their undergraduate experience as having been "good" or "very good" on the Senior Survey. Critical as they may be with respect to one or another aspect of their education, many of them express much affection for the institution providing it.

The negativism of the Unconnected is largely relative and much of it is a function of their more critical frame of mind. Unlike the Strivers who tend to be overly positive, the Unconnected err in the opposite direction. But whatever they say, their performance and behavior clearly show that the Unconnected cannot be cast wholesale into the roles of wastrels, failures, or rebels.

Yet, none of this is sufficient reason to gloss over the problems experienced by the Unconnected or blunt their criticism of the undergraduate experience. If college is to be worth attending, it must be worth engaging oneself in what it has to offer. There is no merit in the failure to connect if what the institution offers is worth connecting to. Any analysis of this group and any judgments of this orientation must, therefore, take into consideration not only the student but also the institutional end of the academic partnership. Keniston (1960) elaborates on the point that alienation has both a personal as well as a social component. One is alienated from something—usually an institution or society at large—and the rift that develops is a function of both the person and the entity he or she is alienated from. Though the Unconnected do not, as a whole, reject the institution, they are relatively alienated from its major educational patterns and themes.

The Unconnected thus pose a special challenge to institutions of higher learning. The standard-issue education that fits the needs of most students does not work as readily with the Unconnected. Some of them are admittedly very hard to reach. They may be in college at the wrong time, or in the wrong college, or may even have no business being in college altogether. No matter how dedicated the faculty or rich the curriculum, such students may fail to connect. But in other cases the students' developmental schedules may be merely out of synchrony with institutional timetables; the sophomore year may not be the right time for them to choose a major, or the junior year to settle on a career choice. Protracted uncertainty in these cases may be preferable to the premature closure of educational or career options. Thus, despite appearances, the Unconnected may be better off in some ways than the prematurely differentiated Careerists, the too easily contented Strivers, and the more otherworldly Intellectuals.

By their refusal to buy into the system uncritically, the Unconnected hold a mirror to the institution's educational ethos. They look beyond academic routines for deeper intellectual purposes. The comments of an Unconnected student that follow are bitter medicine, yet they are also a sobering remedy against complacency and self-satisfaction for even the most distinguished institutions of higher learning.

"There is a lot more to life than studying . . . My goal is learning how to think critically . . . I've been more and more frustrated by the whole approach to education . . . Though we're reading all these great books . . . I expected to discuss them, grapple with issues. But that hasn't happened. They praise Socrates's methods but use the methods of the Sophists that he denounced. I've heeded the advice not to let school get in the way of education."

8

Enhancing the
Undergraduate Experience
for All Students

"Of making many books there is no end," says the Preacher, "and much study is a weariness of the flesh" (Eccles. 12:12).

Having come this far, the reader is naturally led to ask, "So what? What does this broad panoply of findings mean for my institution, for the students I see every day, for the way our undergraduate program operates? How should I change my thinking in light of what I have read here? What should I do different from what I have been doing all along?" The short answer to these questions is quite simple: We cannot offer prescriptions, checklists, or other specific guidelines to translate our findings into institutional policy, and we think it would be presumptuous of us to try to do so. We further realize that few faculty, administrators, or student services officers are likely to change their basic patterns of relating to undergraduates on the basis of a single book. But we think we can make some suggestions about fruitful ways to use our typology of academic orientation and the findings to which it has led us to make improvements in several important dimensions of undergraduate education. That is the focus of this chapter.

The most essential recommendation is best stated at the outset: Institutions of higher education should make serious efforts at self-study in order to understand what their curricular and extracurricular programs mean for their students. The Cohort

Study has revealed a great deal about our students that we did not recognize before. It has helped to confirm or refute various student and organizational beliefs and myths about what a Stanford education is all about. Further, the involvement of senior administrators and staff members in the research program has provided numerous additional benefits by putting them into close personal contact with students to address in an open yet systematic way matters of great significance to their education.

Summary of Study Findings

This work addresses two primary tasks. The first is a description of the basic character of the four undergraduate years and the common features of student life in the university. The second and more central task is the identification of a typology of students based on the intensity of their commitments to career preparation and liberal learning, and exploration of the implications of that typology for students' academic and social activities, major and career choices, and other aspects of their education. We will review briefly the basic findings presented in Chapters Three through Seven before discussing their significance.

The freshman year is a time of *orientation* whereby students make the transition from high school to the arena of higher learning. It is a year marked by excitement and experimentation, exhilaration and anxiety. The sophomore year is burdened by the task of *definition*. It is a time of uncertainty and choice, disillusionment and reaffirmation. The junior year is a period of *consolidation* when tentative directions attain more certainty and greater academic focus adds substance and depth to learning. The senior year calls for *closure* of the undergraduate experience. Residual academic debts are settled, career plans are finalized (or delayed), and ties to the institution are loosened.

How students move through the academic and social systems is partly dependent on which of four academic orientations they follow—whether they are Careerists, Intellectuals, Strivers, or Unconnected. These orientations are defined by the relative emphasis they place on the aims of career preparation and liberal education. Students in these four categories respectively emphasize career preparation, liberal learning, both careers and education, and neither. Their more salient characteristics are as follows:

Careerists. The Careerists are especially likely to be men; the ratio of men to women in this type is higher than for any other. They come from all ethnic backgrounds, but their families are less likely to be of very high socioeconomic status; more commonly they are of upper-middle and middle status. Careerists' fathers are often businessmen or professionals holding master's-level degrees who have done well in their careers and feel that career success is very important. This family emphasis on career success strongly influences the Careerists.

The Careerists' outlook toward careerism and intellectualism is also consistent with their high school backgrounds. They are much less likely than other types to have gone to private high schools, and they tend to have weaker verbal abilities and stronger mathematics abilities. They conform to the general finding that mathematical ability and careerism are closely related.

In college, Careerists tend to pursue pathways that maintain their established attitudes. They do not become as involved with the faculty as other students. They continue to be highly influenced by their families, and they pay a good deal of attention to the job market in making decisions about their majors and careers. They therefore are especially likely to major in departments oriented to major professions, such as economics, biology, and various engineering fields, in order to pursue career interests in business, medicine, and engineering. Throughout college the Careerists are more fixed in their purposes, being less likely than most students to change their career plans between the freshman and senior years. If they do change their career plans, they are more likely than other types to switch to one of the four standard professions of business, law, medicine, or engineering.

Careerists stop out less than other students but are about average in attending overseas study programs. They engage in fewer extracurricular activities than other students, being particularly unlikely to undertake special academic projects, artistic endeavors, and volunteer service; in general, their social and political involvement is quite minimal.

Careerists are less likely to earn awards at graduation than any other type but the Unconnected, and their grades follow an average distribution. They evaluate their own abilities in an average way too, feeling somewhat more competent than other students in technical and mathematical areas that are closely related to their major fields but far less adequate in areas related to the humanities. At the exit point Careerists express only average satisfaction with the university experience. They are more satisfied than most students with their training for graduate or professional school, but they are less satisfied than most with their liberal education, courses, and involvement with the faculty.

Intellectuals. The Intellectuals are especially likely to be women, with the ratio of women to men being higher for this type than any other. Ethnic minority students are least likely to be in this group; when they are high on intellectualism, they are more often Strivers. The Intellectuals' families are generally of very high socioeconomic status and their fathers often hold doctoral-level degrees; many of them are doctors, college professors, or high-level corporate executives. Very rarely do the Intellectuals come from families where the father is not at least a college graduate.

Intellectuals often have very strong high school academic backgrounds and demonstrate strong ability in both the mathematical and verbal dimensions. This is especially true of Intellectual women, but there is also a large segment of Intellectual women who are low in both dimensions relative to their classmates.

Intellectuals tend to become highly involved with the faculty and their courses but are less influenced than most students by their parents. They become more involved with their advisers and are more influenced by faculty and advisers in making their decisions. They are also highly influenced by their experiences with courses, and they seek majors and careers that they think will be intrinsically interesting and rewarding.

The Intellectuals congregate more in the humanities and interdepartmental programs, and they are less likely to major in engineering and the natural sciences. They find it more difficult to settle on career choices than other students, and when they do make up their minds, they make more varied choices. More often they pursue professions in writing, journalism, the arts, and teaching;

they are less likely than others to go into business, law, or medicine. Women Intellectuals show these tendencies more than men; the latter are almost as likely as men of other types to pursue the four standard professions.

Intellectuals stop out far more than other students, but they stop out for shorter periods. They also go overseas far more than other students. They are highly engaged in extracurricular activities, particularly those areas where the Careerists are notable by their absence: special academic projects, the arts, volunteer service, and political activity and discussion.

Intellectuals do very well academically, even though a large segment of them have relatively weak academic backgrounds. They earn more honors at graduation than any other type and they earn the highest grades in all types of courses but engineering. Nonetheless, they assess their competence as lower in technical and mathematical areas than other students.

Intellectuals evaluate their undergraduate experience very highly, particularly their courses, professors, and the quality of their liberal education. The one area where they feel less satisfied is their preparation for professional or graduate school, but they do not feel less satisfied than other students with their career plans, and they leave the university with the self-confidence that their strong liberal education will stand them in good stead no matter what career directions they eventually pursue.

Strivers. The Strivers consist of equal proportions of men and women. Ethnic minority students are more prevalent in this type than any other, and the families of Strivers tend to be of relatively low socioeconomic status, with more of them having fathers in clerical and blue-collar occupations than any other type. But a sizable segment of the Strivers are from the opposite end of the spectrum: The children of doctors are more likely to be Strivers than any other type, and a good proportion of the fathers of Strivers have doctoral-level degrees.

Strivers have weaker high school academic backgrounds than other types. They have generally lower mathematics and verbal test scores, and the students having low scores in both dimensions are more likely to be Strivers than any other type. But the two sexes reveal opposing tendencies: For men a low math score combined with a high verbal score often yields a Striver, but for women a high math score combined with a low verbal score frequently produces a Striver.

Strivers are strongly influenced by numerous individuals and outside forces. Their parents tend to reinforce their careerist tendencies, while the faculty tend to reinforce their intellectual commitments. Strivers also feel highly influenced in their decisions by their course work, fellow students, and the job market. Strivers are often interested in two or even three major fields (though they do not actually change majors more than other students), and in their attempt to choose majors that combine intrinsic interest with good career prospects they end up with a wide variety of major choices. Much the same is true of their career choices: They congregate in business, law, and engineering more than Intellectuals and the Unconnected, but they make considerably more varied choices than the Careerists.

Strivers resemble Careerists with respect to stopping out and going overseas; they are much less likely to pursue either option than most students. But they are quite active in the extracurricular realm, taking on special academic projects and getting more involved in athletics than any other type. They are also quite active in volunteer work.

Strivers earn fewer awards at graduation than any other type, and their grades are lower throughout the four years and across almost the entire range of subject areas than those of other types. Their assessments of their abilities are only about average, but they care more about their abilities and give the highest overall ratings for the importance of the ability items by a good margin.

Strivers also care more about their undergraduate experience than other students and they are highly satisfied with it. They evaluate the academic program highly, and they feel a strong sense of identity and belongingness. They feel well prepared for professional or graduate training and consider themselves well launched on a trajectory leading to involved, busy adult lives.

The Unconnected. The Unconnected are more difficult to summarize than the other three types since they are a more varied group of students; they include potential Careerists and Intellectuals, as well as others who for one reason or another do not connect as readily with available institutional options.

Approximately equal proportions of each sex and ethnic group fall in this category. Their socioeconomic backgrounds are bimodal—both families of very high social status and families of relatively low social status tend to produce Unconnected students, while the middle-status families generally do not. Hence sizable proportions of the children of lawyers, professors, and major corporate executives are of this type, but also many of the children of minor professionals and the owners of small businesses. The largest proportion of the Unconnected comes from families of relatively low income.

The Unconnected have the strongest high school academic backgrounds overall. Students having strong mathematics and verbal ability are more likely to be Unconnected than any other type, and students of strong verbal but weaker mathematics background are also very likely to be of this type.

The Unconnected are much less influenced by parents, faculty, fellow students, or job market considerations than other students. For some of these students this is a deliberate choice: They prefer to insulate themselves from others so they can make their own choices. For others, it is more a matter of lack of initiative and energy.

The Unconnected major in the humanities and natural sciences more than other students while they tend to avoid the interdepartmental programs, and their choices overall are more evenly distributed across the school divisions than those of any other type. Their career choices are likewise quite varied. But they seem to make their choices more by default than active choice, and they feel less certain of their career choices than students of any other type. They also vacillate among alternative career choices more than other types.

The Unconnected are more likely to stop out and are notably less involved in extracurricular activities than other types. They are particularly uninvolved in special academic projects, athletics, volunteer service, and organized campus activities.

The Unconnected earn awards at graduation on a par with other groups (except departmental honors, which requires more individual initiative), and their grades are just about average for all types of courses.

In evaluating the undergraduate experience, the Unconnected are consistently less satisfied than other students. They are the least satisfied with both their liberal education and their preparation for advanced training. Compared to other students, they also attach less importance to most aspects of their education and rate their own abilities lower.

Significance of Study Findings

The Typology. Our typology of academic orientations constitutes the central organizing principle of this book. We see its usefulness in instrumental and pragmatic terms. It is a conceptual lens, one way of filtering the undergraduate educational experience. It must be judged in terms of its utility in helping us understand and improve that experience.

Typologies, as parts of taxonomic systems, have a variety of bases and serve a variety of functions. When Mendeleev discovered that natural elements show a periodic recurrence of properties on being arranged in the order of increasing atomic weight, he laid the foundations of modern chemistry. Yet for a classification to be useful, it need not necessarily elucidate a fundamental natural law. For instance, Linnaeus's botanical arrangements are not based on any natural law, yet they are enormously useful. The same can be said for the diagnostic schemes in medicine and other descriptive classifications in other fields.

Does undergraduate education need its own typology? It depends on how the particular typology will be used. In our case, the four categories we have devised have proven useful in our understanding of careerism and intellectualism. The implications of that understanding are important for the work of admissions officers, curriculum planners, academic advisers, and student services administrators, among others. But our typology has no discernible benefit to those who are concerned, for instance, with alcohol and drug abuse, sexual morality, and a host of other important issues.

The primary significance of a typology such as ours is that it provides a framework and a language for discussion. Instead of telling the admissions office to get "better students," we can discuss more intelligently the assets and liabilities of different academic orientations that students bring to college. Similar considerations apply to discussions of the curriculum and the extracurriculum.

Another benefit of a reliable typology is that it identifies certain *patterns*, which permit *predictions* and facilitate the laying of *plans*. Much of institutional policy making is typically reactive. A clearer and better-controlled direction can be established by a more active approach that has a firm empirical foundation. Instead of prescribing more humanities or science courses for all, we can be more selective in tailoring educational remedies to specific needs.

If we could have true and reliable profiles of student types with respect to variables that are significant to the educational process, our ability to anticipate how these students are likely to behave academically would be greatly enhanced. That in itself does not constitute an excuse or license to manipulate and shape their lives. But to the extent that institutions have a right and a responsibility to plan for the best possible educational environment for their students, the ability to predict with reasonable certainty (which is all one can hope for) would be most useful. Similar considerations would apply to the likely course of each of the four undergraduate years with respect to their tasks and challenges.

Some knowledge of who they are and what they can expect of college is apt to be most useful to the students themselves. For example, if Careerist freshmen were to know that the path they have embarked on is likely to interfere with their liberal education, they may have second thoughts before charging headlong down this path. The possibility that Careerism may not be the best route to true career success may be even more sobering. Similar lessons could be drawn for each of the other academic orientations.

The sort of information we have generated makes possible a certain measure of academic forecasting. Like weather forecasts, academic predictions do not always come true. The expectation of rain will not help prevent it, but at least one can take along an umbrella. Similarly, if students and advisers know what lies ahead, they may be able to cope better with what they will have to face.

Background Variables. We are not the first to discover that background variables like gender, ethnicity, social class, and SAT scores have an effect on students' college experiences. But we have been able to relate such effects to a particular set of student types, thus obtaining further insight into how these variables operate.

Being a man or a woman makes for fundamental differences in the college experience, and *gender* is probably the single most important variable influencing academic and career orientations. But the gender variable never operates singly; no one behaves a certain way simply by virtue of being male or female. We must, therefore, understand the impact of background variables not in isolation but within a complex tapestry.

Our finding that women place greater emphasis on liberal education, and men on career preparation, is hardly surprising, but it is revealing to find that women outnumber men more than two to one among Intellectuals, while the ratio is even greater in the opposite direction among Careerists. This suggests that efforts to stimulate interest in liberal education need to be directed more toward men than women, while women may well need more guidance regarding their career planning.

On the other hand, the equal proportion of the sexes among Strivers belies the common perception that men are more ambitious and hard-driving. By the same token, the overrepresentation of men among the Unconnected contradicts the notion that women are more likely to be undirected in their career interests and less involved with the institution as a whole. Among today's college students, women may be different from men in their orientations toward education and careers, but they are not less concerned to develop at least one of these two important aspects.

Ethnicity clearly affects the orientations students manifest, with minority students being especially likely to be Strivers and unlikely to be Intellectuals. These results are understandable; minority students come from generally lower socioeconomic backgrounds, and their greater emphasis on career success signals their desire to get their share of material rewards and prestige in the larger society. Yet it is also the case that many Strivers have difficulty in preparing for a career and becoming educated at the same time, and minority students need to be aware that by taking on so much they may well be assuring themselves of some degree of frustration and sense of inadequacy at the end of the college years.

The impact on student orientations of *father's occupation, father's education,* the *socioeconomic status and income* of the family, and similar factors shows that how students approach college is heavily influenced by factors outside their control. Even more important, these factors are outside the control of the institution. It is thus important for the institution to recognize the limits of what it can accomplish with its students. Student intellectualism may be heightened if the faculty become more highly involved in students' lives. But the prospects of diminishing student careerism are less bright, because parental influence is a primary reinforcing factor for it. How are institutions going to fight that? Should they attempt to?

The use of *SAT scores* has its defenders and detractors. We are aware of the problems with such standardized tests, but we think that they can be useful guides if handled carefully. We have found that mathematics scores are generally related to careerist tendencies, but verbal scores are not so clearly related to intellectualist leanings. And there are important sex differences here; perhaps the most intriguing one is that women who have high math and verbal scores are likely to be Intellectuals, while their male counterparts are likely to be Unconnected. Given the generally lower emphasis on careers among women, the former finding is reasonable; but why are some of the most able men the least motivated? This is a finding that cries out for further investigation, and it also should serve as a warning to faculty and advisers. Some of the most promising students may need special attention and special challenges; otherwise their strong capacities will allow them simply to float through college.

Constancy and Change. As with all phases of life, constancy and change characterize the college years. While students remain relatively constant in some ways, they change in others. Thus, in dealing with college students one must be prepared to live with a good deal of uncertainty and seemingly undirected behavior. This should not be seen as evidence of a lack of academic purpose. "Youth," wrote Aristotle, "is fickle in its desires." And they have good reason to be so, because they often do not know their own minds. Good teachers and mentors know how to wait patiently while the young go on searching. Other adults who are more impatient because time is running out in their lives must remember that youth has plenty of time.

The patterns we have uncovered with respect to shifts in majors and intended careers show that the tendency to change one's mind is a general feature of all students, although the proclivity to change varies from one group to another. Administrative flexibility is thus necessary to encourage students to shape their own education at their own appropriate pace, though limits are also necessary to help keep students from delaying their decisions indefinitely.

If the constant shifting of students exasperates those who would rather have them keep to a steady course, others who would like to change students are frustrated by their seeming fixedness. For the constellation of changes that we have noted takes place around a core of constancy whereby these students basically maintain their career and educational goals intact. We have noted only modest shifts from one type to another: A Careerist is highly unlikely to turn into an Intellectual, and vice versa. Changes are more likely to occur with respect to intensity or magnitude within a given orientation. Thus, a student who is a Careerist at the outset may become interested in a broader education and change into a Striver. Those on the boundary between the Unconnected group and the Careerist or Intellectual categories may slip in and out of those types without wholeheartedly hooking up to any of them.

These observations have important implications. If the educational and career orientations of students are indeed fairly set by the time they come to college, should an institution that wishes to set or alter the character of its student body do so mainly through the admissions process? We see serious problems with that approach, which we shall discuss shortly.

Given a particular mix of undergraduates, institutions can still exert considerable influence since some change is clearly possible. Once the Careerist student has been admitted, it may still be possible to make him less Careerist. Similarly, the Unconnected student need not be left to his or her own resources; means can be found to foster greater connectedness in one or another direction. What seems clear, however, is that such changes are unlikely to occur on their own; the institution will have to make a deliberate effort if it hopes to move students in desired directions.

On a more theoretical plane, a central question that arises is this: Are the changes noted in college the result of some developmental unfolding or do they reflect mainly the effects of academic socialization? Researchers have adopted the latter position quite frequently; Bushnell (1962) distinguishes between the "acculturation" that comes about as students are exposed to institutional values and the "enculturation" that results from the influence of the peer culture. But the relative constancy of our typological categories raises questions about how much impact colleges actually have on their students. The relative lack of impact could be explained by the possibility that academic orientation is lodged in the broader personal and social character of students; as part and parcel of their personality, it is hard to touch. On the other hand, one could argue that students do not change much because they are not challenged much. If parents and faculty vary greatly themselves in their careerist and intellectualist tendencies, it is easy enough for students to find a supportive niche: Careerists can cleave to their parents, Intellectuals can turn to the faculty. If institutions and their faculties have clear and strong educational purposes, they may be able to deflect more students from their established trajectories.

Careerism and Intellectualism. In discussing the four categories of our typology, we have had a fair amount to say about the relative merits and demerits of each orientation. Though we have tried to be evenhanded in our portrayals, there is no denying that we are more positive about some of the orientations than others. On the whole, the interviewers (ourselves included) favored the students who came to be called Intellectuals and Strivers over the Careerists and the Unconnected even though the typology had not yet been devised at the time. As authors we have tried to moderate these tendencies, yet we find ourselves in fundamental agreement with them.

If this constitutes a bias, it is easy to understand the basis for it. We are all members of an academic institution; some of us have done nothing else but work in institutions of higher learning. Liberal learning and intellectual endeavors are at the heart of the enterprise of higher education, in principle if not always in practice. It is, therefore, natural for us to see students who put their emphasis on liberal education and intellectual values as making better use of their educational opportunities than others who single-mindedly pursue career goals or fail to connect to the dual purposes of the institution at all.

There is more to this perspective, however, than the views of those who share common institutional values. There is corroborative support from the student's own perceptions and levels of satisfaction. It is quite clear that Intellectuals and Strivers generally leave the university more contented than the Careerists and Unconnected. Such expressions of satisfaction cannot be taken entirely at face value. Strivers, in particular, tend to be overly optimistic and positive, while the Unconnected have a more critical and negative view of the world. So it is possible that students from these two groups have fundamentally comparable experiences but express their views in disparate ways. Nonetheless, even when one strips away the artifact of style of expression and mind set, there remains enough of a residue of differences to convince us that Intellectuals and Strivers are in fact more contented than Careerists and the Unconnected.

The merits of Striverhood and Intellectualism are further apparent in the fact that the more extreme exemplars of these types do better on both counts—education and careers. The extreme Careerists and the extreme Unconnected show most markedly the liabilities of their orientations—narrowness in the first case and lack of involvement in the second. The extreme Intellectuals and Strivers are outstanding students by any measure; the extreme Careerists or the Unconnected are not.

In the light of all this, we are willing to stand by the proposition that a strong emphasis on liberal education is crucial to a successful college experience, though it need not entail a neglect of career concerns. Yet to place this conclusion in better balance we must restate earlier cautions about the orientations we tend to favor and clarify further our concerns over the orientations we see as relatively less desirable.

It bears repeating that Intellectuals and Strivers are not free of liabilities. While it is true that Intellectuals within the core group show highly promising prospects with respect to careers, there are many in the Intellectual group at large who fail to pay sufficient attention to their career prospects while in college. This often leaves them with few marketable skills at the time of graduation and the prospect of either a life of financial struggle or the need to start over again to develop the vocational skills required to make a decent living. Similarly, the Strivers have their own weaknesses. Some among them do manage to get the best of both worlds; others are spread too thin and come out of college with neither a particularly firm career prospect nor a solid enough liberal education.

The main liability of aspiring to be an Intellectual or Striver is that the aims of these orientations are harder to attain than the others. The difficulty is partly intrinsic to the nature of these orientations. The road to intellectual virtues is more arduous than that to career success, especially if one seeks excellence. This is true not only for students but in the eventual unfolding of these possibilities in adult life. An ordinary professional is likely to accomplish more than a pedestrian intellectual.

Intrinsic difficulties in the way of Intellectualism and Striverhood are compounded by external influences. Parents push too hard toward careerism; faculty do not pull hard enough toward intellectualism. And conventional conceptions of self-interest place survival and material comfort over intellectual enlightenment, making for an unequal contest between these competing aims.

We see the liabilities that burden Careerists and the Unconnected as still more serious. Yet these liabilities, too, must be placed in their proper perspective. It hardly needs repeating that there is nothing wrong with having strong career aspirations in college; vocational preparation has been and remains one of the fundamental purposes of a college education. Problems arise when career objectives compromise the prospects of obtaining a broad liberal education, for two reasons. First, the fruits of a liberal education are worthwhile ends in themselves; they make life richer, more vital, and more meaningful. Second, our evidence suggests that the best way to be highly successful in one's career may not necessarily be through careerism. In the absence of a follow-up study the last word has yet to be said on this issue, but our educated guess is that the Careerists should be forewarned of this possibility. For instance, substantial proportions of engineering students at Stanford and comparable institutions eventually become business executives. Our guess is that the narrower Careerists tend to remain in engineering jobs working for those of their peers who have broader visions and more rounded educations. Similarly, we suspect that Careerists in other fields are likely to end up toiling away as journeyman practitioners of their trades, only rarely achieving true professional success and prominence.

Nonetheless, the alarm over rising careerism needs to be placed in perspective. There is little question that students appear to be more career oriented now than a decade or two ago. Yet the magnitude of this tendency and its significance may well have been exaggerated in the professional literature, as well as in the popular press. In order to rivet the nation's attention, there is a strong tendency to depict a problem that is a legitimate source of concern as an impending if not an actual crisis. The more sensational elements of the public media can then be counted on to fan the flames and generate distorted but catchy images of social trends. Fifteen years ago the nation's youth was going to pot, now they are going to the bank; their idealism has been replaced by materialism; hippies have become yuppies.

There is some basis for all these contentions, but the changes are not as extreme and do not affect as many people as generally assumed; over a few decades the mass of students does not change its orientation so very much. There is also often less to much-publicized changes than meets the eye. Thus, in 1975–76 humanities majors accounted for 24 percent of all bachelor's degrees granted at Stanford; by 1982–83 this figure had dropped to 17 percent. By this measure, the humanities are declining rapidly. Yet if we look at enrollments in humanities courses rather than majors, we see that the mean number of humanities courses for students was 12.3 in 1975–76 and 12.4 in 1982–83. Thus, while students were less attracted to the humanities as majors (most probably for career reasons), they were by no means shunning humanities courses as part of their general education. What students need to understand further is that majoring in history or English or philosophy can also provide an excellent educational background for law, business, and many other professions, in addition to the contributions that courses in these areas make, as such, to a rich liberal education.

We should also note that there are various factors underlying the rise of careerism that have quite varied implications. The typical Careerist has been and remains a white, middle-class male; certainly more such students are Careerists now than earlier. But simultaneously there has been an influx of women and members of ethnic minorities into institutions of higher learning and, to a lesser extent, into professions that until fairly recently were closed to them. When disadvantaged segments of the population are merely claiming their rightful share of the professional job market, their careerism is harder to criticize.

We can also turn this discussion around. Humanities majors have traditionally been enclaves for women. Within this population have been women with deep and abiding intellectual interests in the humanities and women with basically Careerist tendencies whose vocational aspirations have been socially thwarted. If large numbers of these women are now shifting from the humanities to more career-oriented majors that are now opening up to them, their departure can hardly be lamented as a serious loss to the humanities.

The Unconnected present the most puzzling challenges to interpretations of their orientation. We continue to be sobered by the fact that these students have generally strong SAT scores and end up with generally as good grades as the rest. Yet many of them strike us as making rather poor use of their time in college. At the same time, in some ways the situation of the Unconnected is less worrisome than that of other groups. For instance, unlike Careerists, they are more likely to get a fair liberal education. Similarly, their career prospects may prove to be stronger than those of Intellectuals because of family assets or their obvious competence, unexercised as that may be while in college.

It is disturbing to think that the unconnectedness of these students may also be in part an institutional problem. Maybe the failure is with the faculty and established academic programs. Maybe the institutional choices they are failing to connect to leave something to be desired. Being unconnected is in itself hardly a virtue, yet one must respect any serious attempt to remain independent from mainstream values if there is good cause for it. Therefore, it is important to understand better the Unconnected students' own perspective on why their Careerist and Intellectual tendencies do not get ignited like those of their peers.

We would have done a serious disservice to students if our typology were used to typecast them. No category does justice to individuals. Every student is much more than what any of these labels could designate. We must, therefore, keep reminding ourselves that the true value of elucidating these orientations is found in focusing on the underlying processes that characterize all students to varying degrees. We may not like Careerism but we do not dislike Careerists. We should not be out either to exile Careerists or to exalt Intellectuals, to embrace the Strivers or reject the Unconnected, but rather to create the context and the mechanisms of dealing with these tendencies in constructive ways by maximizing their assets and minimizing their liabilities. We not only have to live with diversity but also must learn to use it to better advantage.

Recommendations

Our findings potentially bear on virtually all aspects of undergraduate education, but we will concentrate on six areas: the admissions process; the undergraduate curriculum; educational leadership; advising and academic services; extracurricular life; and research in undergraduate education. The recommendations we make with respect to these areas are offered with an awareness that recommendations as such have little impact on institutional behavior. When a national commission of distinguished educators and citizens proclaims a greater need for emphasis on the humanities, institutions hardly rush to respond in very meaningful ways. When researchers in higher education conduct elaborate studies that lead to specific prescriptions, their reports are more likely to be read by other investigators than by those who are in charge of running institutions. Somewhat more effective are calls for change that emanate from within institutions by the efforts of faculty and administrators, but even they tend to involve arduous processes of change. Nonetheless, institutions do change, and all such efforts are not devoid of value. The work of national commissions helps to create, or at least promote, the climate for change. The findings of researchers provide support for those who are already headed in a given direction. And, in the end, reason usually prevails in faculty deliberations.

Since we are not a national commission, an established research group in higher education, or a faculty senate committee, there is even less reason why anyone would eagerly follow recommendations from us. We do have, however, one thing going for us: What we have to say is based on the real, everyday experiences of a group of live college students.

The Admissions Process. In many institutions there is a curious schism between those who admit students to college and those who educate them—the people who select the timber are not the ones who build the cabin. There are very good reasons for the independence of the admissions process. Particularly where entrance to selective colleges and universities is concerned, the stakes are very high. There is no lack of parents who would buy or bully their children's way into their preferred institutions. Alumni and members of the faculty expect preferential treatment. Some wish to preserve the traditions of their beloved alma mater or to recapture its old glory as they remember it. Others push for admitting more women or members of ethnic minorities.

Against all these pressures the Admissions Office must stand firm; otherwise nothing less than the integrity of the institution will be at stake. But Admissions will be able to stand firm far more easily if the faculty are actively engaged in the admissions process. After all, it is primarily the responsibility of the faculty to set the academic purpose and tone of the institution. If there is not to be a mismatch between the types of students admitted and those that the faculty prefer to teach, the faculty must make their preferences known.

All of this argues for clear and coherent admissions policies that are closely matched with institutional purposes and objectives. To do this, institutions must have thought out their purposes and objectives in the first place. They need to know the sorts of applicants they want to attract and how the various types of students that are admitted fare in their undergraduate careers. This is where our research comes in. A typology like ours provides a meaningful framework for an institution to decide what sort of students it wants, because it characterizes students by the two central purposes of college education, career preparation and liberal learning. Of course, predicting the eventual orientation of any individual student with certainty is well nigh impossible, and even guessing the prevalence of the four types in a set of students whose background characteristics are well known is less than easy. The relationships between background variables and the typology are simply not strong enough to allow this kind of prediction or the generation of precise criteria that could be used blindly by admissions officers. But general guidelines could be developed, particularly if an institution carries out a study of careerism and intellectualism among its own students in order to see how the four types are related to their particular characteristics. Further, knowledge of our typology of academic orientation could aid in a more intuitive sense, in that admissions officers could evaluate students less mechanically and more meaningfully with respect to their background characteristics and academic assets. In other words, the typology can be used as an aid in thinking about what the students are like and what they are likely to achieve in college.

As it stands, admissions officers hear about faculty preferences on an ad hoc basis. The mathematicians yearn for more of the truly gifted in their discipline; humanists are hungry for students who are intellectually excited and exciting. More commonly, faculty members are silent on the issue; some are pleased with the students they encounter, while others smolder in silence. A meaningful typology would provide a more differentiated and precise vehicle for discourse.

However carefully students are chosen, their progress must be monitored and judgments of quality at the entry point must be compared with evaluations of excellence at the exit point. Comparing grades is not enough; even though those who come in with higher grades usually graduate with higher grades, grades do not tell us what sort of education students receive.

What we are arguing for here, then, is a firm empirical base for making admissions judgments informed by knowledge of the academic orientation of students, their performance in both courses and other activities, and even their lives after graduation. It is up to each institution to decide what mix of Careerists, Intellectuals, Strivers, or the Unconnected should be admitted. If this typology makes no sense for some institutions, they should find a framework that does make sense. There is much to be said for reliance on the intuition of dedicated and informed admissions officers in making judgment calls. But eyeballing has severe limitations in making such serious choices.

Our approach rests on an assumed correlation between characteristics identifiable at admissions and the type of student the selected candidates will become. But we do not mean to imply that we should admit fewer applicants whose typological correlates we dislike. To exercise such control would be self-defeating, if not unethical. Consider some of the possible consequences of such a policy. By weeding out potential Careerists among college applicants, one would interfere with the social mobility of disadvantaged groups; favoring the entry of Intellectuals will lead us back to the days of educating the children of the social elite; too many Strivers will prove too much of a good thing; excluding the Unconnected will eliminate some of the students with the greatest intellectual and career potential; no institution worth its salt could do without its dissenters. So the basic question for us is not who gets in but what we do with them once they are in.

The Undergraduate Curriculum. The Admissions Office is not like a pasta machine that produces strips of dough of uniform size and consistency out of which the faculty chefs produce educated men and women. Neither are incoming students like baked bread that cannot be reshaped any further. Our study reconfirms that students enter college already fairly formed with respect to their academic orientations and career purposes. Yet there is enough room for change to justify institutions taking an active and vigorous role to enhance the educational experience of undergraduates along lines that are compatible with articulated educational purposes.

The primary instrument through which the faculty performs its educational function is the curriculum: the courses of study that are offered and required for graduation. Its etymology (Latin, "to run") is consistent with the pervasive feeling among undergraduates that the curriculum is an obstacle course they must run to get their degrees. Some of the faculty also adhere to this conception when they see themselves as the obstacle setters and monitors of the race. This paradigm enhances competitiveness whereby students are pitted against each other and against the faculty. Competition is an integral part of our culture and cannot be excluded from institutions of learning; to the extent that it encourages excellence it may be all to the good. Yet there is a real danger that this model stifles student initiative and takes the joy out of learning.

The extensive literature on the curriculum of American colleges is littered with the accounts of educational leaders trying to reform the curriculum, usually with little immediate success (hence Hutchins's classic comment that changing the curriculum is like moving a cemetery). A tone of futility is reflected in the anonymous comment, "The curriculum does not matter. If it did matter, we could not do anything about it. If we could do something about it, we would not know what to do" (The Carnegie Foundation for the Advancement of Teaching, 1977).

Much of the learned literature on the curriculum is written by people who do not teach undergraduates and is rarely read by those who do. Contrary to what one might infer from the literature, changes in the college curriculum usually take place in bits and pieces. They are typically initiated by administrators who are adept at mobilizing faculty and then letting them take over. These changes are often reactive to the temper of the times; the loosening of the curriculum in the late 1960s and early 1970s and its more recent tightening are cases in point.

Based on what we have learned from our students, the curriculum fulfills its function best when it offers clearly marked anchor points along with latitude for choice. Different students have different educational needs at different times. To meet such diversity, the undergraduate curriculum must be flexible and offer intelligent choices. At the same time, it should provide direction and coherence to undergraduate education.

The need for direction and coherence is probably greatest among the Unconnected, who have the hardest time making sense out of their college education and integrating it into their lives. Thus, it would be helpful to make sample programs of study available to freshmen and sophomores. Such sample programs should also include guidelines about various forms of liberal education that students might pursue, each of them offering different types of breadth and emphasis and tailored to different general interests. These programs and guidelines would likely be ignored by students who are firmly fixed in their curricular and career choices, but those who need them would have them at hand.

One of the more distressing findings of this study is that for many students there is not enough interaction with faculty outside of the classroom. State universities with mammoth enrollments may not be able to do much about this, but institutions like Stanford can and should. As shown by the Intellectuals and Strivers, there are certainly many students who do develop meaningful and mutually satisfying relationships with their teachers, advisers, and other faculty. The seriousness of educational purpose of the Intellectuals and the enthusiasm of the Strivers help to ensure this. But for Careerists and the Unconnected it is less likely: The Careerists are preoccupied with their vocational goals, so their interaction with faculty is more instrumental; the Unconnected do not seem to find enough common ground between their interests and what they perceive to be the interests of the faculty to allow for much close interaction.

The faculty is generally more than willing to meet students halfway. But few faculty members have either the will or the interest to take an active role in engaging the more passive students. The reasons for this are not difficult to understand. Given the multiple roles and commitments of the faculty, they often have divided loyalties. Everyone agrees that research and teaching should not be competitive but complementary, but the demands of the two are not easy to reconcile.

Many notable exceptions notwithstanding, one could say that the rank ordering of a typical faculty member's interests goes as follows: Dedication to one's own research and scholarship comes first; interest in one's graduate students comes next; this is followed by concern for those undergraduates who are majoring in one's department; serious interest in the teaching of undergraduates at large calls for true dedication; service as general advisers begins to qualify as hardship duty; helping students with whom one does not have any formal affiliation calls for sainthood.

We are exaggerating to make a point, but the thrust of what we say holds true not only in our own institution but in other institutions like it. It is small comfort that one can find some faculty members who are distinguished scholars and researchers, superb teachers of undergraduates, and caring and competent mentors all rolled into one; there can never be enough of them to count on. Nor does the fact that some students seem to be doing fine while hardly crossing paths with their teachers and advisers qualify as an argument to throw in the towel and let students fend for themselves. What we need are neither more heroic faculty nor more self-sufficient students but some effective way of bringing together ordinary faculty with ordinary students, under ordinary circumstances.

Educational Leadership. When we ask students what they think Stanford stands for, we are struck by their general lack of awareness of any institutional purpose. When pressed, they often ascribe their own purposes and aspirations to the institution. Careerists see the university as a place where tomorrow's professionals are trained; those from disadvantaged backgrounds perceive it as a vehicle to improve their socioeconomic lot; Intellectuals point to the intellectual virtues that animate liberal learning (or complain of the lack of such virtues). In the absence of explicit institutional purposes, it is inevitable that college looks like an arena for a free-for-all.

There was a time when university presidents taught courses in moral philosophy that all students had to attend. At their best, these courses gave meaning and coherence to the educational experience. We do not have such courses now, and perhaps we do not need them. Yet surely some other means can be found where an authoritative voice speaks for the basic values for which the institution stands. What is called for is not the endorsement of some particular social and philosophical perspective or monolithic truth but the advocacy of the fundamental principles that are at the heart of the academic enterprise, such as intellectual integrity and the merits of an examined life. The difficulty lies in doing this without sounding grandiose and abstract. We are hard pressed to offer concrete suggestions, but we can at least say that authoritative figures who both believe in and practice what they preach in their own lives can contribute a great deal just by serving as prominent examples of the type of educated persons the students should aspire to become.

To achieve this, senior administrators in the university need to take a more active role in articulating educational purposes and direction to their students. University presidents are usually so pressed by their myriad responsibilities that they are often outside the orbit of undergraduate life. Provosts, who wield so much influence in the critical budgetary and appointment processes, are shadowy figures to undergraduate eyes. School deans have their hands full with their departmental chairmen, and the chairmen with their own faculties. But if these individuals do not set the tone for the faculty to become involved with undergraduates, a major source of motivation and inspiration is lost.

To look after the interests of undergraduates, there are usually deans of the college or administrators with a variety of similar titles. Typically, these university officers have little leverage on departments and the faculty. If they are set up as an independent entity outside of schools, they must derive their power primarily from the person they report to, such as the provost or the president; hence they have no independent base or faculty constituency. If they are cautious and passive in their dealings with those in the true seats of power, they are seen as ineffectual and their office a needless drain on institutional resources; if they are bold and enterprising, they are accused of being intrusive and violating the autonomy of departmental and decanal units. When the administrator with primary responsibility for undergraduate education is placed within a school, many of these problems are obviated—but only at the cost of decreased independence of action and possibly diminished ability to affect the larger and more powerful departments.

There are no pat structural solutions to these problems. Each system has its assets and liabilities. We must recognize that in institutions of higher learning where research and graduate education by necessity dominate faculty priorities, constant attention (and nagging) by some offices and administrators are necessary to keep the interests of undergraduates on the institutional agenda. Yet merely relegating the responsibility for undergraduate education to a single officer is hardly an adequate approach.

Advising and Academic Services. Given the rich array of curricular choices, differing student orientations, and the lack of a centrally articulated set of educational purposes, undergraduates need personalized advice to guide them through college. The main burden for this falls on the academic adviser.

The roles of teacher and adviser are variously bound together. When a student is taught entirely by a tutor, the two functions become inseparable. There is less extensive but still considerable overlap between the teacher and adviser roles when faculty work with majors within their own departments. In these relationships, the adviser and advisee share common academic interests and sometimes common career interests as well. Things usually work out rather nicely.

A greater potential for mismatch characterizes the relationship between general advisers and students who have not yet declared a major. Adviser and advisee are typically less than clear in these situations about their respective expectations and responsibilities. Catalogues and brochures that address these issues provide some guidance but it is simply not possible to spell out all that the advising relationship should accomplish. This may allow for greater flexibility in fashioning a particular relationship but more often the uncertainties entailed result in confusion.

That students are less than satisfied with their general advisers is abundantly demonstrated year after year in our Senior Survey, where students invariably rate most of their general advisers as somewhere between "poor" and "good" while they rate their major advisers as "good" to "very good." In fact, general advising receives lower ratings than any other aspect of the undergraduate program.

As with interaction with the faculty, student relationships with advisers (most of whom at Stanford are faculty members) vary greatly depending on the students' career and educational orientations. Intellectuals and Strivers get more involved with their advisers and get more from them. Careerists may have good relationships with advisers but they tend to be instrumental in nature, while the Unconnected more often have little adviser contact at all. In this area an awareness of the typology and its implications could be particularly helpful. By alerting advisers to the tendency of the Unconnected to avoid faculty and adviser contact and by making it clear that such avoidance contributes to the Unconnected students' general neglect of their liberal education, we might increase adviser concern and willingness to make the extra effort required to reach these students. By pointing out to advisers that Intellectuals may be charming and delightful by virtue of their educational commitments but often risk their own futures by too nonchalant an attitude about career preparation, advisers may be more likely to take these students in hand and push them to face the economic and occupational realities that await them after graduation.

The situation is complicated by the fact that advisers themselves have their own career and intellectual orientations. This creates a dilemma. When freshmen interested in engineering, medicine, and the humanities are assigned to professors in the respective fields, there is a good match with respect to common interests. Yet, these faculty members tend to reinforce the very directions on which these students are already set, for better or for worse. When the assignments get scrambled, student and adviser both complain that they have nothing to say to one another. Where does one find engineers who could be good mentors to humanists, or humanists who could be mentors to engineers?

Academic advisers are not the only sources of advice. Students themselves are an excellent resource. In our Advising Associates program, they facilitate and complement the primary advising relationships of Stanford freshmen. Other sources of guidance are available through academic information offices, career counseling and placement centers, and more psychologically oriented counseling services.

If this whole array of advising services could become more attuned to the different academic orientations of students, there would be much to be gained. As it stands, advisers, counselors, placement advisers, and others start knowing next to nothing about the students; nor are they likely to learn a great deal in their sporadic meetings with them, which are often dominated by discussions of practical issues. The operations of a service like the career placement center could also be improved with a more systematic knowledge of the types of students who go there. We find, for instance, that Careerists are least likely to be highly influenced by the services offered by the placement center. Is that because Careerists do not need career advice? Or do they get it elsewhere? Strivers, by contrast, are most susceptible to such influence in their career decisions. Those who work in these settings need to learn a good deal more about these patterns and use such findings to help orient their activities accordingly.

Advisers need to approach their advisees with an open but not an empty mind. We think that the lack of information about students and the problems advisers have in getting to know them are largely responsible for their all-too-common disinterest in their students. The experiences of the interviewing team with the Cohort subjects are highly instructive in this regard. Virtually all of us had been advisers and carried out our advising duties in the standard fashion. But as interviewers of Cohort subjects, we became highly engaged in our subjects as we got to know them. It is amazing how much you can learn in a matter of hours when you approach a student with forethought, guidance as to what to ask, and a willingness to listen. If advisers could be prevailed upon to do the same, even in more modest form, the knowledge they would gain of their advisees would make them much more effective as advisers and their interactions would be much more rewarding.

Extracurricular Life and Learning. The educational process in college can only be meaningfully understood in the larger context of the student's broader life experiences. Intellectual development makes little sense if decoupled from its psychosocial matrix. The point we are making here was articulated forcefully by Nevitt Sanford in research done at Stanford and elsewhere three decades ago (Sanford, 1962, 1967). His call to make "the development of the individual as a whole" the primary aim of college is far from having been implemented. Though that vision may be utopian, the basic lesson remains valid: Treating students as disembodied intellects makes no sense.

The interview reports make it amply clear that there is nothing peripheral, so far as the students themselves are concerned, about extracurricular life and learning. For quite a few of them, what goes on outside the classroom is of more central interest than what goes on inside. Students are often more important for each other than is the faculty. This is true not only socially but with respect to the fundamental educational experience itself.

College brings together individuals of different gender, ethnicity, socioeconomic status, political and religious beliefs, and geographical origin. The confrontation with such diversity at such a level of intimacy is an experience that most students have never had before. The effect is generally quite broadening and enriching. But it can also be anxiety provoking and academically distracting.

Music and sports claim an enormous share of the energies, time, and attention of college men and women, sometimes becoming the dominant focus of the college years while relegating academics to the periphery. Other social interactions, which may be romantic, sexual, political, or religious, or simply involve having a good time (with or without alcohol and drugs), may become the dominant themes during various stretches of students' lives. Distinctly in the minority are students who essentially do nothing much but study in college.

While students may not be primarily responsible for setting the intellectual tone of an institution, they are highly influential in sustaining it. If a strain of antiintellectualism runs through the peer culture, it can have a chilling effect on the life of the mind. If students engage each other in serious intellectual discourse only in the classroom but not outside it, and only with respect to topics that they are assigned but not in connection with what is happening in the world around them, they will end up with a contrived education. Unless the college can link up the classroom with life outside it, much of its fundamental intellectual purpose will be vitiated.

The most common way that universities and colleges like Stanford make this link is through their residential education programs. Rather than allowing student dormitories and residences to be places for students simply to hang their hats, residential education programs attempt to make them extensions of the academic arena. This may involve faculty members living with the students, lecture series presented in student lounges, small seminar courses held in dormitory conference rooms, cultural or political awareness campaigns and events, and a host of other activities. But the one curious feature of most residential education programs is that they rarely attempt to take into account differences among students; they usually treat students as if they were all the same (except that gender and ethnic differences are often accommodated). This is not only inappropriate but self-defeating, or at least self-limiting. Instead, programs could better be developed in more varied ways to take into consideration the career and educational orientations of students. This becomes especially important when we realize that student residences tend to have characteristic profiles. Some residences become havens for Intellectuals; others are hotbeds of Careerist solidarity; still others are populated largely by Unconnected students. Clearly enough, the Intellectual residences have relatively little need for still more academic outreach efforts by the residential education staff, while the Careerist residences are less in need of career placement speakers and programs; efforts in the opposite direction would be more appropriate.

As with the issue of advising, faculty have a crucial role to play in this area. Even in the best systems of residential education, only a small and dedicated group tends to labor mightily. A few may attain fame as legendary masters, but most go unrecognized. Staff members who are responsible for residential education and extracurricular life more generally bring many strengths to their tasks, yet they often feel like and are treated as second-class citizens in the academic enterprise. As with the admissions staff, there is a schism between one important segment of the university and the other. Differences in educational perspective, territoriality, and other unworthy motives further interfere with effective collaboration. But whatever obstacles there may be, if the faculty truly want to educate undergraduates, they need to work with them outside the classroom as well as within it.

Some faculty and students appear to have a natural gift for establishing relaxed and rewarding personal relationships with each other. In other cases, external circumstances facilitate such orientations, as, for example, when students rent rooms in faculty houses, do yardwork, watch their children, and so on. But otherwise, there are many obstacles in the way of fostering social interactions, let alone closer friendships.

If a faculty member (or spouse) begrudges the time and effort required for taking a more personal interest in students, or if students act as if they have their fill of the faculty in the classroom and laboratory, not much can be done to bring them closer. But if there is reasonable interest on both sides, some of the more artificial hindrances can be readily overcome.

A common mistake made by the faculty is overestimating the magnitude of effort necessary to have frequent social contact with students. For instance, inviting a student to dinner may be thought to require a special meal. In fact, most students are grateful to partake of the regular family dinner or to visit for a cup of coffee or tea. Just being inside the house of a faculty member is interesting to most students because it provides a glimpse of the professor's personal surroundings and thus a window into the student's own future circumstances if he or she is interested in the same field.

As teachers, faculty members often feel burdened by the necessity of making weighty and incisive comments every time they open their mouths. Yet what students are yearning to hear are not pearls of wisdom but more casual comments about everyday events that make it possible to connect to the professor on a personal level. Especially useful are biographical tidbits about the faculty member's education and career, for example, how he or she chose a major or decided on a career. It is comforting for students to learn that highly successful professionals have also gone through periods of uncertainty, have had to backtrack, or sometimes have failed outright.

Personal relationships with students can be maintained at very little cost and effort. Such relationships often work best when they develop spontaneously and in keeping with the ways students routinely run their lives. A chance meeting on campus can be parlayed into a short walk (in the professor's direction, no doubt) that ends with an ice cream treat or a curbside chat. Going to a public lecture, play, or concert with a student, or taking along a small group of students and then discussing the event afterward will be refreshing and enriching for all concerned. Faculty members need only bear in mind the possibility of involving students in the normal activities of their lives and endless opportunities will present themselves for cultivating that special relationship that can mean so much to a student's college experience. And the students are not the only beneficiaries of these associations.

Research in Undergraduate Education. Even institutions that thrive on research do little to investigate the educational experiences of their own students. Those who are concerned with renewal and reform must realize that the real enemies of undergraduate education are apathy and ignorance. It is our experience at Stanford that one of the best ways of combating them is to provide reliable information in palatable form. Such efforts keep undergraduate education on the institutional agenda. The more we know about our students, the more likely we are to care; and from such caring comes the will to do the best we can—hence the plea for more institutional research on undergraduate education.

With respect to the work reported in this book, a number of further questions are raised that may be as useful as whatever answers we have provided. Our list of areas where we have fallen short, and where we need to do further work, includes the following:

It would be important to know with more certainty the distribution of the four types in the undergraduate population at large. As we explained earlier, the method we used to construct the typology precluded our discovering the relative proportions of the four types. Through the interview material we made an attempt to get at least an approximate picture of how large these four groups are, but we have made at best only an educated guess. What we now need is an entirely new study that will use its own appropriate instruments and predetermined criteria with which to examine a sample of the undergraduate population. While we think this is feasible and worth doing, we do not expect it to lead to a clear and precise set of findings because we are not dealing here with mutually exclusive entities; there is bound to be a good deal of overlap. Precise figures in such a situation are only possible at the cost of a great deal of arbitrariness.

A more serious gap is the isolation of the career and education variables from other personality and social dimensions. Because the original intent of our research was to explore patterns of curricular choice and because we knew we could investigate only a limited set of variables, we made a deliberate decision to leave out of our inquiry issues of personality development. Through their responses, our subjects have taught us once again the important lesson that the academic side of life cannot be viewed in isolation from the rest of human existence. Thus, an important extension of this research would be to relate the typology to broader personality features of these students. If such an integration between personality factors and academic styles can be achieved, we would not only have advanced our understanding of college students but also have understood better the developmental phase of young adulthood. To accomplish this fully, we must, of course, also investigate the extent to which the formation of these academic orientations and the other changes manifested while going through college are related to the college experience itself rather than being a part of the larger process of development in general.

We have also not taken into sufficient account the prevailing national social climate during the time that the study was carried out. If personality elements propel students internally, prevailing social circumstances, such as the state of the economy and the political mood of the country, are external constraints that also influence student orientations and choices.

It is quite clear that the academic orientations of students are already fairly well formed by the time they come to college. It would be important, therefore, to know about antecedent factors and the process by which students' attitudes toward liberal learning and career preparation are produced, at least during high school and possibly earlier.

Perhaps the most significant additional work that needs to be done is a follow-up study of these students after they have settled down in their career paths. Given the long gestation period of some of the professions such as medicine, a ten-year period past graduation would be optimal for such a follow-up. After all, the true significance of the credits and debits we have assigned to these orientations will only be revealed in the context of adult experiences and outcomes.

We have expressed confidence that our typology, at a basic level, should be applicable to college students elsewhere. But this needs to be confirmed through the replication of our study in other institutions. Even if our typology is broadly useful, there will no doubt be differences among institutions with respect to the relative prevalence of the four types, which will be of great interest to uncover.

The Silent Partnership

Students now exist largely as silent partners in the educational enterprise. Their motives, aspirations, and patterns of academic choice are generally unknown to those who teach them and are supposed to guide them. Even though they pay substantial sums of money for their education, students have little to say about the quality of the education they get in return. Though they are willing to work hard to meet the institution's academic require-ments, it is all too often not made clear to them what the larger institutional goals are and how best to attain them. Undergradu-ates' educational experiences and the quality of education offered by the institutions that they attend would be much improved if this silent partnership were to be replaced by a more active engagement.

Institutions do a fine job of controlling the quality of the faculty with respect to research and scholarship. But there is less willingness to exert comparable efforts to ensure the quality of teaching at the undergraduate level. Students cannot be the final arbiters of an instructor's performance. Popularity contests are not the best way of judging quality. Just as peer review is the ultimate test of assessing scholarship, the same is ultimately true for assessing faculty teaching. Nonetheless, students can play an indispensable role in this regard. After all, if a teacher is not getting through to students, there is little point in the classroom exercise. Students have a right to be heard and they can contribute greatly to the evaluation and improvement of the teaching that is so big a part of their academic experience.

We need to inform our students with far more clarity and specificity what to expect from college. This requires that institutions explicitly state their purposes and the reasons for them. Rather than letting students find their way through trial and error, the student grapevine, or the cryptic prose of college catalogues, they can be informed much more directly about the likely consequences of what lies ahead through publications and programs that use interesting formats to tell students about the institution and the experience of their predecessors.

Students represent an enormous untapped resource. We must find ways to engage them and help them relinquish the role of the passive learner so they take more responsibility for their own education. Along with providing them with the freedom to make choices, we need to present them with choices that are intellectually exciting and engaging, and provide ample opportunity to link up what they want to do with their lives with the demands of society that they will have to face eventually. We should also challenge their choices so they will examine their motives and interests fully and be sure that their choices are really their own.

Students can be superb caretakers of each other (as well as highly deleterious influences on each other). Institutions often do not realize that students will do a great deal for each other in institutionally endorsed settings just as they do informally all the time. Undergraduates at Stanford function quite effectively in a variety of roles—as advising associates, peer tutors, peer counselors, resident assistants, and in some programs as teaching assistants. We do not mean to suggest that students should do the job of the faculty, but they can complement the faculty in the exercise of some of their functions. The beneficiaries of these interactions are not only those for whom these services are performed but also those who perform those services. By helping others they help themselves.

Institutions that have the resources and facilities must make the undergraduate experience far more of a partnership between students and faculty than is often the case. Having worked hard in high school and taken on enormous financial burdens, students deserve something more than a seat in a classroom. A great many students already fulfill this ideal of working closely with faculty members in partnerships as junior colleagues; it is in these experiences that tomorrow's researchers and scholars are spawned. But we need to broaden the opportunities so that such experiences become part of the normative process of college life for as many students as possible. It is a good thing that so many Intellectuals are able to attain close working relationships with faculty. But we also need to worry about the many fine intellects among the Unconnected who are left to coast along without getting the benefits of being fully engaged.

Students need to take a more active role in the governance of their institution in areas that directly affect their lives. If colleges are going to produce enlightened citizens and leaders, the place to start learning the necessary political skills, social graces, and ideals of service is right in college (if not before). Surely there must be alternatives to the radical rejection of the institution on the one hand and the unquestioning compliance with its values on the other.

The issue is sometimes cast in terms of who "owns" institutions of higher learning and the right of its "consumers." For us, the issue is not ownership but understanding, empathy, respect, and responsibility on the part of all concerned. It is only then that, in Whitehead's words, "the connection between knowledge and the zest of life will be preserved by linking the young and the old in the imaginative consideration of learning."

Appendix I: Background Information on Stanford University

Stanford University (founded 1885) is located near Palo Alto, California, about thirty miles south of San Francisco. Its 13,000 students are about equally divided between undergraduate and graduate students. The 1,300 members of the faculty are distributed among seven schools. Four of these are graduate schools in Business, Education, Law, and Medicine; three schools— Humanities and Sciences, Engineering, and Earth Sciences—offer graduate and undergraduate programs. The School of Humanities and Sciences encompasses departments in three areas: humanities, mathematical and natural sciences, and social sciences. Undergraduates, therefore, can major in one of five units—the three subdivisions within the School of Humanities and Sciences, engineering, or the earth sciences.

Stanford is a highly selective private university, admitting only about 15 percent of the applicants for the freshman class each year. As a result, the students have very strong high school backgrounds, including very high grade point averages and SAT scores. No set formula is used in the admissions process; the Admissions Office looks for a diverse range of exceptional abilities and talents in incoming freshmen. The admissions process is "needs-blind"; that is, students are considered for admission without regard for their ability to pay for their education, and student financial aid is administered entirely independently of the Admissions Office.

Virtually all of the freshmen come to the university straight from high school; only a few of them work for a year or two before continuing their education. All freshmen are required to live on campus, and the vast majority of undergraduate sophomores, juniors, and seniors also live on campus. Faculty members and some staff serve as Resident Fellows and live in the dormitories. They are assisted by student Resident Associates in their supervisory support and educational activities within the residences.

Academic advisers are drawn primarily from the faculty, although some staff members also serve as advisers. Students can also seek advice and counsel from such university offices as the Academic Information Center, the Career Planning and Placement Center, and the Learning Assistance Center. There is a peer advising system (Advising Associates) organized in the dormitories whereby selected older students act as advisers to freshmen.

The degrees of Bachelor of Arts (A.B.), Bachelor of Science (B.S.), and Bachelor of Arts and Science (B.A.S.) are the three undergraduate degrees conferred by the institution. For graduation, a student must complete 180 (quarter) units of academic work; fulfill the writing, distribution, and language requirements; and complete the curricular requirements of a major in a department or program (a minimum of 60 units of work). The student must have completed at least 45 units (including the last 15) at Stanford and must have been in residence at least three quarters of study.

At the time of the Cohort Study, the distribution requirement was fulfilled by taking a minimum of three courses in each of three substantive areas—the humanities, social sciences, and natural sciences and mathematics. Subsequently, a more extensive and rigorous set of requirements has been adopted whereby each student must now take one course from seven designated sets of offerings and one three-quarter sequence in the Western Culture program.

Freshmen are admitted without regard to their intended major field, although students are free to declare a major as soon as they wish after matriculating. The major need not be declared until fall of the junior year, so students have a long time to settle on a major choice, and in many cases a student can change departments even as late as spring of the junior year and still complete the requirements on time. There is no provision for a minor field to complement the major. Some students (currently almost 10 percent of the total) declare two different majors, although not all of them complete the requirements for the second major.

Faculty members within the schools of Humanities and Sciences, Engineering, and Earth Sciences teach both undergraduate and graduate students. Some of the faculty from the professional schools are also actively engaged in undergraduate education. Academic policy is set by the faculty senate on the recommendations of the Committee on Undergraduate Studies and the Committee on Academic Appraisal and Achievement. Departments are largely autonomous in the conduct of their academic programs. During the Cohort Study, the Vice-Provost and Dean of Undergraduate Education was responsible for academic advising and extradepartmental programs. In 1981, responsibility for those and related activities was transferred to the Associate Dean for Undergraduate Programs in the School of Humanities and Sciences.

Appendix II: Methodology of the Cohort Study

The Cohort Study Sample

The original sample consisted of 20 percent of the freshman class entering in 1977, selected at random. The class contained about 1,600 students, the sample 320 students. Of these, two students never arrived at Stanford, six declined to participate in the study, and one was excluded because she was not a first-time Stanford student. The final sample thus contained 311 members of the class of 1981.

The sample matched exactly the entire class in sex composition (44 percent women) and ethnic distribution (5 percent Asian Americans, 6 percent Blacks, 78 percent Caucasians, 6 percent Chicano or Hispanic, 5 percent foreign or other ethnicity). It also closely matched the undergraduate population in terms of high school background (public versus private), SAT scores, and rank in high school class. In addition, the preliminary academic interests expressed by students in the sample were almost identical with those of the entire class:

Academic Interest	Sample	Entire Class
Humanities	11%	12%
Social sciences	30	30
Natural sciences	24	25
Engineering	13	13
Premedical	17	18
No preference	4	2

Hence, by all available measures the students in the sample were highly representative of the entire population. We made similar comparisons between the sample and the entire class in the sophomore and junior years, comparing such factors as attendance rates, attendance at an overseas campus, stopping out, and so on, and consistently found very close matches.

In the second and third years of the study, transfer students were sampled randomly and added to the study population, including fifty sophomores and fifty juniors. The sophomore additions were 54 percent of ninety-three transfers, and the junior group represented 69 percent of seventy-two transfers. Of the sophomores selected, one never enrolled at Stanford and a second declined to participate; among the juniors, five declined to participate. We therefore had forty-eight sophomore and forty-five junior transfers added to the sample. They, too, showed a close match with their respective populations.

Our final sample of participating students consisted of 311 freshmen, 48 sophomores, and 45 juniors, or a total of 404 students. Of the freshmen, whom we call the original cohort, seventeen students left the university permanently at some point before graduation and one died, while four of the transfer students either left the university or decided not to complete the study. We therefore had an active sample of 292 students who entered as freshmen and 89 transfers. For these students, the participation rates in the study were very good. The response rates for the questionnaires were as follows:

	Original Cohort	*Transfer Students*
Freshman year	98%	—
Sophomore year	97	98%
Junior year	88	93
Senior year	81	77

Interviews were completed at a slightly lower rate than the questionnaires, especially in the junior and senior years (75 percent). The net effect is that fully 78 percent of the original cohort that did not leave the university completed all four questionnaires, and 70 percent completed all four of the interviews. Our review of the demographic characteristics of the students in this group revealed that they too were highly representative of the entire entering freshman class, so that analyses based on this set of 227 students are generalizable to the entire class. About 70 percent of the transfer students completed all of the relevant questionnaires and interviews. This is a somewhat lower questionnaire response rate than for the original cohort, but about the same for the interviews.

Interviews

The interview team consisted of upper- and middle-level university administrators, most of whom have regular contact with undergraduate students. Their names and positions at the time of the study are listed in the Acknowledgments. While not all the interviewers had had experience in research interviewing methods, all of them were experienced in working with students and many of them were themselves Stanford graduates. They were chosen in part with the thought that their participation in the Cohort Study would help them to learn about students in a way that they normally would not be able to. This hope was amply fulfilled.

Interview Formats. In the freshman year the interviews were generally unstructured. The interviewers were very familiar with the purposes and structure of the study and had been informed of the topics they should pursue in the interviews, but no formal interview schedule was prepared. For the sophomore year, and partly in reaction to the looseness of the interview format for the freshman year, a more structured approach was employed, using the following detailed outline:

Sophomore Interview Outline

A. *Events/People/Context*
  1. Personal
     a. Health
     b. Family members
     c. Friends
     d. Work

    2. Academic
        a. Faculty—classes
        b. Faculty—advising and other interactions
        c. Intellectual issues
    3. Institutional
        a. Knowledge of resources
        b. Responsiveness, helpfulness
        c. Consciousness of the sense and purpose of Stanford
        d. Sense of identification and belonging

B. *Decisions*
    1. Academic and intellectual progress
        a. Broad areas of interest
        b. Choice of major
        c. Thoughts on career
        d. Social/cultural commitments
    2. Interpersonal
        a. Choice of friends
        b. Bases—dorm, major sports, political, romantic/sexual/companion
    3. Living arrangement
        a. Nature of change
        b. Availability/adequacy
        c. Impact on academic life
        d. Impact on social life

C. *Two-Year Comparison*
    1. Academic
    2. Time management
    3. Quality/level of satisfaction; "sophomore slump"

D. *Junior-Year Plans or Expectations*

E. *Other Comments and Observations*
(Including remarks concerning study—questionnaires, interviews, and so on.)

F. *Interviewer's Global Observations*
    1. Appearance and demeanor
    2. Clarity and seriousness of academic purpose
    3. Scope of intellectual development
    4. Maturity

5.   General level of contentment/satisfaction

This outline was accompanied by a lengthy guide that discussed each segment of the interview and emphasized the specific types of probing to be done. The result was considerably greater uniformity in the interview reports than was obtained in the freshman year, but a corresponding loss of vividness.

For the junior and senior years the general format of the sophomore year was retained but somewhat greater leeway was given to the interviewers in terms of the topics to be explored in depth with the students. The senior interview also contained a section asking for students to make a retrospective assessment of their entire undergraduate careers, and another section concerning their lives five and ten years after graduation. The latter paralleled a segment of the senior questionnaire that asked about their ten-year outlook on jobs, education, marriage, having children, and the like. These two sections of the interview schedule are reproduced here:

Senior Interview Guidelines

(Retrospective and Future Plans Sections)

Overview of Stanford Experience

6.   *Overall evaluation*
Possible questions: How do you evaluate your time at Stanford overall? What were the high and low points of your years here? In a general sense, what are you taking away with you? In what ways has being at Stanford made a difference for you? If you had (have) a younger sibling, would (will) you advise him or her to attend Stanford? Why or why not?
7.   *Retrospective evaluation of decisions made*
Possible questions: With the wisdom of hindsight, how do you feel about the choices you made along the way? Knowing what you know now, would you have done anything differently in terms of choosing courses or your major, or making plans for a career? What about other kinds of opportunities— are there any you wish you'd taken advantage of?

8.   *Impact of external events*
      Possible questions: Looking back over your four years, what
      are the major nonacademic events that have had an impact
      on your education here? (This may include relationships
      with parents or family events, relationships with friends,
      health problems, money problems, events connected with eth-
      nic group membership, and so on.)

9.   *Future Plans*
      Inquire about both immediate and longer-term plans, as well
      as hopes for the future. As a guide to thinking about the
      longer-run future, ask the student to focus on a time approxi-
      mately five years hence, and then approximately ten years
      hence. What do they imagine or predict their lives will be like
      at those points? The emphasis will be on educational and ca-
      reer plans, but other aspects of life should be discussed as
      well. In what ways will personal concerns and relationships
      affect the student's career plans, and vice versa? What sort of
      philosophy or strategy is guiding the student in making these
      plans?

The Interview Reports. The interviewers were asked to
prepare reports each year as soon after completing the interviews as
possible; most of the interviewers completed all of their reports
eventually. The excerpts and biographies we present in the text
often rely on the more thorough and colorful reports, because such
reports make for more interesting reading and those reports indicate
better understanding and insight into the students' character and
thinking.

Questionnaires and Questionnaire Coding

Questionnaires. A comprehensive questionnaire was
administered to students each spring of the four years. Students who
did not graduate in four years received the senior questionnaire in
the middle of their last quarter before graduation; those who did not
graduate by the end of fall quarter of their sixth year since
matriculation (December 1982) were not given the senior
questionnaire, as we closed the data-gathering portion of the study
at that point. Students who stopped out long enough to fall behind
their classmates were given a special interview to learn about their

experiences away from campus and reintegrate them into the study. They generally filled out the questionnaires at the same time as their classmates, except in a few cases where the students stopped out for a full year or more and the current year's questionnaire was inappropriate.

The questionnaires sought information on a wide range of topics, by no means all of which have been used in this book. The senior questionnaire, which was the most comprehensive of all, had the following outline form:

Senior Questionnaire Outline

Section A: Senior-Year Experiences
I.   Academic Interests
    A.   Academic concentration
    B.   Major(s)
    C.   Primary academic interest
    D.   Factors influential in choice of courses (twenty-three items, asked separately for courses within the major and courses outside the major)
II. Academic Advising and Other Influences
    A.   Frequency of consulting faculty members within major department
    B.   Sources of advice on courses, graduate or professional school plans, career planning, personal problems, and academic difficulty (six items): how much advice sought, helpfulness of advice
    C.   Individuals who were particularly significant during the year
    D.   Courses that were particularly significant during the year
    E.   Other forces that shaped their academic experiences during the year
III. Academic Problems
    A.   Types of academic assistance needed (six items)
    B.   Degree to which courses were demanding during the year
    C.   Reasons for difficulties with courses (twelve items)
IV. Employment

A.   Amount of time spent working during the year, paid or unpaid

B.   Reasons for working (seven items)

V.   Time Allocation and Activities

A.   Frequency of engaging in various activities, ranging from "go to the movies" to "political activities" to "serious discussion of personal concerns or relationships" (eighteen items)

B.   Time spent in class and studying

C.   Non-course-related reading done during the year: magazines, books, journals, and so on (nine items)

D.   Retrospective view of frequency of engaging in various activities during the freshman year (parallel to section V.A)

VI. Junior-Senior Year Comparison

Rating of senior year and junior year on a scale from 1 = not at all satisfied to 5 = very satisfied on nine dimensions, including interaction with instructors, interest in courses, sense of belonging, and overall level of contentment.

Section B: Overview of Stanford Experience

I.   Residential History: listing of all on-campus or off-campus residences while a student

II. Overseas Experiences

A.   Overseas program attended

B.   Factors influencing decision to go overseas and level of satisfaction (eight items, ranging from "exposure to people and life-styles of another country" to "have a break from school")

III. Stopping Out

A.   Length of stop-out period

B.   Description of activities while stopped out

C.   Factors influencing decision to stop out (ten items, ranging from "financial difficulties" to "desire to travel")

D.   Level of satisfaction with experience and reasons for this response

IV. Financial Planning

    A.   Assessment of how college education was financed; changes student would make in hindsight

    B.   Level of personal indebtedness for educational expenditures

V.   Academic and Nonacademic Activities and Accomplishments

    A.   Honors, prizes, or other recognition for academic or nonacademic accomplishments during college years

    B.   Activities to which student devoted a significant amount of time during the college years: nonclassroom academic work, the arts, athletics, volunteer service, organized university activities, organized off-campus activities, other

VI.   Overall Assessment

    A.   Characterization of each of the undergraduate years (open-ended question, seeking adjectives and more lengthy descriptions)

    B.   Three people who know the student well and could be contacted later to talk about the student's experiences at the university

Section C: Future Plans

I.   Graduation and Beyond

    A.   Date of graduation; reasons for graduating late, if applicable

    B.   Plans for year following graduation

    C.   Eventual academic degrees to be pursued

    D.   Scores on standardized tests taken for graduate or professional school

II.   Career Plans

    A.   Long-run career interests (up to three, with degree of certainty of each)

    B.   Factors influential in choice of career (twenty-one items)

    C.   Characteristics desired in occupation or profession (twelve items)

    D.   Types of activities involved in likely eventual career, ranging from teaching to management to applying artistic skills (seven items)

   E.   Factors that will influence development of career, ranging from preference for a geographical area to career
commitments of spouse (seven items)

III.   Overview of Future Plans

   A.   Projection of life ten years from now

   B.   Expectations concerning marriage or children within
ten years

   C.   Expectations concerning children ever

Section D: Family Background

I.   Marital Status of Parents

   A.   Father

   B.   Mother

   C.   If divorced, length of time

II.   Occupation and Education of Parents

   A.   Father

   B.   Mother (includes detailed information on how much
mother worked during student's childhood)

III.   Overall Family Status

   A.   Family income

   B.   Self-designated social class, choosing from categories for
lower, working, lower-middle, middle, upper-middle,
and upper class.

Three sections not included in the senior questionnaire were
asked in earlier years. One is a series of twenty-three items related
to the student's reasons for going to college, ranging from "learning
to think critically" to "future financial security" to "developing a
sense of personal identity." The second is a series of eighteen
sources of influence on the choice of a major, parallel to the sources
of influence on choice of career. The final section is a set of eleven
items representing possibly desirable characteristics of a major,
ranging from "interesting subject" to "useful in career field" to
"department's national reputation." These sections were omitted
from the senior questionnaire because they were no longer relevant.

One thorny methodological problem arose in comparing the freshman questionnaire responses to those of later years—the scales, and sometimes the items themselves, were changed between the freshman and sophomore questionnaires in order to solve problems with the initial questionnaire. In some cases only the labels on the scales were changed; for example, the five-point scales for "reasons for attending college" in the freshman year were labeled 1 = not at all influential and 5 = extremely influential; in the sophomore and junior years the labels were 1 = not influential and 5 = very influential, a change that probably produced more extreme responses. In other cases the items themselves were modified. For example, "general education" as a reason for attending college became "general liberal education," and "encourages me to be creative and original" as a desired characteristic of an occupation became "requires creativity and originality," a change that probably produced lower responses. A third problem was that some four-point scales used in the freshman year were transformed into five-point scales. One example is the section on desired character- istics of a career, where responses ranged from 1 = very important to 4 = not at all important in the freshman year but from 1 = not important to 5 = very important in later years.

Such problems affected over half of all the items using ordinal scales on the freshman questionnaire, making exact comparisons between that year's responses and later responses impossible. However, the rank-order of importance of the various items was not affected by changes in the scales, so that comparisons of this rougher sort could still be made. Further evidence that these problems were not prohibitively great appeared when we found that the correlations between the freshman and sophomore intellectual- ism scales, and between the freshman and sophomore careerism scales, were higher than the correlations for all other sets of years, indicating that the numerous small problems of noncomparability did not produce a large general problem. In combining the freshman and sophomore items to produce these and other scales, we weighted the freshman items more heavily when necessary to compensate for the fact that they used maximum values of four instead of five, but we also found that with or without the weighting the results obtained in data analyses using these scales were quite similar. In short, the noncomparability of the freshman questionnaire with other questionnaires did not pose insurmountable difficulties, but in a number of places we have had to introduce corrections to produce appropriate and meaningful results.

As seniors the students were also given the Senior Survey questionnaire, an instrument that is mailed every year to all graduating students just before they leave the university. This questionnaire seeks student views on a number of aspects of the undergraduate program, including faculty teaching, teaching assistants, the courses they have taken, their liberal education, academic advising, and so on. It also asks students to rate themselves on a large number of ability and knowledge dimensions, including writing English; using a foreign language; understanding mathematics, the natural sciences, social institutions, technology, government, Western culture; and so on. The items on the Senior Survey instrument provided us with much of the material we used to assess student satisfaction with the university experience and their views on their own academic accomplishments. These items all use five-point ordinal scales; the scales that ask for basic student assessments range from "very poor" to "excellent," while the scales that ask about the importance of the items range from "very slight" to "very great." The students completed the Senior Survey questionnaire at the same time as the senior questionnaire, that is, during the quarter immediately preceding graduation.

Questionnaire Coding. Most of the questionnaire coding was completely straightforward; responses were entered onto code sheets and then checked by a separate coder. A number of items required special category schemes; they were coded as follows:

(a)   School divisions. According to the long-standing practice of the university, the school divisions group major departments as follows:

Humanities: Art, Chinese and Japanese, Classics, Comparative Literature, Drama, East Asian Studies, English, French and Italian, German Studies, History, Humanities Special Programs, Music, Philosophy and Religious Studies, Slavic Languages, and Spanish and Portuguese

Social Sciences: Anthropology, Communication, Economics, Political Science, Psychology, Sociology

Natural Sciences: Biology, Chemistry, Mathematics, Physics

Engineering (combined with Earth Sciences): Chemical, Civil, Electrical, General, Industrial, and Mechanical Engineering; Applied Earth Sciences, Geology, Geophysics, and Petroleum Engineering

Interdepartmental Programs: African and Afro-American Studies, American Studies, Human Biology, Human Language, International Relations, Latin American Studies, Mathematical Sciences, Public Policy, and Values, Technology, and Society

Other: Medical Microbiology, Individually Designed

(b)   Career interests. In analyzing student career choices we used a purely nominal coding scheme, grouping professions as follows:

Business: executive, manager, entrepreneur, accountant, and so on

Law: attorney, judge; includes international law

Medicine: doctor, dentist, veterinarian, and so on

Engineering: engineer, computer programmer, inventor, technical fields of all sorts

Humanities-related careers: writing, entertainment, the arts, communication, journalism

Teaching: elementary, secondary, junior college, or college where the emphasis is on teaching rather than research

Public administration and social science fields: public planning, policy analysis, politics, social work, social research, psychology

Natural science fields and other health professions: chemist, biologist, physicist, nurse, nurse practitioner, and so on

Because less than half the students planned to have careers in the wide variety of areas outside the four standard fields of business, law, medicine, and engineering, some small number of categories was necessary to be able to perform meaningful statistical analyses. Hence the latter four categories each combines a broad range of types of occupations. Such simplification of the vocational world is inevitable when dealing with a sample of this size.

(c)   Educational level. To code for students' educational aspirations, ambiguity arises with respect to dividing advanced degrees into two separate categories—master's-level degrees and doctoral-level degrees. We settled on the following:

Master's level: M.A., M.S., M.B.A.

Doctoral level: Ph.D., M.D., D.V.M., J.D., Ed.D., Doctor of Divinity

(d)   Construction of the Socioeconomic Status (SES) Index. To provide a single overall measure of the students' socioeconomic status, we combined four separate indicators drawn from the senior questionnaire. They include father's occupation, father's education, family income, and self-designated social class. Mother's educational level and occupation were not included for two reasons. First, family socioeconomic standing is related primarily to characteristics of the father rather than the mother, though some change has occurred in this respect in the past two decades. Second, about half of the mothers were homemakers without paid occupational positions. Thus the number of cases that could be measured using mother's occupation was quite low.

Specific details for coding the four variables making up the Socioeconomic Status (SES) Index are as follows:

(i) Occupations. For father's occupation we used Hollingshead's (1958) categories, which include the following, ranked from high status to low:

1. Higher executives of large concerns, proprietors, and major professionals
2. Business managers, proprietors of medium-sized businesses, and lesser professionals
3. Administrative personnel, owners of small businesses, and minor professionals
4. Clerical and sales workers, technicians, and owners of little businesses
5. Skilled manual employees
6. Machine operators and semiskilled employees
7. Unskilled employees
    For coding mother's occupation, homemakers and students were coded 8.

(ii) Educational level. Educational level was coded in conventional terms: high school graduate or less; some college; college graduate; advanced (graduate) degree. Advanced degrees were separated into master's-level and doctoral-level degrees, as described earlier, because so many fathers had advanced degrees that further differentiation was necessary.

(iii) Family income. An item on the senior questionnaire asked for family income in a series of categories, ranging from less than $10,000 to more than $100,000. The variable ranged from 1 to 8.

(iv) Self-designated social class. Students were also asked on the senior questionnaire to indicate their social class, choosing from the terms lower (coded 1), working, lower-middle, middle, upper-middle, and upper class (coded 5). Unfortunately (but predictably), the great majority clustered in the upper-middle class, but there was enough useful variation to include this variable.

The sum of these variables, the SES Index, has a theoretical range of 4 to 27. The actual variable had a minimum of 6 (one student) and a maximum of 27 (five students), with 26 percent of the students scoring below 20 and 30 percent above 23. There was thus considerable clustering in the range from 20 to 23. In using the SES Index we have employed it both as an ordinal variable and as a recoded grouped variable, splitting students into three roughly equal groups: 6 to 21, 22 to 23, and 24 to 27. We also tried some analyses in which we employed somewhat different cutting points and found that substantive conclusions were not altered significantly by these changes.

(e) Construction of the Extracurricular Involvement Index. A major section of the senior questionnaire asked students to indicate the "academic and nonacademic activities and accomplishments" of their years in college. The section specified that students should describe activities that "reflect significant commitment or achievement on your part," not just casual involvement. Five categories of activities were identified, as follows:

1. Academic experience beyond the classroom (independent research, honor's work, projects, papers, symposiums, academic internships, and so on)

2. Arts (dance, drama, music, film, broadcasting, creative writing, journalism, publications, forensics, studio art, and so on)
3. Athletics (intramurals, club sports, varsity or other organized athletic activity)
4. Service-oriented involvement (resident assistant, teaching assistant, volunteering, advising, counseling, tutoring, panels/ committees, and so on)
5. Organized Stanford activities (student or residence government, clubs, societies, and so on)

Students were free to indicate as many activities in each category as they wished; however, we coded only two items for each category. We thus had a total of ten variables measuring significant extracurricular activity. The Involvement Index then was computed as the sum of the ten separate variables, each one treated as either present or absent. Thus, a highly active student might indicate one activity in each of four areas, and a second activity in three of the four, for a total of seven significant activities and a score of 7 on the Involvement Index, while an inactive student might indicate only one activity in each of two areas, for a score of 2 on the Index. The maximum score is then 10, the minimum 0. The mean for all students was 4.0 activities, with 25 percent of the students reporting two or fewer activities and 24 percent reporting six or more activities.

Construction of the Typology

Items from three sections in the questionnaires were used to construct the intellectualism and careerism scales. These sections are (a) reasons for attending college (not asked in the senior year), (b) characteristics desired in an academic major (also not asked in the senior year), and (c) characteristics desired in a career. Because two of these sections were not included on the senior questionnaire, we concentrated our analyses on the three earlier questionnaires. In selecting items for the scales we initially analyzed items from each questionnaire separately, performing factor analyses of all items from each of these three sections to identify the items that formed the most cohesive sets of indicators. The factor analyses usually produced three factors, one of which was clearly related to intellectual challenge and development and a second that entailed career preparation and career success. The third (and sometimes fourth) factors, always less important than the other two, were highly varied in character.

Not all of the items used in these analyses loaded well on either the intellectualism or careerism factor; such items were omitted from further analysis. Conversely, some items that did not have obvious theoretical relevance to one or the other concept but loaded highly on one of the factors were included in the scales. This was done to increase the number of items used and thereby improve scale reliability. The items finally selected for analysis are given in Table 1.

We then computed summary indexes using all relevant variables that loaded highly on each scale for each year (the freshman, sophomore, and junior questionnaires), producing three intellectualism scales and three careerism scales. The intellectualism scales were highly correlated with each other, with the correlations ranging from .60 to .73 (for example, the correlation between the freshman intellectualism scale and the sophomore intellectualism scale was .69). The careerism scales were also highly intercorrelated, with coefficients in this same range. Each scale was also highly correlated with a summary scale that included all items from all four questionnaires; that is, each year's intellectualism scale was highly correlated with a summary scale that included all items from all four questionnaires, and each year's careerism scale was highly correlated with a summary careerism scale.

We were then faced with the decision of selecting a scale or scales for use in constructing the typology. Two conflicting criteria determined the choice. First, the scales should be stable and highly reliable. Because scale stability and reliability improve as the number of items increases, the overall summary scales using items from all four questionnaires would be most appropriate. But, second, the scales should maximize the number of cases available for analysis, especially since many of our background and outcome variables are categorical in nature and would involve cross-tabulations producing tables with a large number of cells. From this point of view, selecting scales from only one questionnaire (either the freshman or sophomore questionnaire) would be most desirable. We decided to compromise by combining the freshman and sophomore scales, thereby producing stable and reliable scales that also had close to the maximum available cases (nearly all of the students who completed the freshman questionnaire also completed the sophomore questionnaire). Further, the correlations between the two intellectualism scales for the freshman and sophomore years were higher than for any other pair of years, and the same was true of the careerism scales for the freshman and sophomore years; there thus appeared to be a natural affinity between the two years.

The net result was an intellectualism scale containing a total of twenty-nine variables and a careerism scale containing twenty-six variables. Most of the items used in the scales had a range of 1 to 5 (usually labeled "not important" to "very important"), while a few had a range of 1 to 4. Hence, the intellectualism scale had a theoretical range of 29 to 142 while the careerism scale had a theoretical range of 26 to 126. The lowest intellectualism score actually indicated by any student was 73, or an average of about 2.5 on a five-point scale, and the maximum was 139. The lowest careerism score was 43, an average of about 1.7 on a five-point scale, and the maximum was 126, the theoretical maximum. There is thus a much higher "floor" for the intellectualism variable; a student who considers the intellectually related variables to be uniformly of only moderate importance in his goals and decisions is very low in intellectualism compared to his fellow students.

The intellectualism and careerism scales, based on freshman and sophomore questionnaire responses, formed the basis of the typology used in the text. The correlation between the two scales was very low ($r = .10$, $p = $ n.s.), so a simple cross-tabulation of the scales allowed us to produce a four-category typology that could be used to study the impact of intellectualism and careerism on students' college experiences. We have already described in Chapter Two the procedure we followed in establishing the four types and using the questionnaire and interview material to study them. We refer the reader to that chapter for more details.

Appendix III: Tables Describing Choice and Change in the Undergraduate Years

Appendix III, Table 1. Career Choice by Year in School.

	Freshman	Sophomore	Junior	Senior
Business	16.7%	20.8%	24.1%	28.8%
Law	19.5	17.0	17.9	17.0
Medicine	20.7	17.0	16.0	15.1
Engineering	10.3	11.3	10.4	6.6
Writing/communication/arts	13.2	10.8	9.0	11.3
Teaching	5.7	5.7	6.6	10.4
Public administration/ social sciences	5.7	8.5	7.5	6.6
Natural sciences/other health professions	8.0	9.0	8.5	4.2
Don't know or homemaker	17.9	---	---	---

Note: Constant cases (N = 212); 38 freshmen said "don't know" or "homemaker."

Appendix III, Table 2. Major Choice by Year in School.

	Freshman	Sophomore	Junior	Senior
Humanities	14.4%	16.7%	19.4%	18.1%
Social sciences	26.4	27.8	24.5	25.9
Natural sciences	24.1	20.4	16.7	16.7
Interdepartmental programs	16.2	15.7	20.4	20.8
Engineering/earth sciences	18.5	18.1	17.6	16.7
Other	0.5	1.4	1.4	1.9

Note: Constant cases; N = 216.

Appendix III, Table 3. Senior Career Choice by Sex, Ethnicity, and Socioeconomic Status.

	Sex		Ethnicity			Socioeconomic Status		
	Men	Women	Black/Chicano	Asian American	Caucasian	Lower	Middle	Higher
Business	29.4%	28.0	29.2%	7.1	29.4	20.6%	31.5	33.3
Law	20.2	12.9	20.8	14.3	16.5	17.5	22.2	11.9
Medicine	16.0	14.0	8.3	35.7	14.7	12.7	9.3	23.8
Engineering	8.4	4.3	8.3	21.4	5.3	15.9	1.9	2.4
Writing/ communication/ arts	10.1	12.9	12.5	7.1	11.8	9.5	16.7	7.1
Teaching	9.2	11.8	12.5	7.1	10.6	14.3	7.4	7.1
Public administration/ social sciences	3.4	10.8	8.3	7.1	6.5	6.3	3.7	9.5
Natural sciences/ other health	3.4	5.4	0.0	0.0	5.3	3.2	7.4	4.8

Note: Constant cases; 119 men, 93 women; 24 Black/Chicano, 14 Asian American, 170 Caucasian students; 63 lower socioeconomic status, 54 middle status, 42 higher status.

Appendix III, Table 4. Change of Major, Freshman to Senior Year.
(N = 238)

(A) Stability and movement out

| | Senior major | | | | | |
Freshman major	Humanities	Social sciences	Natural sciences	Interdept. programs	Engineering/ earth sciences	N
Humanities	68%	12%	12%	9%	0%	34
Social sciences	11	67	2	14	3	63
Natural sciences	9	11	59	14	7	56
Interdepartmental programs	15	18	0	63	3	40
Engineering/ earth sciences	5	5	5	9	75	44

(B) Movement in

| | Freshman major | | | | | |
Senior major	Humanities	Social sciences	Natural sciences	Interdept. programs	Engineering/ earth sciences	N
Humanities	54%	16%	12%	14%	5	43
Social sciences	7	68	10	11	3	62
Natural sciences	10	3	83	0	5	40
Interdepartmental programs	6	18	16	51	8	49
Engineering/ earth sciences	0	5	10	3	83	40

Appendix III, Table 5. Senior Major Choice by Sex and Ethnicity.

	Sex		Ethnicity	
Humanities				
	Men	14.3%	Black/Chicano	13.6%
	Women	18.6	Asian American	7.7
			Caucasian	17.6
Social sciences				
	Men	25.9	Black/Chicano	50.0
	Women	27.9	Asian American	15.4
			Caucasian	25.2
Natural sciences				
	Men	17.9	Black/Chicano	4.5
	Women	14.0	Asian American	30.8
			Caucasian	16.4
Interdepartmental programs				
	Men	21.4	Black/Chicano	4.5
	Women	20.9	Asian American	15.4
			Caucasian	23.9
Engineering/earth sciences				
	Men	18.8	Black/Chicano	22.7
	Women	16.3	Asian American	30.8
			Caucasian	15.1

Note: Constant cases; 112 men, 86 women; 22 Black/Chicano, 13 Asian American, 159 Caucasian students.

Appendix III, Table 6. Influences on Choice of Career.
(Means, based on 1-5 scale)

	Freshman[a] (N = 242)	Sophomore (N = 291)	Junior (N = 257)	Senior (N = 242)
Academic advisor	1.4	1.7	1.9	2.0
Other faculty	1.6	1.9	2.1	2.3
Parents	2.8	2.8	2.8	3.0
Siblings	1.6	1.7	1.7	2.0
Roommates	1.2	1.6	1.6	2.0
Dorm/house resident asst.[b]	---	1.3	1.3	1.5
Other students	2.0	2.3	2.5	2.9
Alumni	1.2	1.3	1.4	1.7
Career Placement Center	1.2	1.5	1.5	1.8
Coursework[b]	---	3.1	3.2	3.5
Work experience outside SU[c])	2.6	3.0	3.1	3.4
Work experience at SU)		2.6	2.8	2.9
High school teacher	2.0	1.7	1.7	1.7
Knowledge of job trends	2.8	2.8	2.6	2.5

[a] Originally a 1-3 scale, converted to 1-5 scale to facilitate comparison.
[b] Not asked freshman year.
[c] Work experience at and outside Stanford not differentiated freshman year.

Appendix III, Table 7. Sources of Advice About Various Topics.

	Sophomore (N = 282)	Junior (N = 259)	Senior (N = 242)
Advisor			
Current courses	59%	62%	62%
Career planning	52	55	45
Personal problems	34	27	19
Academic difficulty	44	38	30
Other faculty			
Current courses	57	62	57
Career planning	42	50	45
Personal problems	27	24	17
Academic difficulty	47	43	27
Parents			
Current courses	47	40	27
Career planning	82	82	74
Personal problems	91	90	80
Academic difficulty	57	55	31
Fellow students			
Current courses	94	93	91
Career planning	70	75	71
Personal problems	93	94	88
Academic difficulty	83	74	61

Appendix IV: Tables Describing Determinants and Outcomes of the Typology of Academic Orientation

Appendix IV, Table 1. Effects of Demographic Variables.

	Careerists	Intellectuals	Strivers	Unconnected	N
Gender					
Men	29.0%	15.3%	25.2%	30.5%	131
Women	16.2	34.3	25.7	23.8	105
	Chi-square = 14.0		$p < .01$		
Ethnicity					
Blacks and Chicanos	24.1	13.8	34.5	27.6	29
Asian Americans	21.4	14.3	35.7	28.6	14
Caucasians	23.7	26.9	22.0	27.4	186
	Chi-square = 4.8		p = n. s.		
Socioeconomic Status Index					
Lower SES group	28.8	13.7	27.4	30.1	73
Middle SES group	28.1	26.3	22.8	22.8	57
Upper SES group	20.0	36.4	18.2	25.5	55
	Chi-square = 9.7		p = n. s.		

Father's Occupation

	%	%	%	%	N
Skilled manual to lesser professionals, executives	29.9%	14.9%	26.9%	28.4%	67
Skilled manual	9.1	9.1	63.6	18.2	11
Clerical, sales	40.0	0.0	40.0	20.0	5
Minor professionals	25.0	16.7	8.3	50.0	12
Lesser professionals, executives	35.9	17.9	20.5	25.6	39
Major professionals, executives	23.2	28.8	23.2	24.8	125

Chi-square = 30.3 $p < .01$

Father's Specific Occupation

	%	%	%	%	N
Doctor	12.1	30.3	39.4	18.2	33
Lawyer	22.2	22.2	11.1	44.4	9
Corporate executive	34.1	27.3	6.8	31.8	44
College professor	22.2	33.3	11.1	33.3	18
Engineer	15.4	7.7	30.8	46.2	13
Blue collar worker	11.1	0.0	66.7	22.2	9
Own small business	27.3	36.4	9.1	27.3	11

Appendix IV, Table 1. Effects of Demographic Variables, Cont'd.

	Careerists	Intellectuals	Strivers	Unconnected	N
Father's Subordinates					
None	28.6%	14.3%	20.0%	37.1%	35
1-10 people	24.7	21.9	30.1	23.3	73
11-50 people	16.3	32.6	27.9	23.3	43
51 + people	38.5	26.9	11.5	23.1	26
	Chi-square = 11.5		p = n. s.		
Father's Education					
Less than college education	24.2	9.1	33.3	33.3	33
Less than high school	0.0	20.0	20.0	60.0	5
Completed high school	38.5	0.0	38.5	23.1	13
Some college	20.0	13.3	33.3	33.3	15
College graduate	27.5	27.5	20.3	24.6	69
Lower advanced degree	39.5	16.3	16.3	27.9	43
Higher advanced degree	10.0	34.0	32.0	24.0	50
	Chi-square = 25.1		p < .05		

Mother's Occupation

Minor professionals, clerical, sales	17.8%	13.3%	35.6%	33.3%	45
Clerical, sales	16.7	4.1	37.5	41.7	24
Minor professionals	19.0	23.8	33.3	23.8	21
Major, lesser professionals, executives	31.0	29.3	20.7	19.0	58
Lesser professionals, executives	30.2	27.9	20.9	20.9	43
Major professionals, executives	33.3	33.3	20.0	13.3	15
Homemakers	28.4	22.7	23.9	25.0	88

Chi-square = 17.5 p = n. s.

Length of Mother's Career

Less than five years	23.1	23.1	33.3	20.5	39
Six years or more	22.6	22.6	22.6	32.3	62
Homemakers	28.4	22.7	23.9	25.0	88

Chi-square = 3.2 p = n. s.

Mother's Education

High school or less	23.3%	6.6%	26.7%	43.3%	30
Some college	22.0	22.0	26.8	29.3	41
College graduate	28.6	26.0	22.1	23.4	77
Advanced degree	23.5	31.4	27.5	17.6	51

Chi-square = 14.3 p = n. s.

Appendix IV, Table 1. Effects of Demographic Variables, Cont'd.

	Careerists	Intellectuals	Strivers	Unconnected	N
Family Income					
Less than $39,999	23.2	11.6	33.3	31.9	69
Less than $10,000	14.3	14.3	42.9	28.6	7
$10,000 to $19,999	21.4	14.3	50.0	14.3	14
$20,000 to $29,999	32.1	10.7	17.9	39.3	28
$30,000 to $39,999	15.0	10.0	40.0	35.0	20
$40,000 to $74,999	31.7	33.3	15.0	20.0	60
$40,000 to $49,999	25.0	20.0	25.0	30.0	20
$50,000 to $74,999	35.0	40.0	10.0	15.0	40
More than $75,000	24.2	27.4	22.6	25.8	62
$75,000 to $99,999	28.6	28.6	14.3	28.6	28
More than $100,000	20.6	26.5	29.4	23.5	34

Chi-square = 30.6   p < .10 (individual categories)
Chi-square = 14.3   p < .05 (grouped categories)

	Careerists	Intellectuals	Strivers	Unconnected	N
Self-Described Social Class					
Lower to middle class	26.5	11.8	33.8	27.9	68
Working class	16.7	0.0	33.3	50.0	6
Lower-middle class	23.1	15.4	38.5	23.1	13
Middle class	28.6	12.2	32.7	26.5	49
Upper-middle, upper class	25.1	29.9	18.9	26.0	127
Upper-middle class	25.6	29.9	19.7	24.8	117
Upper class	20.0	30.0	10.0	40.0	10

Chi-square = 13.8   p = n. s. (individual categories)
Chi-square = 11.6   p < .10 (grouped categories)

Appendix IV, Table 2. Effects of Student Academic Characteristics.

High School Type	Careerists	Intellectuals	Strivers	Unconnected	N
Public	25.7%	24.6%	22.8%	26.9%	171
Private	16.9	21.5	32.3	29.2	65
	Chi-square = 9.6		p = n. s.		
Verbal SAT Score					
200 thru 610	26.3	25.4	29.8	18.4	114
611 thru 800	20.8	21.7	20.8	36.7	120
	Chi-square = 10.0		p < .05		
Math SAT Score					
200 thru 600	18.9	25.5	29.2	26.4	106
601 thru 800	27.3	21.9	21.9	28.9	128
	Chi-square = 3.5		p = n. s.		

Appendix IV, Table 2. Effects of Student Academic Characteristics, Cont'd.

	Careerists	Intellectuals	Strivers	Unconnected	N
Cross-Tabulated SAT Score					
High verbal, low math	15.0%	20.0%	25.0%	40.0%	40
Low verbal, high math	33.3	20.8	27.1	18.8	48
High verbal, high math	23.8	22.5	18.8	35.0	80
Low verbal, low math	21.2	28.8	31.8	18.2	66
	Chi-square = 14.3		p = n. s.		
Cross-Tabulated SAT Score for Men					
High verbal, low math	21.4	7.1	42.9	28.6	14
Low verbal, high math	45.2	16.1	16.1	22.6	31
High verbal, high math	29.8	14.0	17.5	38.6	57
Low verbal, low math	14.3	21.4	39.3	25.0	28
	Chi-square = 15.0		p < .10		
Cross-Tabulated SAT Score for Women					
High verbal, low math	11.5	26.9	15.4	46.2	26
Low verbal, high math	11.8	29.4	47.1	11.8	17
High verbal, high math	8.7	43.5	21.7	26.1	23
Low verbal, low math	26.3	34.2	26.3	13.2	38
	Chi-square = 17.3		p < .05		

Verbal SAT Score for Men

200 thru 610	30.5	18.6	27.1	23.7	59
611 thru 800	28.2	12.7	22.5	36.6	71

Chi-square = 2.8   p = n. s.

Verbal SAT Score for Women

200 thru 610	21.8	32.7	32.7	12.7	55
611 thru 800	10.2	34.7	18.4	36.7	49

Chi-square = 10.4   p < .05

Math SAT Score for Men

200 thru 600	16.7	16.7	40.5	26.2	42
601 thru 800	35.2	14.8	17.0	33.0	88

Chi-square = 10.2   p < .05

Math SAT Score for Women

200 thru 600	20.3	31.3	21.9	26.6	64
601 thru 800	10.0	37.5	32.5	20.0	40

Chi-square = 3.4   p = n. s.

Appendix IV, Table 3. Effects of Sources of Influence.

	Careerists	Intellectuals	Strivers	Unconnected	N
Total Family Influence					
Low influence	15.2%	29.1%	19.0%	36.7%	79
High influence	34.0	15.5	29.9	20.6	97
	Chi-square = 15.9		$p < .01$		
Total Faculty Influence					
Low influence	26.6	12.8	23.4	37.2	94
High influence	23.3	29.1	29.1	18.6	86
	Chi-square = 12.1		$p < .01$		
Total Student Influence					
Low influence	23.8	22.6	19.0	34.5	84
High influence	27.2	20.7	28.3	23.9	92
	Chi-square = 3.5		p = n. s.		
Total Job Market Influence					
Low influence	17.3	25.5	20.4	36.7	98
High influence	33.3	16.7	33.3	16.7	78
	Chi-square = 15.2		$p < .01$		
Total Work Experience Influence					
Low influence	30.1	17.2	23.7	29.0	93
High influence	19.0	23.8	29.8	27.4	84
	Chi-square = 3.8		p = n. s.		
Total Coursework Influence					
Low influence	24.2	18.2	20.5	37.1	132
High influence	21.0	31.0	32.0	16.0	100
	Chi-square = 16.2		$p < .01$		

Appendix IV, Table 4. Major and Career Choice and Change.

| | School Division of Major | | | | | |
	Humanities	Social sciences	Natural sciences	Interdept. programs	Engineering/ earth sciences	N
Freshman Major Choice						
Careerists	4.0%	30.0%	28.0%	12.0%	26.0%	50
Intellectuals	34.6	25.0	7.7	19.2	13.5	50
Strivers	7.3	18.2	25.5	23.6	23.6	55
Unconnected	16.9	27.1	27.1	6.8	22.0	59
		Chi-square = 38.2		p < .01		
Major at Graduation						
Careerists	5.9	35.3	17.6	17.6	23.5	51
Intellectuals	31.4	23.5	7.8	27.5	7.8	51
Strivers	12.3	24.6	15.8	26.3	21.1	57
Unconnected	27.3	23.6	18.2	16.4	12.7	55
		Chi-square = 25.8		p < .05		
Major at Graduation by Gender						
Careerists						
Men	2.9	35.3	20.6	14.7	26.5	34
Women	11.8	35.3	11.8	23.5	17.6	17
		Chi-square = 2.9		p = n. s.		
Intellectuals						
Men	31.6	21.1	15.8	31.6	0.0	19
Women	31.3	25.0	3.1	25.0	12.5	32
		Chi-square = 5.7		p = n. s.		
Strivers						
Men	12.9	22.6	19.4	22.6	22.6	31
Women	11.5	26.9	11.5	30.8	19.2	26
		Chi-square = 1.11		p = n. s.		
Unconnected						
Men	18.6	25.0	18.8	18.8	15.6	32
Women	39.1	21.7	17.4	13.0	8.7	23
		Chi-square = 3.6		p = n. s.		

Appendix IV, Table 4. Major and Career Choice and Change, Cont'd.

Major Department at Graduation, Men Only

	International relations	Electrical engineering	Industrial engineering	Human biology	Biology	Economics	English	History	N
Careerists	0.0%	5.9%	11.8%	8.8%	17.6%	26.5%	0.0%	0.0%	34
Intellectuals	15.8	0.0	0.0	10.5	10.5	0.0	15.8	10.5	19
Strivers	6.5	9.7	9.7	16.1	12.9	12.9	6.5	6.5	31
Unconnected	3.1	3.1	3.1	12.5	9.4	12.5	6.3	9.4	32

Major Department at Graduation, Women Only

	International relations	Industrial engineering	Human biology	Biology	Communication	Economics	English	N
Careerists	5.9%	11.8%	11.8%	11.8%	11.8%	17.6%	0.0%	17
Intellectuals	6.3	0.0	15.6	3.1	12.5	9.4	15.6	32
Strivers	15.4	7.7	11.5	11.5	7.7	11.5	3.8	26
Unconnected	0.0	0.0	8.7	17.4	8.7	4.3	17.4	23

Educational Aspirations Over Time

	Freshman year				Senior year			
	BA/S	MA/S	Ph.D, MD/JD	N	BA/S	MA/S	Ph.D, MD/JD	N
Careerists	12.0%	34.0%	54.0%	50	4.0%	46.0%	50.0%	50
Intellectuals	29.8	21.3	48.9	47	13.0	52.2	34.8	46
Strivers	13.6	30.5	55.9	59	6.3	50.0	43.8	48
Unconnected	30.9	32.7	36.4	55	10.2	51.0	38.8	49

Freshman year: Chi-square = 11.9 p < .10

Senior year: Chi-square = 4.5 p = n.s.

Educational Aspirations by Gender, Senior Year

	Men				Women			
	BA/S	MA/S	Ph.D, MD/JD	N	BA/S	MA/S	Ph.D, MD/JD	N
Careerists	5.9	41.2	52.9	34	0.0	56.3	53.8	16
Intellectuals	13.3	20.0	66.7	15	12.9	67.7	19.4	31
Strivers	4.2	62.5	33.3	24	8.3	37.5	54.2	24
Unconnected	10.0	50.0	40.0	30	10.5	52.6	36.8	19

Men: Chi-square = 8.1 p = n.s.

Women: Chi-square = 9.1 p = n.s.

Career Categories

	Business	Law	Medicine	Engineering	Humanistic professions	Teaching	Public admin., social sci.	Natural sci., other health	N
Freshman Career Choice									
Careerists	20.8%	22.9%	22.9%	16.7%	6.2%	0.0%	2.1%	8.3%	48
Intellectuals	16.3	16.3	20.9	4.7	16.3	9.3	14.0	2.3	43
Strivers	21.3	21.3	17.0	10.6	12.8	4.3	4.3	8.5	47
Unconnected	6.0	14.0	22.0	10.0	14.0	10.0	8.0	16.0	50
					Chi-square = 30.3	p = n. s.			
Senior Career Choice									
Careerists	39.2	19.6	21.6	11.8	2.0	2.0	2.0	2.0	51
Intellectuals	27.3	11.4	9.1	2.3	22.7	13.6	9.1	4.5	44
Strivers	36.7	18.4	8.2	10.2	8.2	8.2	8.2	2.0	49
Unconnected	19.6	17.6	11.8	5.9	15.7	13.7	9.8	5.9	51
					Chi-square = 32.0	p < .10			
Senior Career Choice by Gender									
Careerists									
Men	37.1	20.0	22.9	17.1	0.0	2.9	0.0	0.0	35
Women	43.8	18.8	18.8	0.0	6.3	0.0	6.3	6.3	16
				Chi-square = 10.0	p = n. s.				
Intellectuals									
Men	20.0	20.0	20.0	0.0	13.3	20.0	0.0	6.7	15
Women	31.0	6.9	3.4	3.4	27.6	10.3	13.8	3.4	29
				Chi-square = 9.3	p = n. s.				
Strivers									
Men	41.7	20.8	4.2	8.3	12.5	8.3	4.2	0.0	24
Women	32.0	16.0	12.0	12.0	4.0	8.0	12.0	4.0	25
				Chi-square = 4.5	p = n. s.				
Unconnected									
Male	22.6	19.4	9.7	9.7	16.1	9.7	6.5	6.5	31
Female	15.0	15.0	15.0	0.0	15.0	20.0	15.0	5.0	20
				Chi-square = 4.6	p = n. s.				

Appendix IV, Table 4. Major and Career Choice and Change, Cont'd.

Career Choice (Grouped Version)

	Four standard professions	Four non-standard professions	Undecided	N
		Freshman Choice		
Careerists	74.0%	14.9%	11.1%	54
Intellectuals	45.4	32.8	21.8	55
Strivers	55.9	23.8	20.3	59
Unconnected	40.6	37.5	21.9	64
		Senior Choice		
Careerists	92.0	8.0	--	51
Intellectuals	50.0	50.0	--	44
Strivers	73.4	26.6	--	49
Unconnected	57.9	42.1	--	51

Note: Standard professions include business, law, medicine, and engineering.

Certainty of Senior Career Choice by Gender

	Mean	S.D.	N
Careerists (all)	4.02	0.91	51
Men	3.91	0.98	35
Women	4.25	0.68	16
Intellectuals (all)	3.82	0.99	44
Men	3.87	0.83	15
Women	3.80	1.08	29
Strivers (all)	4.12	0.99	49
Men	4.38	0.65	24
Women	3.88	1.20	25
Unconnected (all)	3.71	1.27	51
Men	3.71	1.37	31
Women	3.70	1.13	20

$F = 1.6$ (differences among typology groups), p = n. s.

Amount of Change of Major and Career Choice

	Change of major		Change of career		
	Mean	S.D.	Mean	S.D.	N
Careerists	0.93	0.92	0.65	0.82	55
Intellectuals	0.88	0.99	1.07	0.85	56
Strivers	0.90	0.84	0.82	0.93	60
Unconnected	0.74	0.78	0.89	0.81	65

$F = 0.56$ $F = 2.23$
$p = $ n. s. $p < .10$

Stability of Major and Career Choice

	Careerists	Intellectuals	Strivers	Unconnected	Total
Major choice					
Stayed in original school division	69.6%	62.5%	75.0%	57.1%	66.8%
Career choice					
Stayed with original career	61.7	42.4	59.0	34.1	50.6
Stayed within standard fields	97.4	72.2	78.6	66.7	81.9
Stayed within non-standard fields	42.9	73.3	45.5	60.0	58.5
Changers joining a standard field	90.5	44.8	64.0	47.2	58.6
Undecided freshmen later joining standard fields	100.0	50.0	77.8	55.6	66.7
Undecided freshman percentage	10.0	23.3	18.8	18.0	17.3
N =	50	43	48	50	191

Appendix IV, Table 5. Overseas, Stop-Out, and Extra-Curricular Activity.

	Attended overseas campus	Stopped out for one or more quarters	Length of stop-out period				
			One quarter	Two quarters	Three quarters	One year or more	N
Careerists	36.4%	12.7%	66.7%	16.7%	16.7%	0.0%	6
Intellectuals	55.4	35.7	85.7	7.1	7.1	0.0	14
Strivers	33.3	16.7	50.0	16.7	16.7	16.7	6
Unconnected	27.7	30.8	58.3	25.0	8.3	8.3	12
Chi-square	10.7	11.4			10.5		
Probability	< .05	< .01			n. s.		

Grouped Extra-Curricular Involvement Index

	0 - 2 Activities	3 - 4 Activities	5 - 9 Activities	Mean	N
Careerists	23.5%	41.2%	35.3%	3.73	51
Intellectuals	21.7	21.7	56.5	4.59	46
Strivers	22.0	36.0	42.0	4.24	50
Unconnected	32.7	38.5	28.8	3.38	52

Chi-square = 9.8 $F = 3.39$

$p = $ n. s. $p < .05$

Activity Variables

	Academic activities outside class	Arts	Athletics	Service oriented activities	Organized Stanford activities	Organized activities outside Stanford	Means	N
Careerists	45.1%	41.1%	60.8%	45.1%	66.7%	13.7%	2.73	51
Intellectuals	65.2	65.2	63.0	71.7	65.2	26.1	3.57	46
Strivers	74.0	48.0	74.0	62.0	62.0	20.0	3.40	50
Unconnected	40.4	48.1	51.9	48.1	53.8	15.4	2.58	52

Social and Political Involvement

	Volunteer hours/week, sophomore year	Community service frequency, senior year	Political discussion frequency	
			Junior year	Senior year
Careerists	0.27	1.61	3.59	3.76
Intellectuals	0.91	2.11	4.21	4.28
Strivers	0.62	1.92	3.91	3.78
Unconnected	0.98	1.86	3.78	3.58
Mean	0.71	1.87	3.87	3.84
F-statistic	1.78	1.29	3.44	4.26
Probability	n. s.	n. s.	< .05	< .01

Appendix IV, Table 6. Marital and Child Status, by Gender.

	Not married or equivalent within 10 years			Will have children within 10 years			Will ever have children		
	Men	Women	Total	Men	Women	Total	Men	Women	Total
Careerists	10.0%	0.0%	6.5%	62.5%	66.7%	63.8%	84.4%	78.6%	82.6%
Intellectuals	15.4	0.0	4.5	71.4	82.8	79.1	92.9	96.3	95.1
Strivers	4.0	0.0	2.1	66.7	56.0	61.2	100.0	96.0	98.0
Unconnected	3.6	5.3	4.3	80.0	78.9	79.5	93.1	94.7	93.8
Probability	n. s.	n. s.	n. s.	n. s.	n. s.	$< .10$	n. s.	n. s.	$< .05$

Appendix IV, Table 7. Satisfaction with the Senior Year.

	Interaction with instructors	Intellectual discussion	Social interaction	Interest in courses	Desired grades	Career plans	Time management	Sense of belonging	Overall contentment
Careerists	3.65	3.67	3.86	3.65	3.41	4.02	3.35	3.90	3.82
Intellectuals	3.70	4.04	3.89	3.96	3.58	3.98	3.61	3.85	3.98
Strivers	3.52	3.90	3.82	3.88	3.46	4.24	3.60	4.04	4.20
Unconnected	3.35	3.35	3.73	3.56	3.66	3.52	3.38	3.58	3.94
Mean	3.55	3.73	3.82	3.76	3.53	3.93	3.48	3.84	3.98
F statistic	1.20	5.77	0.25	1.95	0.65	4.31	0.92	1.59	1.98
Probability	n. s.	$< .01$	n. s.	n. s.	n. s.	$< .01$	n. s.	n. s.	n. s.

Appendix IV, Table 8. Senior Survey Evaluations.

Evaluation of the Undergraduate Program

	Overall education quality	Course quality within major	Adequacy of professional training	Adequacy of liberal education	Contribution of living arrangements to intellectual life
Careerists	4.19	3.72	4.07	3.63	3.54
Intellectuals	4.36	4.11	3.67	4.16	3.41
Strivers	4.31	4.05	4.10	3.76	3.64
Unconnected	4.26	3.81	3.74	3.59	3.27
Mean	4.28	3.92	3.90	3.78	3.46
F-statistic	0.68	2.94	2.56	3.47	0.91
Probability	n. s.	< .05	< .10	< .05	n. s.

	Advisor while undeclared	Major advisor	Faculty as researchers	Faculty as teachers	Faculty accessibility	Quality of teaching assistants	Individual work with faculty
Careerists	2.19	3.16	4.29	3.55	3.83	3.14	3.61
Intellectuals	3.02	3.43	4.26	3.80	3.67	3.36	3.91
Strivers	2.61	3.15	4.52	3.57	3.48	3.29	3.77
Unconnected	2.50	3.25	4.30	3.33	3.25	2.93	3.83
Mean	2.58	3.25	4.34	3.56	3.55	3.17	3.79
F-statistic	2.98	0.49	1.16	2.84	3.91	2.36	0.49
Probability	< .05	n. s.	n. s.	< .05	< .01	< .10	n. s.

Appendix IV, Table 8. Senior Survey Evaluations, Cont'd.

Importance of Different Aspects of the Undergraduate Program

	Overall education quality	Course quality within major	Adequacy of professional training	Adequacy of liberal education	Contribution of living arrangements to intellectual life
Careerists	4.21	4.02	4.14	3.80	3.61
Intellectuals	4.41	4.32	3.18	4.30	3.45
Strivers	4.50	4.10	4.05	3.86	4.10
Unconnected	4.38	3.91	3.49	3.73	3.39
Mean	4.37	4.09	3.72	3.92	3.63
F-statistic	1.26	2.05	8.88	4.02	3.74
Probability	n. s.	n. s.	< .01	< .01	< .01

	Advisor while undeclared	Major advisor	Faculty as researchers	Faculty as teachers	Faculty accessibility	Quality of teaching assistants	Individual work with faculty
Careerists	3.16	3.32	3.43	4.40	3.48	3.40	3.71
Intellectuals	3.27	3.65	3.67	4.52	3.56	3.57	3.94
Strivers	3.44	3.58	3.60	4.43	3.40	3.38	3.55
Unconnected	2.93	3.20	3.21	4.29	3.28	3.29	3.41
Mean	3.19	3.44	3.48	4.41	3.43	3.41	3.67
F-statistic	2.04	1.71	2.17	0.89	0.77	0.96	2.15
Probability	n. s.	n. s.	< .10	n. s.	n. s.	n. s.	< .10

Appendix IV, Table 9. Academic Success and Difficulty.

Awards and Academic Difficulty

	Phi Beta Kappa	Departmental honors	Graduation with distinction	Formal academic difficulty
Careerists	5.9%	7.8%	19.6%	1.8%
Intellectuals	13.7	13.7	29.4	3.6
Strivers	3.5	7.0	12.3	5.0
Unconnected	9.1	5.5	18.2	6.2
Chi-square	4.3	2.7	5.1	1.5
Probability	n. s.	n. s.	n. s.	n. s.

Total Grade Point Average by Year

	Freshman	Sophomore	Junior	Senior	Mean
Careerists	3.33	3.36	3.36	3.33	3.34
Intellectuals	3.40	3.50	3.46	3.49	3.46
Strivers	3.26	3.29	3.29	3.27	3.28
Unconnected	3.26	3.30	3.39	3.39	3.34
Probability	n. s.	< .05	n. s.	< .10	< .05

Appendix IV, Table 9. Academic Success and Difficulty, Cont'd.

Grade Point Average in Courses of Each School Division

	Humanities	Social sciences	Natural sciences	Engineering	Human biology	All other
Careerists	3.47	3.31	3.28	3.20	3.08	3.02
Intellectuals	3.56	3.44	3.48	3.09	3.51	3.16
Strivers	3.42	3.27	3.29	3.05	3.21	3.15
Unconnected	3.44	3.30	3.28	3.25	3.21	3.04
Mean	3.51	3.34	3.32	3.17	3.24	3.09

Number of Courses in Each School Division

	Humanities	Social sciences	Natural sciences	Engineering	Human biology	All other
Careerists	12.4	10.6	12.4	7.3	1.6	5.8
Intellectuals	19.5	9.1	7.3	2.7	2.4	5.5
Strivers	13.5	10.1	10.7	6.2	2.4	6.2
Unconnected	15.9	9.0	10.3	5.2	2.0	5.6
Mean	14.5	9.5	9.8	4.9	2.0	5.6

Appendix IV, Table 10. Self-Assessments of Abilities.

Self-Assessments of Abilities, Absolute Scale

	Write English prose	Use a foreign language	Understand Western culture	Understand non-Western culture	Understand literature, fine arts	Understand philosophy, religion	Understand human development	Understand social processes
Careerists	4.26	3.14	3.09	3.00	3.44	3.63	3.68	3.76
Intellectuals	4.09	3.46	3.45	2.95	3.67	3.55	3.50	3.90
Strivers	4.02	3.19	3.05	3.19	3.63	3.59	3.86	3.85
Unconnected	4.02	3.23	2.88	2.85	3.41	3.51	3.58	3.52
Mean	4.10	3.27	3.13	2.99	3.54	3.57	3.65	3.76
F-statistic	0.88	0.57	2.25	0.59	0.90	0.12	1.25	1.79
Probability	n. s.	n. s.	< .10	n. s.	n. s.	n. s.	n. s.	n. s.

	Understand mathematical sciences	Understand natural sciences	Understand technology	Make use of computers	Understand workings of government	Evaluate international problems	Absorb, analyze information	Use creative faculties
Careerists	3.71	3.79	3.59	3.54	3.58	3.87	4.49	4.00
Intellectuals	3.07	3.24	2.87	3.00	3.70	3.89	4.39	4.07
Strivers	3.57	3.70	3.50	3.35	3.60	3.72	4.39	4.07
Unconnected	3.29	3.64	3.20	2.94	3.36	3.40	4.14	3.71
Mean	3.41	3.59	3.29	3.22	3.56	3.71	4.35	3.96
F-statistic	3.50	2.13	3.15	2.29	0.98	2.28	2.43	1.95
Probability	< .05	< .10	< .05	< .10	n. s.	< .10	< .10	< .10

Appendix IV, Table 10. Self-Assessments of Abilities, Cont'd.

Importance Attached to Abilities

	Write English prose	Use a foreign language	Understand Western culture	Understand non-Western culture	Understand literature, fine arts	Understand philosophy, religion	Understand human development	Understand social processes
Careerists	4.32	3.29	3.26	3.15	3.45	3.40	3.43	3.59
Intellectuals	4.52	3.66	3.55	3.54	3.86	3.75	3.61	3.86
Strivers	4.57	3.53	3.42	3.54	3.78	3.66	4.00	3.83
Unconnected	4.11	3.33	2.95	3.03	3.30	3.28	3.35	3.23
Mean	4.38	3.46	3.30	3.32	3.60	3.52	3.60	3.62
F-statistic	2.98	0.96	2.78	2.85	3.05	1.97	3.34	4.37
Probability	< .05	n. s.	< .05	< .05	< .05	n. s.	< .05	< .01

	Understand mathematical sciences	Understand natural sciences	Understand technology	Make use of computers	Understand workings of government	Evaluate international problems	Absorb, analyze information	Use creative faculties
Careerists	3.42	3.41	3.51	3.62	3.53	3.71	4.56	4.36
Intellectuals	2.72	3.21	3.05	3.19	3.70	4.16	4.72	4.39
Strivers	3.24	3.58	3.65	3.51	3.61	4.05	4.71	4.50
Unconnected	2.95	3.53	2.95	3.08	3.14	3.51	4.45	4.14
Mean	3.09	3.43	3.29	3.36	3.49	3.86	4.61	4.34
F-statistic	3.50	0.83	3.12	1.90	2.39	3.60	1.87	1.81
Probability	< .05	n. s.	< .05	n. s.	< .10	< .01	n. s.	n. s.

References

Adorno, T. W., Frenkel-Brunswick, E., Levinson, D. J., and Sanford, R. N. *The Authoritarian Personality.* New York: Harper & Row, 1950.

Allport, G. W., and Vernon, P. E. *Study of Values: Manual.* Boston: Houghton Mifflin, 1931.

Allport, G. W., Vernon, P. E., and Lindzey, G. *Study of Values: Manual.* (3rd ed.) Boston: Houghton Mifflin, 1960.

American Council on Education. *National Norms for Entering College Freshmen.* Washington, D.C.: American Council on Education, 1966–1970.

American Council on Education. *The American Freshman: National Norms.* Washington, D.C.: American Council on Education, 1971–1972.

Antler, J. "Culture, Service, and Work: Changing Ideals of Higher Education for Women." In P. Perun (Ed.), *The Undergraduate Woman: Issues in Educational Equity.* Lexington, Mass.: Lexington Books, 1982.

Astin, A. W. *The American Freshman, 1966–1982: Some Implications.* Washington, D.C.: National Committee on Excellence in Education, 1982. (ED 227 070)

Blackwell, J. E. *Mainstreaming Outsiders: The Production of Black Professionals.* Bayside, N.Y.: General Hall, 1981.

Boli, J., Katchadourian, H. K., and Mahoney, S. "Analyzing Academic Records for Informed Administration: The Stanford Curriculum Study." *Campus Report,* Stanford News Service, Oct. 19, 1983, pp. 1–20.

Bouwsma, W. J. "Models of the Educated Man." *American Scholar,* 1975, *44* (2), 195–212.

Bowen, H. R. *The State of the Nation and the Agenda for Higher Education*. San Francisco: Jossey-Bass, 1982.

Boyer, E. L., and Levine, A. *A Quest for Common Learning: The Aims of General Education*. Washington, D.C.: The Carnegie Foundation for the Advancement of Teaching, 1981.

Bronson, W. C. *The History of Brown University, 1764-1914*. Providence, R.I.: Brown University, 1914.

Bushnell, J. H. "Student Culture at Vassar." In N. Sanford (Ed.), *The American College*. New York: Wiley, 1962.

The Carnegie Foundation for the Advancement of Teaching. *Missions of the College Curriculum: A Contemporary Review with Suggestions*. San Francisco: Jossey-Bass, 1977.

Clark, B. R., and Trow, M. "Determinants of College Student Subcultures." Unpublished paper, Center for the Study of Higher Education, Berkeley, Calif., 1960.

Clark, B. R., and Trow, M. "Determinants of the Sub-Cultures of College Students—The Organizational Context." In T. M. Newcomb and E. Wilson (Eds.), *College Peer Groups*. Chicago: Aldine, 1966.

Clark, B. R., and others. "Students and Colleges: Interaction & Change." Berkeley: Center for Research and Development in Higher Education, University of California, 1972. (ED EJ 069 255)

Commission on the Humanities. *The Humanities in American Life*. Berkeley: University of California Press, 1980.

Cooperative Institutional Research Program. *The American Freshman: National Norms*. Los Angeles: Cooperative Institutional Research Program, University of California, 1973-1983.

Dressel, P. L., and Mayhew, L. B. *General Education: Exploration in Evaluation*. Washington, D.C.: American Council on Education, 1954.

El-Khawas, E. *Campus Trends, 1984*. Higher Education Panel Reports, no. 65. Washington, D.C.: American Council on Education, 1985.

Ellis, R. A., Parelius, R. J., and Parelius, A. P. "The Collegiate Scholar: Education for Elite Status." *Sociology of Education*, 1971, *44*, 27-58.

Elton, C. F. "Male Career Role and Vocational Choice: Their Prediction with Personality and Aptitude Variables." *Journal of Counseling Psychology,* 1967, *14* (2), 99–105.

Feldman, K. A., and Newcomb, T. M. *The Impact of College on Students.* San Francisco: Jossey-Bass, 1969.

Flacks, R. "Adaptations of Deviants in a College Community." Unpublished doctoral dissertation, Department of Sociology, University of Michigan, 1963.

Folsom, C. H., Jr. "An Investigation of Holland's Theory of Vocational Choice." *Journal of Counseling Psychology,* 1969, *16* (3), 260–266.

Gaff, J. G., and others. *General Education: Issues and Resources.* Washington, D.C.: Association of American Colleges, 1980.

Galambos, E. C. "The Search for General Education: The Pendulum Swings Back." *Issues in Higher Education,* No. 15. Atlanta, Ga.: Southern Regional Education Board, 1979. (ED 179 169)

Gamson, Z. F., and Associates. *Liberating Education.* San Francisco: Jossey-Bass, 1984.

Gordon, M. S. "The Changing Job Market for College Graduates in the United States." Paper presented at conference on youth, Ditchley, England, Nov. 1, 1976.

Gottlieb, D., and Hodgkins, B. "College Student Subcultures: Their Structure and Characteristics in Relation to Student Attitude Change." *School Review,* 1963, *71,* 266–289.

Heist, P. A., and Yonge, G. *Manual for the Omnibus Personality Inventory, Form F.* New York: Psychological Corporation, 1968.

Hendrix, R., and Stoel, C. "Improving Liberal Education: A Report on Fund Projects, 1973–81." *Liberal Education,* 1982, *68* (2), 139–159.

Holland, J. L. *Psychology of Vocational Choice.* Waltham, Mass.: Blaisdell, 1966.

Holland, J. L. *Making Vocational Choices: A Theory of Careers.* Englewood Cliffs, N.J.: Prentice-Hall, 1973.

Hollingshead, A. B., and Redlich, F. C. *Social Class and Mental Illness.* New York: Wiley, 1958.

Hutchins, R. M. *The Higher Learning in America.* New Haven, Conn.: Yale University Press, 1936.

Jencks, C., and Riesman, D. *The Academic Revolution.* New York: Doubleday, 1968.

Johnson, D. G. *Physicians in the Making: Personal, Academic, and Socioeconomic Characteristics of Medical Students from 1950 to 2000.* San Francisco: Jossey-Bass, 1983.

Katchadourian, H., and Boli, J. "The Stanford Senior Survey: Five-Year Trends in the Evaluation of the Undergraduate Program." Stanford, Calif.: Office of Undergraduate Research, Stanford University, forthcoming.

Keller, M. *Class, Bureaucracy and Schools: The Illusion of Educational Change in America.* New York: Praeger, 1971.

Keller, P. *Getting at the Core: Curricular Reform at Harvard.* Cambridge: Harvard University Press, 1982.

Keniston, K. *The Uncommitted: Alienated Youth in American Society.* New York: Harcourt Brace Jovanovich, 1960.

Keniston, K. "The Faces in the Lecture Room." In R. S. Morison (Ed.), *The Contemporary University: U.S.A.* Boston: Houghton Mifflin, 1966.

Korn, H. A. "Differences in Student Responses to the Curriculum." In J. Katz and Associates (Eds.), *No Time For Youth: Growth and Constraint in College Students.* San Francisco: Jossey-Bass, 1968.

Lasch, C. *The Culture of Narcissism.* New York: Norton, 1979.

Levine, A. *Handbook on Undergraduate Curriculum: Prepared for the Carnegie Council on Policy Studies in Higher Education.* San Francisco: Jossey-Bass, 1978.

Levine, A. *When Dreams and Heroes Died: A Portrait of Today's College Student.* San Francisco: Jossey-Bass, 1980a.

Levine, A. *Why Innovation Fails: The Institutionalization and Termination of Innovation in Higher Education.* Albany: State University of New York Press, 1980b.

Meyer, J. W. "The Effects of the Institutionalization of Colleges in Society." In K. Feldman (Ed.), *College and Student: Selected Readings in the Social Psychology of Higher Education.* Elmsford, N.Y.: Pergamon Press, 1971.

Mirrielees, E. R. *Stanford: The Story of a University.* New York: Putnam's, 1959.

National Center for Education Statistics. *Digest of Educational Statistics.* Washington, D.C.: National Center for Education Statistics, 1982.

Newcomb, T. M., Koenig, K. E., Flacks, R., and Warwick, D. P. *Persistence and Change: Bennington College and Its Students After Twenty-Five Years.* New York: Wiley, 1967.

Osipow, S. H., Ashby, J. D., and Wall, H. W. "Personality Types and Vocational Choice: A Test of Holland's Theory." *Personnel and Guidance Journal,* 1966, *45,* 37–42.

Pemberton, W. A. *Ability, Values, and College Achievement.* University of Delaware Studies in Higher Education, no. 1. Newark, Del.: University of Delaware, 1963.

Perun, P. J. (Ed). *The Undergraduate Woman: Issues in Educational Equity.* Lexington, Mass.: Lexington Books, 1982.

Peterson, R. E. "On a Typology of College Students." Research Bulletin RB–65–9. Princeton, N.J.: Educational Testing Service, 1965.

Report of the Harvard Committee. *General Education in a Free Society.* Cambridge, Mass.: Harvard University Press, 1945.

Riesman, D. *On Higher Education: The Academic Enterprise in an Era of Rising Student Consumerism.* San Francisco: Jossey-Bass, 1981.

Roemer, R. E. "Vocationalism in Higher Education: Explanations from Social Theory." Paper presented at annual meeting of Association for the Study of Higher Education, Washington, D.C., Mar. 1980. (ED 187 200)

Rudolph, F. *The American College and University.* New York: Knopf, 1962.

Rudolph, F. *Curriculum: A History of The American Undergraduate Course of Study Since 1636.* San Francisco: Jossey-Bass, 1977.

Sanford, N. (Ed.). *The American College: A Psychological and Social Interpretation of the Higher Learning.* New York: Wiley, 1962.

Sanford, N. *Where Colleges Fail: A Study of the Student as a Person.* San Francisco: Jossey-Bass, 1967.

Shulman, C. H. *Revamping Core Curricula.* AAHE-ERIC Higher Education *Research Currents.* Washington, D.C.: American Association of Higher Education, 1979.

Steering Committee, Study of Education at Stanford. *Report to the University.* Vol. 10: *Government of the University.* Stanford, Calif.: Study of Education at Stanford, 1969.

Theodore, A. "The Professional Woman: Trends and Prospects." In A. Theodore (Ed.), *The Professional Woman.* Cambridge, Mass.: Schenkman, 1971.

Thomas, G. E. "Race and Sex Group Equity in Higher Education: Institutional and Major Field Enrollment Statuses." *American Educational Research Journal,* 1980, *17,* 171-181.

Thomas, L. *The Medusa and the Snail: More Notes of a Biology Watcher.* New York: Viking Press, 1979.

U.S. Department of Health, Education, and Welfare. *Earned Degrees Conferred.* Washington, D.C.: Dept. of Health, Education, and Welfare, 1961.

Warren, J. R. "Patterns of College Experiences." U.S. Dept. of Health, Education, and Welfare Cooperative Research Project S-327. Claremont, Calif.: College Graduate School and University Center, 1966.

Warren, J. R. "Student Perceptions of College Subcultures." *American Educational Research Journal,* 1968, *5,* 213-232.

Whitehead, A. N. *The Aims of Education and Other Essays.* New York: Macmillan, 1929.

Yale Report. *Reports on the Course of Instruction in Yale College by a Committee of the Corporation and the Academical Faculty.* New Haven, Conn.: Yale University, 1828.

Index

Careerists (cont'd)
ences among, 92, 95, 111; and
graduate study, 101-102; and
institutional purpose, 244; Intellectuals compared with, 119, 120,
121, 129-130, 131, 134, 135, 137,
138, 144, 145, 146, 150, 151, 225;
interviewer impressions of, 90-
92, 96-97, 98, 99, 103-104, 107,
108-109, 110-111, 113-115; and
liberal education, 93, 106-109;
major and career choices of, 100-
106; and marriage, 111; and
overseas study, 108-109; parents
and, 95-97; peers of, 99, 111;
potential, Unconnecteds as, 190-
192, 226-227; prevalence of, 38;
profiles of, 84-89; satisfaction
among, 113-117; self-assessments
by, 112-113; significance of, 233-
238, 241; social life of, 109-111;
socioeconomic status of, 92-95;
stopping out by, 109; Strivers
compared with, 153-154, 161,
162, 165, 166, 167, 168, 169, 170,
171, 174, 177-178, 179, 226; Unconnecteds compared with, 182,
183, 184, 196, 198, 202, 209, 212,
213, 220; value orientation of,
102-103
Carmen, 218
Carnegie Commission on Higher
Education, 13
Carnegie Council on Policy Studies
in Higher Education, 10, 13
Carnegie Foundation for the Advancement of Teaching, 10, 242,
312
Carol, 49; Unconnected, 99
Charlene, 53
Cheryl, 173
Chris, 52
Christina, 132
Christopher: Careerist, 84; Uncon-
nected, 216-217
Clark, B. R., 39-40, 41, 42, 43, 312
Cliff, 110
Clint, 103

Cohort Study: data sources for, 23-
25; described, 21-25, 261-278;
findings of, summarized, 222-
228; interview formats for, 263-
266; interview reports for, 266;
interviews for, 24-25, 35-36;
purposes of, 23; questionnaire
coding for, 272-276; questionnaires for, 23-24, 30-34, 266-272;
recommendations from, 238-254;
sample for, 26-28, 261-263; significance of findings from, 228-
238; typology for, 28-39, 276-278
Coleen, 103
Commission on the Humanities, 6-
8, 312
Cooperative Institutional Research
Program, 13, 14n, 312
Cornell, E., 7
Curriculum, recommendations on,
241-244
Cynthia, 87-88

D

Dana, 49
Daniel, 157-158
David, 48; Striver, 163; Uncon-
nected, 189-190
Dawn, 180
Debby, 93
Debra, 28
Diana, 51
Diane, 115
Donald, 180
Donna, 127
Dressel, P. L., 9, 312
Drue, 132

E

Edward, 4, 88-89, 102
Eileen, 91
El-Khawas, E., 2, 312
Ellis, R. A., 39, 312
Elton, C. F., 42, 313
Emily, 84
Eric, 142